Rescued

Adventures with Down and Out Dogs

Jenni Williams

This is a true story. Some names and minor identifying details about individuals have been changed.

For Eve and Jess

CHAPTER 1

HOWLING MAD

February 2012

IT WAS JUST after 8:00 a.m. and I had no idea that my best friend was about to humiliate me on live radio. Jess and I were sat in the studio of WFRE 99.9 FM, a popular country music station in Frederick, Maryland. I'd never been on the radio before, however it was difficult to enjoy the experience because I was acutely nervous over how Jess would cope. She didn't like people very much but we were due to be interviewed about her search for a new best friend, so it was important that she gave a good impression.

Jess was lying uncharacteristically quietly at my feet, gently chewing her beloved tennis ball. She was a black and white husky mix with gorgeous brown eyes set in a beautiful face that could switch from happy and excitable to nervous and fearful all too easily.

The news announcer finished his bulletin and Tom, the breakfast presenter, smoothly took over.

"So folks, it's time for 'Shelter Pet of the Week'," intoned Tom in a rich Southern drawl. "Here with me is Didi Culp, education officer at Frederick County Animal Control. And we also have Jenni, who we'll be hearing from in a moment, and her foster dog Jess who's looking for a home of her own."

Tom turned to Didi, an attractive woman with long white hair and twinkling blue eyes. She was a dog behaviourist who I'd consulted for advice many times over the past months. And Didi had mostly figuratively scratched her head and told me I was doing everything she would suggest and Jess had her stumped too.

"So Didi, I understand that Jess isn't actually a resident at the shelter but is one of the dogs in your foster care programme," said Tom. "Tell us a bit about that."

"Sure," said Didi, "This is such an important programme that does so much for the homeless pets of Frederick County."

Didi went on to explain that the foster care programme provided temporary loving homes, often long-term, for dogs and cats who needed extra training and rehabilitation before they were ready to be adopted or who didn't do well in the shelter environment – both in Jess's case. Foster carers would work on behavioural issues or tend to medical needs and give the dog the extra care and attention that they needed. Didi sensitively pointed out that FCAC was aiming to be a no-kill shelter but that meant relying on foster carers to take the difficult cases. As the county shelter, FCAC was obliged to take in every domestic animal surrendered to them and therefore sometimes had to make hard choices. Without the foster care programme, dogs and cats considered extremely hard to rehome might otherwise be euthanised in order to free up finite space and resources. So what I'd long suspected was true; I'd been Jess's last chance.

Then Didi told the listeners about Jess and stressed she was non-aggressive but extremely nervous around people. She clarified that despite this, Jess was able to form an incredibly close bond with someone she loved and she explained how I'd worked hard to rehabilitate and socialise her and help her trust people again. In a master class of understatement and brevity that belied the worst five weeks of my life, Didi admitted that Jess once got loose at the shelter and they had to call on me to get her back.

Tom then turned to me.

"So Jenni, you're Jess's foster mom. Thank you so much for what you do. Tell me, how long have you been a foster carer?"

"About sixteen months now," I replied. "Jess was my fourth foster dog but I've had her for nine and a half months so a long time. And I've also fostered ten puppies whilst I've had her."

"Wow, that's great," said Tom smiling at me. "You must be a true believer in the cause! Now I can't help but notice something – you have an accent?"

I laughed obligingly. "Yes I do, I'm British. My husband and I have been living here in the US for a couple of years but we're going back to England soon. And that's why we need to urgently find a forever home for Jess."

Then Tom asked me to describe Jess. I'd been debating how to answer this question – I wanted to do her justice without attracting people with unreasonable expectations.

I launched into a heartfelt speech about what a wonderful dog Jess was, how she was so well behaved in the house and loved curling up on the sofa with me. I explained how she also loved the outdoors, needed a lot of exercise and deserved someone who was as active as she was. I reiterated what Didi had said about the incredibly close bond we had and assured the listeners that although Jess was nervous of people she didn't know, she was fully capable of epic levels of love and was the most affectionate of all my foster dogs. Finally I said that Jess was my dream dog and it broke my heart that we couldn't adopt her ourselves but our life in the UK simply wasn't compatible with Jess's needs.

Tom nodded sympathetically. "And I'm guessing it must be so hard to give these dogs up?"

"It's incredibly hard," I agreed. "I've fallen in love with every single one of my dogs. But that's the job of a foster carer – love the dog as if they're yours and then give them up to their forever home. And keep doing that over and over again."

Didi and I both thought it would help make Jess more memorable if I got her to perform her party trick live on air so Didi had told Tom to ask me about it.

"So Jenni, I understand Jess is true to her husky heritage and likes to have a howl with you and your husband?"

"Yes she does," I replied, "One of us will start howling and she'll join in. It's a great family bonding exercise!"

"That sounds fun, I think we want to hear that. Will she howl for us now?"

"Sure she will, I'll just start her off!"

I smiled at Jess who against all the odds was still lying calmly on the floor. I leant down to give her a treat to make her sit up in the correct position for optimum howling. Then I bent my head back and howled my best howl, confidently expecting Jess to join in.

She didn't. I howled again, with more feeling. Jess remained silent but looked at Tom and Didi with a bemused look on her face. Her expression said, "Don't look at me guys, I have absolutely no idea what Jenni's doing."

I decided to give Jess one more opportunity so I howled my heart out for a third time; I howled alone. This was excruciatingly embarrassing and I wanted to leave town immediately. I had howled like a wolf on live radio and my dog had simply looked at me like I was mad.

"So no howling today," stated Tom flatly whilst Didi tried, almost successfully, to suppress a laugh.

"Er, well she usually does," I said sounding completely delusional.

Tom finished up the interview by explaining how to go about adopting Jess and then put on a song. In the break, Tom thanked us for coming in and said he hoped Jess would get adopted soon. Despite the howling incident, it had been a great experience.

The plan after the interview was for one of the station staff to take some video of Jess outside to go on WFRE's website and Facebook page. It was a disaster. Jess had surprisingly held it together inside the station, however as soon as we got outside she reverted to her usual deranged self. She took an instant dislike to Video Guy and leapt around frantically, straining and biting at her lead in a bid to get away from him. This was totally routine Jess behaviour around someone she didn't know but it wasn't quite the impression we wanted to give.

Video Guy was determined to get his footage and kept trying to get closer to Jess. The result was a video of her looking like the kind of dog you definitely wouldn't adopt if you wanted a normal life.

As soon as Video Guy went back inside, Jess calmed down. I opened the boot of my 4 x 4, or SUV in American-English, and she jumped in happily. I stroked her and gave her a few treats and congratulated her on her first radio appearance, even though she'd left me to do all the talking. Didi felt the interview had been a success; maybe this was the fifteen minutes of fame that Jess needed and her future forever family were currently phoning the shelter in eager anticipation. Jess and I drove home via the Dunkin Donuts drive-thru as I felt I deserved some caffeine, some sugar and some fat after my mortifying solo howling performance.

For the rest of the day, Jess rubbed my nose in my humiliation. She'd look at me with a wicked glint in her eye and then burst out 'laughing' into one of her huge tongue-lolling grins. Then she'd come and nuzzle her head in to me as if to say sorry and then laugh at me again. I've heard it said that dogs don't have a sense of humour in the way we do. Anyone who thinks that has obviously never been pranked by their dog on live radio. And of course when my husband and I howled with her that evening, she joined in as enthusiastically as ever.

Yet despite the undeniably funny side of this incident, I was intensely worried. Jess was an incredibly challenging dog and only a few months previously I'd been told that she was unadoptable. And unadoptable dogs didn't have a long life expectancy as Didi had gently explained to the radio listeners. Our bond, my love for her and my patience with her behaviour had saved her life but I was leaving soon and taking Jess back to England was not an option, mainly for her sake.

The radio interview was the latest initiative in a long and so far unsuccessful campaign to get Jess adopted; I had run out of ideas and she was running out of time. Had I done her justice? Had I said the right things? Had I saved her life?

*   *   *

Almost four years later I found myself on the radio again and this time I was the spokesperson for someone even more important to me than Jess had been – my daughter Eve. Classed as 'severely disabled' in medical terms, she is also loving, independent, determined and stubborn. She has a developmentally advanced sense of humour and is the best company in the world. She reminds me of someone.

Eve was born a couple of months after we returned from the US. She arrived a month prematurely via an emergency C-section due to a plummeting heart rate. She was tiny, weighing only 3.5 lbs, and when the nurse placed her on my chest and I looked at her for the first time I had an overwhelming sense that something was 'wrong'. I was right; when she was three weeks old, Eve was diagnosed with an extremely rare chromosome condition. We were told she would almost certainly never talk, possibly never walk and would require life long care.

And now, three and a half years later, Eve and I had been invited to feature on BBC Radio 4's 'Ramblings' programme together with our beloved female Golden Retriever, Scout. The format of 'Ramblings' is deceptively simple; the presenter, Clare Balding, interviews someone during the course of a walk, or in Eve's case, during a ride in her pushchair. That initial prognosis had so far proved correct and Eve still couldn't walk or talk but she made up for it with cheeky grins and a vibrant personality. The theme of the series we appeared in was 'Walking with a Purpose' and I was talking about life with Eve and how my daily dog walks with my two favourite girls in beautiful countryside helped me deal with the worry of caring for a severely disabled child.

Clare is one of Britain's best-loved TV and radio presenters, known for her warm and engaging style. Happily, I discovered she was just as genuine and sensitive in real life. It's an odd experience, meeting someone who is a complete stranger on a personal level, who you nevertheless feel you know due to her celebrity status. It grants you the detachment to speak freely coupled with the familiarity to share deeply buried thoughts.

As I led Clare on one of my favourite walking routes through woodland near our house, I found it easy to open up about Eve and the highs and lows our family had faced. I explained how important Scout was to me – how she was a life-enhancing antidote to the constant worry and how our twice daily walks ensured I had regular time out doing something physically and mentally beneficial. I likened her to an oxygen mask on a plane and as anyone who's ever listened to the pre-flight safety brief knows, you must fit your own oxygen mask before helping others. I had to have a dog in my life; it was non-negotiable.

Unsurprisingly the subject of my foster dogs came up. With her typical insight, Clare suggested that rehabilitating dogs like Jess no doubt taught me the value of non-verbal communication and noted this must have helped me with Eve. Not only did I agree with this observation but I was touched that someone else recognised the connection between fostering down and out dogs and caring for a severely disabled child.

My dogs kick-started a fiercely protective streak in me, forced me to embrace my nurturing side and uncovered a well of patience I didn't know I had. They taught me that caring for someone vulnerable is more rewarding than I ever imagined and that surprisingly, I was good at it.

They gave me confidence in my instincts and showed me that non-verbal communication is just as valid and meaningful as the verbal kind. And most importantly of all I learnt that life is better, the world is less frightening and I am more resilient with a dog by my side. They made me the mummy Eve needed and I owe them a debt I can never repay.

This is their story.

CHAPTER 2

GOING TO THE DOGS

MY HUSBAND AND I moved to the USA in July 2010. Steve was an officer in the Royal Army Medical Corps and had been seconded to the US Army on a two-year military exchange programme. He was posted to Fort Detrick in the city of Frederick in Frederick County, Maryland, about an hour north of Washington DC. We both loved the USA and had visited iconic tourist destinations like the Grand Canyon and Yosemite National Park on holiday. Two years living in one of our favourite countries was a dream come true and we were determined to make the most of it.

We'd never been to Maryland before but we loved our new home immediately. Founded in 1745, Frederick is Maryland's second largest city after Baltimore yet looks and feels more like a picturesque and historic town enclosed by more modern suburbs. It is surrounded by forest, hills and farmland and the famous Appalachian Trail lies only thirteen miles away, winding its way between the Potomac River and Pennsylvania. Despite its location just south of the Mason-Dixon line, Maryland fought for the Union during the American Civil War. Frederick was an important strategic thoroughfare between North and South and became a 'hospital city' for the wounded on both sides that poured in from nearby battlefields such as the famous Gettysburg in southern Pennsylvania.

At 1,200 acres, Fort Detrick is a relatively small US army base but the biggest employer in Frederick County. It is home to the United States Army Medical Research Institute of Infectious Diseases (USAMRIID) as well as the National Cancer Institute, the US government's main agency for cancer research. Despite this scientific pedigree, Frederick County is a predominantly rural one whose residents have adopted the tongue in cheek nickname 'Frednecks'.

A few weeks after we arrived, one of Steve's new colleagues kindly gave us tickets to see the Baltimore Symphony Orchestra play in Frederick. Some members of the audience were dressed in black tie and evening gowns and some wore biker jackets and baseball caps. The lead violinist sported a bootlace tie and cowboy boots. This sartorial range summed up Frederick's down-to-earth and diverse vibe; I loved it.

We had opted to live in army housing on base which meant Steve could cycle to work in less than ten minutes. Our house was on First Flight Court, a quiet cul-de-sac. There were twenty modern and spacious houses grouped around a large kidney shaped communal lawn, about 150 yards long, with a summerhouse at one end. Our house had three bedrooms, a double garage and a private patio, and backed on to a large field that separated us from the rest of the residential streets. There were no British style private gardens although some residents had installed their own waist high chain link fencing to create a small yard in order to safely contain their dogs or children.

Beyond the housing on the other side of Large Field lay approximately 120 acres of scrubby grassland with intermittent copses of trees. Wild Field, as we called it, stretched all the way to the other side of Fort Detrick, near Steve's office, and culminated in a couple of softball fields, a family picnic area and a small fishing lake called Nallins Pond. I would end up spending a lot of time on Wild Field.

Fort Detrick was a nice enough place to live. Roughly half the base comprised the residential area, landscaped lawns interspersed with children's playgrounds, an outdoor pool and tennis courts, and Wild Field. The other half contained office buildings and barracks as well as USAMRIID, the National Cancer Institute and a collection of ugly industrial buildings of indeterminate use. There was a sports centre with a gym and indoor pool, a supermarket and the obligatory 'PX' – a small department store operating exclusively on US military bases.

However living on Fort Detrick could sometimes feel claustrophobic. There were armed guards on the entrance gates and you had to show your ID and submit to occasional searches of your car. Nevertheless it was considerably easier to be allocated a military house than find somewhere to rent ourselves. As it was, the first month went by in a blur of admin and there was curiously little support from the British Embassy.

We had to buy a car as the Embassy only paid for a hire car for two weeks, arrange car insurance, get an American bank account, take a Maryland driving test, arrange the internet and mobile phones and so on. To research all these things we really needed the internet but we couldn't set up an internet or mobile phone contract without a bank account. And it was difficult to apply for a bank account, or contact the Embassy to arrange confirmation of our residency status and Steve's job without email, the internet or a mobile phone.

All I will say is thank goodness for neighbours who don't password protect their Wi-Fi. Mr and Mrs Comcast HUB-RT4-K8D, I never found out who you were but you were extremely helpful.

Slowly but surely we began to settle in, enough that we felt able to take off to Montana, Wyoming and Yellowstone National Park in early September for a sorely needed holiday. In the six months before we moved to Frederick, Steve had been deployed to Afghanistan where he'd been responsible for providing medical cover for British and American troops in Helmand Province. Our road trip was the first chance he'd had to relax since his return. It did us both the world of good and made the inevitable stress of moving countries worthwhile.

Whilst out west, I was reminded of a pithy little phrase that I'd heard before on USA vacations – 'Happy Trails.' It's an upbeat way of wishing someone well on their travels and is frequently uttered by hikers, outdoor enthusiasts and National Parks Service rangers. I loved its connotations of exploring the wilderness and noticed it often featured as a cheery sign off in national park leaflets or on trail maps. I once asked someone the origin of the phrase and was told it was an old cowboy saying. Trails might be long and difficult sometimes and you can't change that but you can at least choose your attitude – you can resolve that each trail will be a happy one. Oddly enough this friendly valediction would come to have huge meaning for me over the next couple of years.

Our return from vacation marked when Frederick began to feel like home. Having the 21st century essentials of life sorted meant that we could spend our evenings and weekends exploring our new town and discovering Frederick's numerous bars, craft breweries and restaurants. Firestones Culinary Tavern, a popular bar and restaurant situated on Frederick's historic Market Street, became a regular haunt as did Baker Park, a 50 acre parcel of green in downtown Frederick that I'd end up knowing intimately. The park was a picture perfect city oasis boasting well maintained lawns, children's playgrounds, tennis courts and a lake. Baker Park was bisected by a tree-lined stretch of Carroll Creek, an eight mile tributary of Frederick County's Monocacy River. The creek's shallower sections were a popular cooling off point in summer for dogs and their people.

Settling in to life in Frederick also meant it was time for me to focus on what I was going to do for two years. Steve had been specially selected for this posting due to his professional skills and experience; in contrast I was surplus to requirements. I was designated a 'dependent alien' by the US Government and wasn't allowed to work. This may have bothered some people but I saw it as a unique opportunity to enjoy a career break and undertake some interesting voluntary work. And top of the list was something to do with dogs.

I had wanted a dog all my life, for as long as I could remember. It was my deepest wish as a child and the feeling was at times overwhelming. I loved books and TV programmes about dogs, especially 'Lassie' and 'The Littlest Hobo'. Both of those eponymous canine heroes were trustworthy and intelligent companions, even though the Littlest Hobo seemed somewhat fickle in his affections and moved on to a new person at the end of each episode. I'll be forever grateful to Lassie and Hobo for planting the notion in my childhood psyche of dogs as friends and equals; it was a belief that remained ingrained and was to prove vital decades later.

Although I was an outwardly confident and sociable child, inwardly I was quite sensitive. Teasing upset me and I sometimes found the twists and turns of childhood friendships bewildering. I often felt like an outsider who had to make a constant effort to fit in. In contrast, dogs seemed to offer steadfast loyalty and unwavering friendship. They didn't judge, they didn't tease, and they didn't have any expectations of you. They simply wanted to be your friend and go on adventures with you, even if that adventure was a just a walk in the woods.

However books and television programmes were the closest I got to a canine companion because despite what seemed like constant pleading, I wasn't allowed a dog. Neither of my parents liked dogs and my mother was actively scared of them, to the extent that my siblings and I were warned to stay away from dogs because they could 'turn' in an instant. She also didn't want the inevitable mess and dirt or the obligation of daily walks. My father agreed.

Looking back from an adult perspective I have to admit my parents were right to stand firm. For the dog's sake, the adults in the house have to be completely supportive of having a muddy, expensive, high maintenance individual join the family. Many an unhappy dog has ended up in a shelter or worse because parents gave in to their children's incessant requests and then subsequently regretted it.

But I didn't see the situation that way at the time. My mum would frequently reply to one of my speeches about why we should get a dog with the statement that when I had my own house I could have as many dogs as I liked. I resolved to do just that. This book is testament to the only time I've ever taken my mother's advice.

Despite my latent respect for my parents' position, I genuinely feel sorry for people who don't understand the dog-human bond. Dogs have lived alongside us in a way that no other animal has and our friendship goes back an awfully long way.

The most recent research theorises that humans and the now extinct wolf species that is the ancestor of modern wolves and the domestic dog became friends approximately 30,000 years ago, much earlier than previously thought. Furthermore some researchers assert that dogs and humans evolved together and actually influenced each other's development. Or to put it another way, dogs have made us who we are today.

One of the most intriguing pieces of archeological evidence is the ancient footsteps of a small child discovered in the Chauvet Cave in France. Next to the child's footprints are the paw prints of a large canine. The dog is walking alongside the child, not stalking it, indicating that they're friends, not hunter and prey. Those fossilised tracks have been dated at 26,000 years old.

So how did early wolves become dogs? Whilst there is disagreement over the geographical location and even whether there was more than one domestication event, the broad consensus is that a slightly braver than average (and for whatever reason, possibly hungrier than usual) group of wolves essentially domesticated themselves by approaching a roaming hunter-gatherer group or settled human camp in search of food. This is the 'survival of the friendliest' theory and seems a more likely scenario than humans suddenly opting to waste precious time and resources taming a large and predatory carnivore. The process of full domestication was a long one but by 7,000 years ago dogs were found all over the world, wherever humans had settled. Both species had decided the dog-human relationship was a mutually beneficial one and the rest is history.

Of course I didn't know all this when I was a child but I suspect I sensed it, as do all dog people. The ancient friendship between dogs and people had been going on for tens of thousands of years and I simply wanted to join in. I resolved that I was going to get a dog when I was a grown up and no one was going to stop me. Thankfully the person I've spent almost my entire adult life with loves dogs nearly as much as I do.

Steve and I had met as officer cadets at the Royal Military Academy Sandhurst. I'd decided to join the army as an officer in my final year at university. I had absolutely no experience of military life – I hadn't done anything like the cadets whilst I'd been at school or the Officer Training Corps at university. But having no experience of something had never stopped me before and an office-based graduate job didn't appeal in the slightest. The army seemed an intriguingly different proposition.

Steve and I met after the first few weeks and immediately became friends and then rather more than that. We were both slightly rebellious, questioned authority and often found ourselves equal parts bemused and exasperated at the army way of doing things. Steve nevertheless went on to commission but I was medically discharged with a training injury half way through the course.

One of the things that attracted me to Steve was his love of animals, especially dogs. He'd grown up with black Labradors and his family still had two Labs, Kim and Tanny. Tanny was Steve's childhood dog and a distinguished old lady by the time I knew her. She was friendly but with a dignified and slightly aloof bearing.

Kim was another matter. Kim was the first dog I ever properly got to know and I couldn't have asked for a better introduction to the dog world. Good-natured, silly and affectionate, Kim and I became firm friends. She soon realised that I was a soft touch and would sneak her a piece of bacon at breakfast time. In return she let me share the rug when she occupied her rightful place in front of the fire.

By our early thirties Steve and I had moved to Dorking, a market town in the heart of the Surrey Hills in south-east England. We were surrounded by beautiful countryside and our weekends were filled with walking, running and mountain biking. However with both of us working full time and living in a flat, the rest of our lifestyle wasn't conducive to having a dog. It was something we talked about frequently but both accepted it couldn't happen for a while.

Yet now I found myself with two years of free time on my hands. One of the volunteering opportunities I was interested in was raising a puppy for a guide dog association. I had researched it before we left England and it sounded perfect. The volunteer was responsible for raising the puppy for its first eighteen months, ensuring it was well socialised and implementing a preliminary training schedule.

However when I contacted the puppy coordinator for the Maryland area I was frustrated to discover that the criteria had changed and the requirement to attend weekly training sessions for eighteen months with only one week off allowed in the first year meant it wasn't something we felt we could commit to, bearing in mind we had a few vacation plans. I couldn't help but feel a bit despondent. I had wanted a dog for so long and this was the first time in my life when the stars were aligned and I was in the perfect position to give a dog a home. Yet it still didn't look like it was going to be possible.

A couple of days later Steve came home with some interesting news. One of his colleagues volunteered at the county animal shelter, Frederick County Animal Control. The shelter was coincidentally situated on Rosemont Avenue, which ran alongside Fort Detrick's western boundary and was less than a five minute drive from our house.

The shelter had an established foster care programme for dogs and cats who needed some extra attention or training before they were considered adoptable. Steve's colleague suggested that I look into it. This sounded perfect. I had no idea that there was such a thing as fostering dogs (I'm afraid I wasn't interested in the feline side, sorry cats!) and assumed you would have to have extensive experience to do something like that. Nonetheless I decided to find out more.

The following day I drove down to Frederick County Animal Control. FCAC housed the uniformed and armed officers responsible for investigating the abuse and neglect of animals within Frederick County and enforcing county and state laws. It also encompassed the Pet Adoption Centre where stray and unwanted animals, mainly cats and dogs, were held. As the county shelter, FCAC was obliged to take in any animal surrendered by members of the public who had decided for whatever reason, however dubious, that they wanted to rehome their non-human family member. Other members of the public on the lookout for a new dog or cat could walk around and view the animals and meet any they were interested in adopting.

I remember the first time I entered the dog adoption floor, the area of cages side by side that housed anything up to twenty dogs at a time. Whilst the staff prided themselves on keeping the cages clean there was obviously a strong doggy scent in the air and I loved it. I felt like I'd come home. That feeling never left me – every time I walked onto that adoption floor I took a deep, contented breath and felt a wonderful sense of peace and calm.

I walked along the line of cages containing homeless and unwanted dogs and fell in love several times over. How on earth I was going to get through two years without adopting several of them I didn't know. After tearing myself away from the dogs I went to speak to one of the receptionists and explained I was interested in fostering. The young woman behind the desk asked me a few preliminary questions, gave me a form to fill in and explained that someone would be in touch.

I was pleasantly surprised at not being rejected immediately and was filled with hope a couple of days later when I had a phone call from an Officer Luther. She explained she was one of the animal control officers and had been asked to interview me and Steve and assess whether we'd be suitable foster carers. We fixed a time for the following afternoon when Steve would be home from work.

The next day I cleaned and tidied everywhere in the house, including upstairs. I thought Officer Luther might want to look around the whole house and I was determined to give the best possible impression. I was so nervous that I honestly thought we'd be rejected if she thought a foster dog might trip on a dangerously discarded sock or inhale an errant piece of fluff. Steve got home right on time and I made him stay in uniform as I thought that gave a good impression. He laughed at me but I really wanted to do this more than anything. I couldn't imagine a better way to spend my time than fostering dogs.

Officer Luther turned out to be one of those authority figures that exude professionalism and competence without being intimidating. A few years younger than us, she apologised for wearing civilian clothes and explained she was a uniformed officer but had recently injured her knee whilst out pursuing a stray dog and was restricted to light duties for the time being. I suspected that interviewing prospective foster carers must have been a rather dull assignment for Officer Luther but she didn't show it and seemed genuinely interested in why we were in the US and what our plans were.

We soon got on to the subject of why I wanted to foster. I told Officer Luther how much I loved dogs but wasn't able to have one back home as we both worked full time and lived in an apartment. I explained that I wasn't allowed to undertake any paid employment during my time in the US but wanted to do something worthwhile and not simply sit around watching daytime TV. Fostering seemed like a great way to have a dog for a period of time whilst also doing some good.

Officer Luther nodded understandingly and then asked us about our experience with dogs. This was an easy question for Steve – his family had always had dogs whereas I had to admit that I'd never had a dog of my own but had wanted one for as long as I could remember. I said how much I always enjoyed spending time with Steve's family dogs and he loyally chipped in and said how much they loved me back.

Officer Luther explained it might be months before we got a call and the foster situations would all be different. Some might be puppies that needed fostering until they were old enough to be adopted as Maryland state law decreed that a puppy couldn't be sold or adopted until it was eight weeks old. There might be some medical cases but most were instances where the dog had certain behavioural problems that needed working on before they could be adopted. She asked if there were any situations where I wouldn't be interested.

I admitted that as I had never had a dog of my own, I didn't feel confident dealing with medical issues or behavioural problems just yet. I'm not sure whether Officer Luther simply didn't write that down or if she had greater confidence in my abilities than I did but three of my first four foster dogs were medical and behavioural cases.

Officer Luther told us she had no hesitation in recommending us and asked me to go in to FCAC the following day as there would be some paperwork for me to fill in on reception. I was overjoyed and thanked her for her faith in me. We said goodbye and then I hugged Steve in relief and delight. This was a dream come true and it seemed only fitting to crack open a couple of beers from Frederick's own Flying Dog brewery to celebrate.

The next day I went in to the shelter and explained to the receptionist who I was and that I needed to sign some paperwork.

"Oh right, the British couple. I've been expecting you. Officer Luther said she thinks you're the best foster carers she's ever met."

I beamed inwardly to hear what Officer Luther thought of us and guessed this endorsement meant I'd get to foster at least one dog during our time in Frederick. I thanked the receptionist and headed home, hoping it wouldn't be too long before I received the call I was longing for.

CHAPTER 3

FIRST DOG

TWO DAYS LATER my phone rang and the woman introduced herself as Linda, the kennel manager at Frederick County Animal Control.

"Jenni, I have an injured foxhound who needs eight weeks of crate rest. Would you be interested in fostering him?"

My heart leapt. Of course I was interested in getting my first dog; I'd been interested for the last thirty years. Linda told me that the dog was currently being treated at Kingsbrook Animal Hospital, a local veterinary practice that FCAC used. He was believed to be a stray and had been picked up a few days ago after being hit by a car. He didn't have a collar, wasn't micro chipped and no one had contacted FCAC to report a missing foxhound. Although he didn't have any broken bones, he had suffered soft tissue and ligament damage and his back leg was in a cast. He wouldn't be able to go on long walks and my job would be to keep him as comfortable as possible whilst enforcing his crate rest and transporting him back and forth to Kingsbrook for regular check ups.

I felt a slight pang of disappointment that I wouldn't be able to walk my first dog or play fetch with him. However that couldn't be helped and I resolved that Mr Foxhound would have a life worth living whilst he recovered from his injuries.

I rang Steve and excitedly informed him that we were getting a four-legged houseguest for a couple of months. He was surprised it had happened so quickly but was delighted for me. Linda and I had agreed that we'd pick the dog up from Kingsbrook just before 6:00 p.m. as it would be easier if Steve was there too. He promised to be home in good time.

I then went to PetValu, our nearest pet store, and bought a couple of bowls for food and water and a squeaky toy. Linda had told me she'd provide me with a big bag of dog food so I didn't bother buying any but I did pick up a few treats to welcome Mr Foxhound to his new home.

On the way back I called in at FCAC to sign the foster care paperwork and pick up the food, a pile of towels and the all-important crate. Linda explained that as the foxhound was a stray, we had the honour of naming him. I nipped back home to set up the crate and lined it with a couple of the towels so that our patient would have a comfortable space to recuperate in.

As soon as Steve got home from work we set off to collect my first dog, a moment I'd dreamed of for thirty years. All the way to Kingsbrook Animal Hospital we discussed names. It had to be something suitably American and robust sounding; however Steve didn't like any of my choices and I didn't like any of his. I hoped a name would leap out at me when I saw my dog in the flesh.

When we arrived at Kingsbrook the receptionist was expecting us. She mentioned that they'd started calling the foxhound 'Hank' but said they understood if we wanted to change it. Steve and I grinned at each other, both thinking the same thing. Our surname was Williams so he'd be Hank Williams; as there was a famous country music star of the same name I decided that 'Hank' was perfect. The staff were genuinely pleased that Hank would remain 'Hank' and I realised that they were all extremely fond of him. He'd clearly been in good hands.

One of the veterinary technicians came out to brief us on Hank's injuries and treatment. She explained the damage to his leg and reiterated how important it was to make sure he rested it.

Hank was allowed a maximum of six walks a day of no more than ten minutes each. The vet tech explained that he was allowed out of the crate at other times if he'd lie down calmly but if not then it was more important to keep him in there. She also explained it was important to keep his bandage as dry as possible otherwise a wet bandage could cause an unpleasant fungal infection.

She then showed us an ingenious waterproof 'bootie' – an empty IV fluid bag with the top cut off and holes pierced around the open end with a long strip of cotton gauze threaded through. Every time we took Hank outside we would need to put his IV bag bootie on and tie it around his leg. This would prevent his bandages getting wet and soggy. Then we'd need to take it off when he came back inside to allow his paw to breathe. That sounded simple; how hard could it possibly be to put an IV bootie on a foxhound? I would soon find out.

The vet tech also went through Hank's medication with me. There were painkillers and anti-inflammatories for him to take three times a day. She suggested hiding the tablets amongst his kibble or in a piece of bread. She told us he was really sweet natured and still a bit subdued by his experience. I listened to the briefing carefully, not wanting to forget anything and possibly hinder Hank's recovery.

And then finally the vet tech spoke the words I'd been longing to hear. "Ok, let me go get Hank for you!"

As Hank came round the door to the treatment area I let out a little gasp. He was perfect – handsome, long-legged and lean and had a bright yellow bandage covering the cast on his left back leg. Amusingly there was a fabric sticker of a cartoon Frankenstein's Monster adorning the bandage. It was late October and Halloween was coming up. The vet tech explained that Kingsbrook liked to be creative with their bandages and the bright colours and seasonal stickers were all part of the service.

I was slightly concerned that Hank might not want to leave Kingsbrook and the lovely staff but he willingly followed us out to the car and allowed us to lift him on to the back seat. I sat in the back with him in order to keep him company and ensure he wasn't unduly worried at what was going on.

During the drive home Hank didn't stop gazing out of the car window. He seemed to want his face to be in the early evening sun and he had a dreamy, faraway expression in his eyes. I guessed he was a dog who loved the outdoors and I promised him there and then that he'd always get the maximum number of walks that he was allowed.

"Welcome home Hank," I said as we pulled into our garage. I carefully lifted him out of the car and led him into the house. I showed him where his crate was and where his food and water bowl were, essential doggy orientation. But there was something I should have done immediately and didn't. I didn't show him where the toilet was.

So it really wasn't Hank's fault that he peed on the floor within a couple of minutes of arriving at our house. He'd been sniffing around the living room when he suddenly yawned, stretched his entire body out and starting making a large puddle on the floor.

"Oh no way!" I exclaimed. "Definitely not house trained then!"

"Er...we probably should have taken him outside first," said Steve, the man who had grown up with dogs.

We obviously didn't get cross with Hank, as his lack of weeing etiquette was entirely our fault. I volunteered Steve for mopping up duties and took Hank outside.

"Ok Hank, this is the toilet," I said gesturing to the whole of Fort Detrick. "Anywhere out here is fine!"

I walked Hank around the area immediately behind our house, letting him have a good sniff around. Steve came to join us and we did a little circuit around our house and then the large communal lawn in the middle of First Flight Court.

Then it happened. Hank had been sniffing the ground and walking around in a tight little circle when he crouched down and pooped. I hadn't told anyone but this was the aspect of having a dog that I was most dreading. I had never picked up dog poo before as it's not the kind of thing you do unless you have to and I really wasn't looking forward to this unavoidable aspect of having a dog.

Steve held the poo bag out to me. "Go on," he said.

"Can you do it? I really don't want to."

Steve laughed at me, probably the most helpful thing he could have done. It was the incentive I needed.

"Oh give it here," I said, grabbing the bag from him. I opened it up, put my hand in and approached the offensive item lying on the grass. Trying not to breathe I tentatively reached out and closed my hand around it. It was surprisingly firm and easy to pick up. I turned the bag inside out and tied a knot in the end.

"Did it!" I announced proudly. "That was easy, not sure why I was ever worried!" Thankfully scooping the poop has never bothered me since.

All too soon Hank's prescribed ten minutes were up and we brought him back inside. We kept him on the lead and walked him round our open plan downstairs to let him see the layout of his new home. Then we took his lead off to see if he'd settle down on a bed of blankets I'd made on the floor. Unfortunately Hank had no intention of settling down when instead he could be running in circles around our kitchen island so there was nothing for it but to put him in his crate so that his leg would get the rest it needed. He went in happily and lay down, gazing at us intently. I took him out for a further ten minutes after dinner and then again just before we went to bed. Both times we tried to give him some time outside the crate but both times Hank showed no intention of resting so sadly back in the crate he went.

The next morning I woke up a bit earlier than normal, slightly nervous that Hank might have had a wee or poo in his crate. He hadn't although he did look relieved to see me and it was a bit of a wrestling match to get his IV bootie on him, so keen was he to go outside. Then it was back inside for breakfast and the first dose of his medication.

So life with Hank settled into an unchanging daily routine. First thing in the morning I'd take him out for his initial walk, then he'd come back in and have breakfast. Then he'd go back in the crate. He'd get another ten minutes mid-morning and then again around lunchtime. He'd eat dinner mid-afternoon followed by his fourth walk, then we'd go out again around 6:00 p.m. and last thing at night.

Obviously we couldn't get far in ten minutes so we either walked on Large Field behind our house or the communal lawn in the middle of First Flight Court. It must have been mind-numbingly boring for Hank but he never showed it; he was always just so pleased to escape the confines of his crate and spend some time outside. I especially enjoyed our walks last thing at night, just me and Hank in the darkness.

Fridays were exciting and a useful break from our routine as every Friday morning I'd take him to Kingsbrook Animal Hospital to have his cast and bandages changed. Hank always seemed overjoyed to see the Kingsbrook staff and they always greeted him like a long lost friend.

On the way to Kingsbrook, I'd often stop at Nallins Pond, the fishing lake and nature area on the other side of Fort Detrick to our house. It was a pleasant spot for a ten minute walk and made for a welcome change of scene. The pond was home to numerous ducks and geese so there were plenty of interesting smells to sniff and hopefully helped to remind Hank that there was a whole other world outside his crate and the immediate environs of First Flight Court.

The best bit about the visits to Kingsbrook was that Hank had to be sedated whilst his bandages were changed and he was always still dozy when I picked him up at 4:00 p.m. This meant that when I got him home he was usually able to have an hour or so out of his crate because he would lie down calmly and snooze rather than run around on his bad leg.

I soon discovered that putting the IV bag bootie on Hank was not an easy task, especially not first thing in the morning when he'd been in his crate all night and was desperate to go out. He frequently broke free from me as I was trying to put the bootie on and would then run round the kitchen island to frustrate my efforts to catch him.

"Hank, mind your leg!" I'd plead with him, terrified that he'd worsen his injury and I'd be sacked as a foster carer. Gradually I became quicker and more skilled at IV boot application and Hank began to realise that the sooner it went on the sooner he went outside. The other challenge of looking after Hank was making him take his medication. He didn't like it and was adept at eating every piece of kibble in his bowl without touching the two little tablets.

I started buying cans of wet food and added a little bit to his kibble every morning and afternoon so that the juice would disguise the tablets. That did the trick nicely. However for his midday meds I'd have to wrap the tablets in a piece of bread or cut a small square of cheese and hollow it out and place the tablet inside. The fact that Hank remained at a stable weight whilst he was with us was little short of a miracle. Limited exercise and daily treats of cheese and bread is not normally a recipe for remaining svelte and trim but Hank managed it.

However there was no getting away from the fact that Hank's life wasn't much fun. He spent the majority of his existence in a crate and he couldn't understand the good medical reasons why. For this reason I felt guilty if I ever had to leave him; I thought the least I could do was give him as much human company as possible.

Consequently those eight weeks were not particularly exciting for me either. An injured dog in a crate that couldn't go on long walks, chase a ball or even follow you around the house wasn't quite the dog experience I'd been hoping for. But conversely Hank's injury was the reason I had the pleasure of his company. And his company truly was a pleasure. I discovered that the simple presence of Hank induced in me a deep feeling of contentment; everything just felt more 'right'. There was a completely different energy in the house and I loved it.

So we made the best of our unusual situation. I'd often sit next to Hank's crate and chat to him and reassure him that his next trip outside was only a couple of hours away. I told him stories of our life back home and described all my favourite places in the Surrey Hills for hiking or mountain biking. I hoped that something in my voice conveyed the spirit of the outdoors and gave him hope that the crate was temporary and better days lay ahead – days filled with forests, new trails and the simple pleasure of choosing which fork in the path to take.

Despite my efforts, being cooped up in a crate with minimal time outside must have been verging on hellish for any dog, especially a foxhound. Unsurprisingly, Hank began to resist going back in his crate after a walk or a meal. I'd have to gently but firmly push him in, at which point he started putting one of his front paws up on the doorway of the crate and pushing back against me. It became a bit of a wrestling match between us until I resorted to simple bribery.

I started to throw a treat in for him, which worked brilliantly for about three days. Then Hank perfected the art of running in, gobbling up the treat and somehow turning round in his crate and running out again in a couple of milliseconds before I had the opportunity to shut the door. So I got faster at shutting him in and Hank reverted to the 'paws on the doorway' technique.

Sometimes he'd simply lie down wherever he was when he realised it was crate time again and refuse to get up. So I had to half cuddle and half slide him along to the crate, at which point he'd usually realise that resistance was futile. Our living room had polished wood flooring which made this much easier.

I will always be astonished that Hank never once snapped or growled at me during these battles. It just goes to show that dogs tolerate an awful lot from us. Hank was definitely not a particularly intelligent dog but perhaps deep down he realised that I was doing what I had to do in order to help his leg get better. I hoped we'd developed a bond, despite the crate between us.

About halfway through Hank's time with us Linda told me that the next time I took Hank in to Kingsbrook they would take the opportunity to neuter him. Frederick

County Animal Control had a policy of spaying and neutering all their animals before they were adopted so that they didn't perpetuate the cycle of unplanned breeding and more unwanted animals. Hank would go in to Kingsbrook on a Friday as usual but he'd return minus a couple of things.

I'm not sure if it was coincidence or not but we noticed a bit of a change in Hank after his neuter operation. He began to be a lot more affectionate with us and also took to carrying around a large cuddly red bone we'd bought him, whenever he was out of the crate. We started called it his 'blankie' and he'd insist on taking it outside with him and on subsequent visits to Kingsbrook, which the staff found highly amusing.

We'd had Hank for six weeks when Linda informed me that Kingsbrook were pleased with his progress and fully expected him to make a complete recovery. This was fantastic news and Linda told me I'd done a great job. Hank's bandages would be removed in a couple of weeks and then Hank would be ready to be adopted.

Linda wanted to start marketing Hank on Petfinder, a website Frederick County Animal Control used to showcase all their animals. I emailed Linda a few photos of him including one of him lying down after a Friday visit to the vet and one of him with his blankie bone. I hoped Hank's personality would shine through and someone out there would fall in love with his goofy face and big brown eyes. I also wrote a brief profile about him to really sell him to potential adopters. Hank couldn't speak for himself; I had to be his voice.

A couple of days after Hank's photos appeared on Petfinder, Linda called me with some good news. Not only had a family applied to adopt Hank but they were an army family and lived on Fort Detrick. She gave me their address and I realised their house was just the other side of Large Field. It was a two minute walk at the most.

The woman was called Penny and Linda gave me her number so that I could get in touch and arrange for them to come and meet Hank. I was slightly nervous as I waited for her to answer – what if I didn't like these people? How could I let Hank go to a new family if I didn't think they deserved him?

However Penny sounded lovely and told me how much they liked the photos of Hank and the profile I'd written. I was right, they did live two whole minutes away. We agreed to meet on Large Field at 4:30 p.m. that afternoon when her husband Trey was back from work so they could get acquainted with Hank and decide if they all suited each other.

At 4:29 p.m. Hank and I left our house and walked on to Large Field where Penny, Trey and their two young children were waiting for us. First impressions were good all round; they made all the right noises, exclaiming that Hank was a very handsome dog.

I started telling them all about him, trying to make him sound as interesting as possible. Then Penny asked if Hank ever barked in the house.

"No, not at all," I replied completely truthfully. "I've never ever heard him bark." Hank looked up at me and then did something he'd never done before. He barked. Three times.

I couldn't believe it. This was the first time that one of my foster dogs made me look stupid but it wasn't to be the last. I was speechless and just stared at Hank in shock.

"Hey, he's making a liar out of you," said Penny laughing.

"No, I promise you, that's the first time he's ever barked. Really!"

I don't think Penny believed me and I couldn't blame her. But for the record, that was honestly the first time Hank barked since I'd started fostering him. Why he chose that particular moment to exercise his vocal chords I'll never know but his comic timing was impeccable.

Unfortunately things went from embarrassing to worse. It was a cold December day and there was a light dusting of snow on the ground. Penny was suitably wrapped up and was wearing an expensive looking scarf around her neck, with one end hanging down her back. Temptingly down her back if you're an unruly foxhound intent on giving the worst possible impression to the people who want to offer you a home for the rest of your life.

Not two minutes after the barking, Hank spied Penny's scarf and jumped up, grabbed the end in his mouth and started shaking it and pulling Penny over.

"Hank! Stop that," I admonished him, frantically trying to extract Penny's scarf from his slobbery jaws.

Thankfully Penny, Trey and the kids were all laughing. Maybe this was meant to be and Hank knew they were his forever family and was simply trying to entertain them.

In any case, Hank's high-risk strategy worked. Penny told me they loved him and were definitely going to put an application in. A few days later Linda rang to let me know that they'd been interviewed and had passed. As soon as Kingsbrook signed Hank off then his new family would be able to take him home.

At our final check up at Kingsbrook, the vet told me that Hank's leg had completely recovered. There was no lasting damage and he would have full use of it in the future. I was over the moon; that news seemed to justify the eight weeks of enforced crate rest. I'll never know how Hank felt about it – I'm not sure dogs think in terms of short term costs versus long term benefits – but I hoped that when he was out running with Trey he'd realise that his foster carer and his veterinary team had always had his best interests at heart.

I was also quietly proud of myself. I'd done my job as a foster carer and looked after Hank in the way he deserved. Whilst I couldn't take any credit for the veterinary care Hank had received, I'd nonetheless been a part of the team that had rescued this stray and injured dog and given him a second chance at life. That felt rewarding in a profound way. I'd always been acutely conscious of the numerous ways that dogs help us, even though I'd never experienced it myself. Now I'd helped one of them and given something back; I was a part of the ancient and enduring bond between dogs and humans in a way I didn't know was possible all those years ago when I was merely a child who wanted a puppy.

The staff at Kingsbrook were all sorry to say goodbye to Hank. They had grown really fond of him and I thanked them all for taking such excellent care of him.

"Come on then Hank, let's get you home. This is a big day for you."

Penny, Trey and the kids were coming to collect their new dog at about 4:30 p.m. when Trey got home from work. This meant Hank and I had an entire, crate-free afternoon together and we made the most of it. The vet had said Hank could start normal walks immediately so I walked him over to Wild Field and back to our house along Fort Detrick's fence line. It was wonderful to forget all about the ten minute time limit and savour Hank's happiness at getting some decent exercise.

Back home I sat on the sofa and enjoyed the spectacle of Hank running round and round our downstairs. He seemed to be making up for lost time on his four perfectly functioning legs. He didn't stop all afternoon but ran circuits of our living room and dining room, occasionally jumping up on the sofa to say hello to me. Then all too soon the doorbell rang; Hank's forever family was ready to take him home. I didn't want a long goodbye and in any case, I knew I'd see him again soon as Penny had invited me round for coffee in the next few days.

I opened the door to four smiling and excited faces, handed over Hank's much-loved cuddly bone and the remainder of his food and knelt down in front of him.

"Be good Hank. Thank you for being my first dog. Take care of that leg."

I couldn't bring myself to say goodbye; it seemed too final. And then I remembered the perfect way to wish someone a lifetime of fun, travel and adventure.

"Happy trails Hank! Happy trails."

I handed the lead to Penny. Hank looked at me, a bit uncertain. But then the promise of another walk proved decisive. The dog I'd waited 30 years for trotted off with his new people, ready to start his future. He didn't even look back at me.

This wasn't quite the meaningful farewell I'd envisaged and Hank's apparent indifference stung a little. I knew our relationship was an unusual one and he was unlikely to feel much affection for someone who shut him in a crate for 23 hours a day. Nonetheless I had a sentimental notion that on some level Hank knew that I'd helped him recover from his injuries and forgave me for what I'd been obliged to do. Yet now I doubted whether we had any bond at all. However in just a couple of months Hank would answer that question by coming to the rescue when I needed him most.

CHAPTER 4

PUPPY LOVE

THAT EVENING STEVE and I went out to Firestones to celebrate the successful end of my inaugural fostering assignment and commiserate that our first, but hopefully not last, foster dog had left home. Steve asked me if I'd enjoyed the experience as much as I thought I would. Despite the fact that my first dog was a crated one, I'd loved it. The routine of having a dog suited me – the daily walks, the constant companionable presence, the placing of another's needs before your own. There was now no doubt in my mind at all that I did want my own dog one day.

However ironically I didn't want my own dog just yet; I'd loved fostering and found it even more rewarding than I'd expected. By making sure Hank took his medication, driving him to and from the vets, and enforcing the crate rest rules, I'd helped him on his way to a new life and that was a wonderful feeling. And as hard as it was to say goodbye, I knew I wanted to foster more dogs.

The next morning was somewhat strange – I had nobody to get up for. I didn't have to wrestle an IV bag bootie on a reluctant paw or feed anyone but myself. By mid-morning I felt lonely. Having Hank certainly restricted what I'd been able to do but now I had total freedom I didn't know what to do with it.

Thankfully it was nearly Christmas, our first one in the USA, and after a few days of post-Hank doldrums I had plenty to be getting on with. We had decided to spend our first Christmas in the US in a log cabin somewhere and we'd found the perfect one near Chester, Vermont. Americans tend to have beef for Christmas as they have turkey at Thanksgiving in late November. However I'd managed to source a frozen turkey from a local organic food company so we could have a traditional British Christmas lunch.

On 23rd December we packed up our car, complete with turkey and all the trimmings in a large cool box, and set out on the seven hour drive to Vermont. We didn't arrive at our cabin until after midnight but it was worth the long journey. The cabin was exactly what we'd hoped for – cozy and rustic but well equipped. It had a wood burning stove and a plentiful stack of wood, although Steve insisted on chopping a whole load more just for the log cabin authenticity of the experience.

We had a wonderful Christmas followed by a few days touring New Hampshire's White Mountains and going cross-country skiing in Bretton Woods. We then crossed back into Vermont for more skiing and drove back to Maryland via the Catskill Mountains in New York State.

After we returned from our Christmas vacation I informed Linda I was keen to foster again. To keep me occupied in the meantime I began volunteering at the shelter – walking dogs, cleaning out their cages, topping up their water or folding laundered towels.

I loved everything about volunteering at the shelter. Obviously I loved walking the dogs but I also enjoyed the more mundane tasks. Whenever I folded laundry I was freeing up a kennel tech to do something more skilled. Whenever I cleaned the windows I was contributing to the shelter's favourable public image, making people content to adopt from there.

I'd previously attended a volunteer induction session where Sean, the volunteer coordinator, had gently urged everyone to do the less glamorous jobs too. Dirty, smeared windows would not give a positive impression of the shelter and this might impact negatively on the animals. If members of the public thought that FCAC was a dirty and unprofessional outfit then they would be less inclined to adopt a dog or cat from there and that animal might lose their chance of a forever home. It was the best justification I'd ever heard for cleaning windows.

However the most enjoyable task at the shelter was supervising the 'meet and greets' between a dog and prospective adopters. Members of the public didn't need to make an appointment; they could stop by any time the shelter was open and view the dogs and cats that were up for adoption. One day I was working on the adoption floor when a mum, her teenage son and younger daughter entered. They started browsing the dogs, spending a few moments at each cage whilst an excited dog inside tried to win their hearts and minds.

I approached them with a smile.

"Hi guys, if you're interested in meeting any of the dogs just let me know and I can take them out to the outdoor enclosures so you can get to know them better."

"Thanks," said Mom, "Our dachshund died recently and we'd really love another one but I don't see any here."

At that exact moment the door from the examination room opened and Lauren, the senior veterinary technician, came out carrying a tiny dachshund with a pink collar around her neck. The kids' faces lit up when they saw her.

"Would you look at that!" exclaimed Mom.

"It's fate!" I said, grinning at the fortunate timing. "Hi Lauren, I think these people would like to meet this little girl."

Lauren smiled. "This is Rosie, isn't she gorgeous?"

The dachshund-loving family immediately surrounded Lauren, cooing over Rosie. Obviously they wanted to get to know her better so we went outside to one of the meet and greet enclosures where it immediately became apparent that this was love at first sight, in both directions. It was especially nice to see Teenage Son besotted with Rosie as a dainty little dachshund isn't necessarily the sort of dog you'd think a teenage boy would be interested in.

After spending about twenty minutes with Rosie the family agreed that she was definitely the dog for them and went back inside and put an application on her there and then. They were interviewed and approved a few days later and duly took Rosie home to her new life. This was the kind of happy ending born of sad beginnings that happened regularly at the shelter although Rosie's story is especially notable as she met her forever family before even setting her paws on the adoption floor.

I realise now that FCAC played an important role in my new life, over and above being the source of my foster dogs. It meant I wasn't simply Steve's wife; I had a role and a purpose that was purely mine. I also felt an immediate connection with some of the staff; people who had decided to make a profession of something that I was just beginning to volunteer at. Their love of animals seemed such an innate part of them; I wanted to be like that too. Back home, I'd never made any secret of the fact that I liked dogs and wanted one of my own one day. But I don't think I'd ever admitted the depth of my obsession, not least because I'd never been in a position to indulge it.

However moving to a new country confers on you the freedom to be a different version of yourself. I didn't have to explain or justify my love of dogs to anyone at FCAC – it was accepted as a given. I found it liberating.

The more I got to know Linda, the kennel manager who ran the foster care programme, the more I liked and respected her. She was patient and approachable although I sensed an air of sadness about her. Unfortunately I wasn't imagining this. Linda always wore a rectangular pendant around her neck of a gold star on a white background with a red border. I had a feeling I'd read about this symbol somewhere and thanks to Google discovered that this identified Linda as a 'Gold Star Mom', an American mother who's lost a child in war. I later found out that Linda's son, Corporal Kurt Shea, had been killed in Afghanistan on 10th May 2010, just five days before Steve flew safely home. There but for the grace of God.

Lauren, the veterinary technician, became a good friend. Always smiling, she was hugely dedicated to the animals in her care and unfailingly helpful to the volunteers. The Director of FCAC was called Mr Domer. A larger than life and commanding character, he had previously been Acting Chief of the Frederick Police Department and had a background in training police dogs.

Mr Domer had been instrumental in establishing a scheme whereby FCAC provided work experience to non-violent inmates in the Frederick County prison system. These guys did the same kinds of jobs that I did as a volunteer – walking dogs, folding laundry, and cleaning the enclosures. They were hard working, friendly and showed genuine affection for the dogs they helped to care for. They were also the 'go to guys' for walking the stronger, more excitable dogs. It struck me that this programme was an innovative way of giving an inmate new skills and a sense of pride in order to maximise their chances of rehabilitation.

Dogs don't know your background and won't judge you for mistakes you've made in your life. They're also a great leveler. On several occasions I found myself – a white, middle class, graduate wife of an army officer – stacking clean towels or mopping out kennels with an African-American inmate who'd probably had none of the advantages I'd had in life. And yet in that setting we were simply two dog lovers, performing an ostensibly menial task with a higher purpose of enabling the shelter to run smoothly and send the incarcerated dogs of Frederick County to new homes. Maybe that was why those men had such an affinity with the shelter dogs; they knew what it was like to lose your freedom.

The human contingent of FCAC was completed by an array of kennel technicians and the animal control officers, uniformed god-like beings who possessed firearms and the power to arrest people who broke Frederick Country's animal welfare laws. I still want to be an animal control officer when I grow up.

At the beginning of February Linda came to see me and asked if I would be interested in assisting in FCAC's on-site spay and neuter clinic. I was unsure about whether I wanted to do this and admitted to Linda that I was pretty squeamish. However after more of Linda's brand of gentle yet unyielding persuasion I agreed to meet with Carol, the volunteer who ran the Monday morning session, in order to find out more.

Carol immediately struck me as a committed and experienced volunteer, albeit a rather intimidating one. It was obvious that she didn't think much of my squeamishness and viewed my reluctance to volunteer in the clinic as a lack of dedication to the shelter. Maybe it was to prove her wrong or maybe it was because I'm often drawn to doing things I have no experience of, but I agreed to give the spay and neuter clinic a try.

My first Monday morning did not go well; I spent the entire time trying not to throw up. I'd never done anything remotely like this before and the literal blood and guts was too much for me. I hardly said a word and I'm not sure how helpful I was. I suspect the team wondered why I was there and so did I. However I persevered and to my surprise, after a few weeks I actually began to enjoy it. Partly it was because I could see that the spay and neuter programme was a crucial way to reduce the number of unwanted puppies and kittens in circulation and partly it was the extremely pleasant and intelligent company of the vet, Dr C, the other volunteer, MaryJane and of course Carol.

MaryJane, an attractive and friendly woman who I liked immediately, was a senior HIV research scientist who worked at the National Cancer Institute on Fort Detrick. As a dog lover who didn't have one of her own, she volunteered in the clinic every Monday morning in order to enjoy a regular 'dog fix'.

Back when Steve and I first moved to Frederick we'd heard frequent adverts on the local radio station for the Sgt David J Smith Memorial Golf Tournament in honour of a Frederick native who'd been killed in Afghanistan in January 2010, halfway during Steve's deployment. I soon learned that MaryJane was Sgt Smith's mother and the organiser of the golf tournament. It struck me as incredibly poignant that there were two 'Gold Star Moms' working at the same small county animal shelter.

Carol was a cartographer and worked for a GIS solutions company. She wasn't intimidating at all once you got to know her and we became firm friends as soon as she realised I was a genuine animal lover. As for Dr C, he was an absolute gentleman. If Hollywood were to make a film about an elderly and genial small town vet then Dr C would be their man. The 'C' stood for something apparently unpronounceable so Dr C insisted on being referred to by his initial, not wanting to put anyone to the trouble of pronouncing his surname. He was patient and kind with both animals and novice volunteers, which made for a relaxed and pleasant atmosphere in the clinic. I consider myself privileged to have worked for him.

As much as I enjoyed my Monday mornings at the spay and neuter clinic, it was hard work. We had to arrive at the shelter for 6:30 a.m. in order to give all the dogs an opportunity for a toilet break outside. Then they were all moved into smaller cages in the recovery room, across the corridor from the operating room. We'd then set up the operating room with all the necessary equipment prior to Dr C's prompt arrival at 7:00 a.m.

We also had to prepare the surgical packs, restrain each animal as they were receiving their injection of anaesthetic and disinfect the operating table between operations. It was remarkable how compliant most dogs and cats were and we rarely had any problems. Did they sense that we were helping, not harming, them?

It was especially gratifying when we had a dog in the clinic that I'd known and walked whilst volunteering. It meant that someone had applied to adopt them, they had passed the interview and the dog was being spayed or neutered prior to going to their forever home.

One aspect of volunteering at the shelter was seeing somewhat eclectic mixes of dog breeds. A dog in one of my early spay and neuter sessions was a pit bull-corgi cross named Spud. Spud's body was unmistakably corgi-like in terms of size and shape but he had a dark brindle coat and a pit bull head. I told the team about the Queen's love of corgis and joked that maybe I could adopt Spud for her. Dr C was particularly tickled to think of a pit bull mix roaming the opulent rooms of Buckingham Palace.

Carol was a prolific volunteer. In addition to running the spay and neuter clinic she was an experienced foster carer, fostering dogs, cats and even ferrets. Getting to know Carol was to prove hugely advantageous for my own fostering career.

One cold, grey and snowy morning in February a couple of days after my first spay and neuter clinic, my phone rang. It was Linda and she had the best news – she wanted to give me a puppy.

"Hi Jenni, I wondered if you'd like to foster a female German shepherd puppy for two weeks."

A puppy, only what I'd always wanted for the past thirty years! We had a friend coming to stay from the UK so I could only take the puppy for three days but Linda agreed that would be fine and another foster carer would take over.

I drove down to the shelter, barely able to contain my excitement. I was finally getting a puppy of my own. Well, for three days anyway. Not only that but like Hank, she'd been picked up as stray so I was allowed to name her. By the time I got to the shelter I'd decided on 'Lily'. I followed Linda into the quarantine room and in one of the cages was the most beautiful creature I'd ever seen. She was a dark fawn colour with a black ring half way down her tail, a black face and bright inquisitive eyes. As far as I was concerned it was puppy love at first sight.

"Oh she's absolutely gorgeous!" I gushed at a smiling Linda. "Hello Lily, would you like to come home with me?"

Linda opened the cage and Lily confidently bounded into my arms. I scooped her up and she immediately licked my face all over as if to tell me not to worry, she was going to take care of me.

Puppy breath is the most amazing smell in the universe. When you first smell it you think it's a bit disgusting but about two seconds after the top notes of Eau de Petit Chien hit you, something switches in your brain and you realise it is in fact that most delicious and life enhancing scent you've ever smelled. Those puppy pheromones definitely triggered an immediate bonding response in me and I felt instantly protective of Lily.

"I think she likes you," smiled Linda.

"Oh I hope so!" I replied. "We're going to have lots of fun Lily, are you ready to come home with me?"

Linda kitted me out with some puppy food, treats, a crate and a pack of puppy pads as Lily obviously wasn't house trained. Lily seemed completely unfazed as Linda and I encouraged her into the crate for the short drive back to my house. I placed my precious cargo lengthways on the front seat and moved the seat forward so the crate was securely held against the dashboard. I was concerned that a car ride with a complete stranger might remind her of being picked up as a stray but Lily seemed perfectly at ease. Hopefully this meant her ordeal of either escaping or being abandoned had been a short one and she wasn't too traumatised by it.

Once home I carried Lily's crate into the living room and let her out. Then I remembered what had happened when we brought Hank home so I put a lead on her and took her straight outside. Happily Lily had both a wee and a poo so I was able to give her a treat and lots of fuss as a reward for going where I wanted her to go.

It was a cold February and we'd had a light dusting of snow in the past few days. I'd taken to wearing fleece lined, moccasin style slippers inside the house and once back inside I took my shoes and socks off and put my slippers on. Being of a slightly untidy disposition I left my discarded socks on the floor which Lily pounced on with glee and tore off around the living room, shaking my poor sock vigorously until it was definitely dead. I couldn't help but laugh and managed to retrieve my sock by exchanging it for a treat.

However Lily then turned her attention to my feet and my bare ankles above the line of my moccasins. She pounced and numerous razor sharp puppy teeth sank into my ankle. She let go briefly and attacked my other ankle. It hurt – I'd just discovered that puppy teeth are surprisingly sharp.

Still, that's no excuse for what I did next. Stupidly I squealed and ran away from this baby velociraptor. This was obviously the worst thing I could have done because Lily instantly decided this was the best game ever and pursued me at full puppy speed which was surprisingly fast. I leapt on the sofa; Lily did too, which was quite impressive considering her size. But I was at least able to grab her and keep her away from my feet.

So I'd just taught my new pup that biting my feet got her a game of chase with exciting high-pitched noises and then a snuggle on the sofa, all within twenty minutes of getting her home. I know I was a novice at practical puppy training but I had done a lot of reading around the theory and I did know better than to squeal enticingly and run away. All puppies nip and I should have been prepared for this scenario and been ready to employ the 'yelp and shun' method; you do exactly as the term suggests – yelp when the puppy nips you and then ignore them for a brief period of time. This teaches them that they've hurt you, you're not enjoying the 'game' and that it won't get them your attention – quite the reverse. In this way, the puppy learns 'bite inhibition', or in other words, stops nipping people.

Of course ideally puppies should mostly have learnt this lesson at the point they leave their litter and become part of a human family. They'd already have a solid grounding in bite inhibition from natural play with their littermates and mum – from their siblings they learn that being nipped hurts and from their mum they learn there'll be a consequence. Although instead of a shun, the mother dog tends to inflict a retaliatory nip which acts as a deterrent. But Lily had been deprived of her canine family far too young and it was up to me to fulfill that teaching role now. Fortunately Lily was a smart girl and we made definite progress in the three days we had her.

There was no way of knowing how long Lily had spent as a stray but the experience hadn't seemed to affect her negatively. She was confident, full of personality and brimming with energy. The next time I took her outside for a toilet break, we went on a short walk around the back of the house and ventured a short way on to Large Field. I kept her on the lead for the first five minutes but once we were at the farthest point from the road I let her off for a run. She was incredibly fast for her size and age and easily kept up with me jogging around.

After about ten minutes we went back inside and she flopped down on the living room rug and watched me sleepily whilst I packed the dishwasher. Linda had told me that getting used to the noise of normal household activities was an important aspect of foster care as it's obviously not something the shelter can replicate. When I'd finished I looked up and my little pup was fast asleep. That was a positive sign as she realised that the sound of clattering plates and cutlery was nothing to be scared of and it was safe to let her guard down and snooze.

After about an hour she woke up so I took her straight outside where to my delight she successfully peed and pooped again.

"Oh good girl Lily! Good girl, you clever thing," I crooned, letting her know that peeing and pooping outside was exactly what I wanted her to do and rewarding her with a couple of training treats. I was determined to make some housetraining progress in the short time I had her, to show Linda that I knew what I was doing and could be entrusted with all future puppies that crossed FCAC's threshold.

Later that afternoon I was sitting on the floor with Lily and playing tug with one of the puppy chew toys Linda had sent with her.

"Steve is going to adore you," I promised her. "I think we'll both want to keep you!"

And then I realised – I hadn't actually told Steve. I'd been so focused on Lily that it hadn't occurred to me to let him know that we had another foster dog. I decided that I might as well keep it a surprise until he got home. I knew my husband well enough to know he wouldn't mind.

Shortly after 5:00 p.m. I heard the whirr of the automatic garage door opening and then the connecting door to the house swung open.

"Hi babe," called Steve from the small lobby area round the corner from the rest of our downstairs.

"Hi babe, guess what!" I replied picking Lily up. "I have a surprise for you!"

Steve came round the corner and saw Lily in my arms. Thankfully but unsurprisingly his face lit up with a big smile.

"Hey, who's this?"

"This is Lily and we're fostering her for a few days. Isn't she gorgeous! Sorry, I've been having so much fun I completely forgot to tell you!"

Lily was wriggling excitedly, longing to greet this new person. I put her down and tail wagging, she happily pounced on Steve's feet. Steve crouched down, clearly as taken with her as I was.

"Hello Lily, let me look at you. You're a beauty," he said, scratching Lily behind the ears and picking her up. He grinned at me. "So just how happy are you today?"

"Pretty happy! Finally got a puppy!"

We both agreed that Lily didn't look exactly like a German Shepherd puppy as she didn't have the typical black cape along her back. I did a Google search and discovered that Lily most resembled a Malinois, one of the four types of Belgian Shepherd.

As any Malinois fan will tell you, they're like German Shepherds only better. In the US they're humorously known as 'landsharks' or 'malligators'. I'm clearly not the only one who's been on the wrong end of razor sharp Malinois teeth. One meme I saw on a Malinois Facebook page had the great quote, "Malinois – because German Shepherds need heroes too." Only a few months later, a Belgian Malinois named Cairo would make the news as a crucial member of the Navy SEAL team that raided Osama Bin Laden's compound in Pakistan.

Steve and I spent the evening playing with our new family member. We lay on the floor whilst Lily happily ran between us, getting petted and fussed over and periodically pouncing on our heads. It was engrossing, strangely intimate and a completely different dynamic to having Hank in the house. Lily playfully demanded our constant attention and we were only too willing to oblige. And although I'd seen Steve with his family's dogs on numerous occasions, I'd never see him with a puppy before. As I watched my husband interact with this vulnerable little animal I saw him through a different prism. There was a new shade of tenderness to him that was incredibly attractive and got me thinking about something that we'd previously discussed but agreed to postpone. Fostering dogs was affecting me in unexpected ways.

That night brought a lot more snow and a welcome surprise for us in the morning when the Commandant of Fort Detrick declared the base closed until lunchtime to allow the maintenance crews time to clear the roads safely. This meant Steve had an unexpected morning off work. He decided to use it productively and build a quinzhee in our back yard. A quinzhee is like an igloo but is made by heaping up snow and then hollowing it out instead of cutting and stacking blocks of snow.

Unsurprisingly Lily took a great interest in Steve's endeavour and took it upon herself to help out. Steve would heap up the snow and Lily would pounce on it, then run around circling the now collapsed mound of snow and then pounce on it again. I'm not sure who was having more fun, Steve or Lily. However after a while Lily and I retreated inside, as I didn't want her to get too cold.

For the rest of the morning Lily and I would periodically go outside for a toilet break and to see how Steve was doing. Lily was having the time of her short life, enjoying this new experience with her new people. I knew I had to be careful not to over-exercise her but I needn't have worried; when Lily grew tired she'd simply sit down and look up at me. That meant she wanted me to pick her up for a break. Then she'd wriggle when she wanted to go down again.

After a few hours Steve had made a surprisingly respectable looking quinzhee. It wasn't massive, just big enough for him to curl up inside with a deliriously happy Malinois puppy. As great as the shelter was, Lily simply wouldn't have had an experience like this there. Man and dog, 'surviving' together in Ice Age-esque conditions.

Lily and I spent the afternoon and the following day playing, walking in the snow, snoozing on the sofa and playing some more. She was getting the hang of house training and would go and sit by the patio door if she needed to go out. I was rigidly following the puppy house training rules and took her out after a sleep, after food, after a bout of playing, plus every twenty minutes. It meant I didn't have time to do anything other than completely focus on Lily but that was fine by me. Every hour that passed was a countdown to giving up my second dog and I didn't want to waste a minute. It had been a wonderful experience, quite literally a childhood dream come true. Almost thirty years previously, I'd promised my parents that I wouldn't get bored of a puppy. My inner child felt vindicated; my love of dogs hadn't been a phase – it had been a premonition.

On our final evening with Lily, Steve and I sat on the floor letting her run between the two of us, pausing only to nibble a toe or an ear occasionally. I didn't want to think about the fact I'd be taking her back to the shelter in only twelve hours. I half-jokingly suggested to Steve that we should keep her and he patiently reiterated the reasons we couldn't get a dog of our own yet – when our two years in Frederick were up we were going home to an apartment and full time jobs. He reminded me that I knew that and that was why I was fostering and hadn't simply gone to the shelter for a one-off visit to choose our own dog.

He was right of course. I was just impatient. Steve promised me we would have our own dog one day and in the meantime fostering was proving a wonderful experience. We'd already fostered two dogs; maybe we'd get lucky and be asked to take a third. I hoped so.

Conscious of the damage a non-housetrained puppy could do to carpets we'd kept Lily downstairs which was a mixture of polished wood and tiled floors. Both were easy to wipe in the event of a housetraining blip. When we went to bed, we put Lily in her crate and she always settled perfectly happily. However on her last morning with us I started to question why we did it this way and the truth is, it was because Steve had grown up with the rule that dogs never go upstairs. I had absorbed that rule without ever challenging it and accepted that when we got our own dog, he or she would remain firmly downstairs.

But that morning I decided it was a stupid rule that didn't meet my needs. I was going to miss Lily hugely and the thought of spending some of the precious time we had left separated by an arbitrary convention that dogs must never experience certain parts of your house seemed ridiculous.

I fed Lily her breakfast and took her outside as usual. But then instead of putting her back in her crate whilst I went back upstairs to shower and dress, I took her up with me. Steve was just getting out of the shower.

"Oh, we have a visitor," stated Steve, a slight frown on his face.

"Yes." I replied, a definite tone of 'this is what's happening' in my voice. "I've decided I don't really understand why dogs can't come into the bedroom and I think it's silly."

I put Lily down and she immediately ran over to Steve and helpfully licked water off his feet and ankles. Then she spied a threatening towel on the floor, attacked it enthusiastically and gave it a vigorous shake in her little jaws.

"See, isn't it lovely having her up here with us," I said to Steve, smiling.

"Er, yes, I'm just not used to having dogs upstairs," replied my husband, the faintest hint of a smile flashing across his face as Lily licked his feet again.

As we got ready together, Lily ran around our bedroom and en suite bathroom, stealing Steve's socks, grabbing the cord on my bathrobe, and generally getting in the way. She was loving every minute of it and it felt completely right to have her there. Steve managed to keep a disapproving look on his face for an entire minute before he crumbled and admitted that Lily's presence made getting ready for work a lot more fun.

Once I was dressed it was time to take Lily back to FCAC. I'd only had her three days but this was as difficult as saying goodbye to Hank and I had to blink back tears during the short drive to the shelter. Another dog I'd fallen in love with and another farewell.

At least Linda had welcome news for us on the adoption front. FCAC operated a waiting list for people who wished to adopt certain breeds and she had already contacted a family about Lily and arranged for them to come and meet her. So my first puppy was going to be someone else's forever dog soon and that was the whole unselfish point of fostering.

I took Lily out of the crate to say goodbye. She nuzzled into me, completely unaware that her world was about to change again. I inhaled her intoxicating puppy smell for the last time.

"Don't worry, we'll take care of her," Linda assured me.

"Happy trails Lily," I whispered and handed her over to Linda.

Although I'd only had Lily for three days, she'd given me a lot to think about. I was struck by how quickly Steve and I adapted to a caring role and how natural it felt to be a family of three. And I'd been fascinated by watching this inquisitive and fearless puppy learn about her world and begin to understand how things worked in our family – simple things such as sitting by the door if she needed to go out and her endearing excitement when Steve came home from work.

I'd also learnt that I didn't need an arbitrary 'human only' space; that concept now seemed irrational to me. If those early humans had insisted on a 'human only' space around the campfire or their sleeping area then I suspect the dog would never have come into existence in the first place. It seemed to me that humans created the dog by doing away with inter-species barriers. Allowing Lily free run of our bedroom felt like the least I could do for the continuation of the greatest friendship in history.

CHAPTER 5

SAM

A COUPLE OF weeks after Lily went back to the shelter, Linda rang me and told me she had a dog who required long term fostering. Sam was an extremely fearful beagle, so fearful that he was a suspected abuse case. He had been surrendered by a woman who'd explained that she was moving and couldn't take him, a sadly common excuse. The shelter environment had not suited him at all and whenever anyone approached his cage he would shrink into the farthest corner and give off 'please leave me alone' vibes. Obviously this was a problem in itself as who wants to go through life that scared. However it also meant that his chances of adoption were poor; prospective adopters tended to pass by the anti-social dog cowering in a corner. The decision had been made to place him in foster care in the hope he would improve once he was out of the shelter. Unfortunately this hadn't worked.

Linda explained that Carol had been fostering Sam for a few weeks and I remembered her mentioning her new foster dog during one of the Monday morning surgeries. Carol was an experienced and doting foster carer but Sam wasn't doing well with her. She had been honest enough to admit that she wasn't making any progress with him and that furthermore, Sam seemed scared of her. She suspected that she reminded him of one of his previous people and assumed those memories were not fond ones.

Sam's situation and probable background showed how Frederick County Animal Control was often at the mercy of limited and unreliable information about their animals. When someone came to surrender their dog or cat, they tended to spend as little time as possible at the drop off desk, which was located to the rear of the shelter, away from the public entrance to the Pet Adoption side. The member of staff at the desk would naturally try and get as much information as possible about the animal and the reasons why they were no longer wanted.

However if someone has abused their dog then they're unlikely to admit that to the institution with the power to take legal action against them. If it subsequently became clear that the animal was displaying signs of having been abused then the person that did it was long gone and had possibly given a false name and address anyway. And so it fell to FCAC staff and foster carers to do their best to decipher what an animal was telling them.

In Sam's case, both Linda and Carol felt that it was worth trying him with a different foster carer, ideally one who was at home during the day. Linda suggested me and as Carol knew me from the spay and neuter clinic, she readily agreed. A useful lesson that the more you volunteer for, the more opportunities come your way.

Obviously I told Linda I'd love to foster Sam. It was a Friday and Carol wanted to spend a final weekend with him so we agreed that she'd bring him to the spay and neuter clinic on Monday morning and I'd take him home from there.

Over the weekend I did a lot of reading about nervous and fearful dogs and a lot of thinking. I was conscious that this fostering assignment represented a step up for me and the kind of task I was being trusted with. Hank had required a friendly jailer and reliable taxi driver. Puppies – whilst not easy – are straightforward in terms of what they need. But Sam would be different. I was going to have to gain his trust, understand his fears without reinforcing them and teach him that some people could be trusted and were worth spending time with.

Furthermore I was aware that an experienced and skilled foster carer had made no progress with him. Linda had hinted that Sam was on the verge of being considered unadoptable before Carol took him on. Frederick County Animal Control was not a no-kill shelter and it didn't have infinite space and resources. I knew that as a last resort, animals deemed unadoptable were sometimes euthanised. I was possibly Sam's last chance.

In recent weeks I'd done a lot of reading about the 'positive reinforcement' method of dog training, a gentle and humane technique that works by rewarding the behaviour you want and ignoring undesirable behaviour. In simple terms, the theory is that a dog is more likely to repeat behaviour that earns them a reward and will stop doing anything that costs them your attention. This methodology appealed to my belief that dogs are our friends as opposed to subordinates that humans have a right to dominate. It struck me that positive reinforcement would be key to getting through to Sam and I resolved to reward him for any sociable or otherwise positive interaction with me.

On Monday morning I woke up feeling excited, conscious that I was on the verge of a new experience in fostering. Luckily we had a short list at the clinic that morning and they were all males – neuter operations are considerably quicker than spays as the parts being removed are outside the body. So after only a couple of hours Carol took me into the quarantine room to meet Sam.

There in a crate against the back wall was a gorgeous tri colour beagle. He was curled up on his bed, which took up half of his crate, but as soon as we opened the door and went in he sprang up and then backed himself into a corner as best he could. His head was down and he could barely look at us. Then as we approached he started to tremble slightly. My heart went out to him immediately. A human had made him this way and now it was this human's job to undo the damage.

The crate belonged to the shelter but Carol had bought the bed; she kindly told me to keep it so that he had something he was used to. She reported that his crate was the place he seemed most comfortable and encouraged me to continue using it. I didn't say anything but I immediately wondered whether enabling his fears by letting him hide away was actually doing more harm than good.

Carol explained that it always took a while to entice Sam out of his crate so we decided against getting him out now. It would be better for me to take him straight home and I privately thought it might be easier to get him out at my house rather than the shelter. So I carried his crate to my car and Carol carried the bag of food and his lead that she was also kindly donating. I placed Sam's crate in the boot and stepped back to let Carol say goodbye. I could see she was upset. In her mind she'd failed Sam. In actual fact she'd saved him once and had just saved him again by being generous spirited enough to admit defeat so that he got another chance. I thanked her for the opportunity and promised I'd do my best for him.

When we got home I carried Sam's crate with him in it into the living room and set it down in a corner against the wall and near the sofa. Then I opened the door. Sam was cowering in the corner again, his eyes almost popping out of his head in fear. It was such a shame that his demeanour was so off putting to potential adopters because he was a handsome dog – a classic tri colour beagle with a black back trimmed with brown, and a white chest and legs with brown speckles. He had deep brown eyes in a brown face dissected by a white strip that ran from the tip of his nose to the top of his forehead. I imagined he could look rather distinguished in the right circumstances.

But these were not the right circumstances and Sam was desperately unhappy. I decided the best thing to do was ignore him for a while, not as a punishment for undesirable behaviour but to avoid stressing him any further. I left the crate door open and busied myself bringing in his food and filling a water bowl for him. Then I pottered around doing a few chores so that Sam could get used to me. He remained sitting up tensely in his crate, eyeing me warily.

Under normal circumstances I would have taken Sam out as soon as we got home to let him have a wee and poo if he needed one, and to establish that wees and poos happened outside. But given his fear I felt it was wiser to let him decompress for a while and show him that I presented no threat. An accident in the house could be easily rectified; making him scared of me within minutes of getting him home would not be as easy to clear up.

After almost an hour Sam still showed no signs of wanting to leave the safe environment of his crate. He did however seem slightly less petrified. I decided enough was enough and he had to come out at some point. I'd stocked up on dog treats over the weekend and Carol had told me that Sam loved cheese most of all so I'd also bought a packet of pre-cut cheese cubes. I grabbed a couple from the fridge, picked up his lead and sat down a couple of feet away from him.

"Come on Sam, time for a walk."

Sam stared at me, his eyes telling me he didn't trust me at all. I slowly leaned forward and placed a piece of cheese just outside the door of his crate. Sam ignored it, his eyes fixed on me, the threat deemed more of a priority than the treat. I got up slowly and went upstairs for a couple of minutes so Sam could eat the cheese without worrying that I was going to pounce on him. When I came back down it had gone.

"Ok Sam, good boy! I'm glad you do actually eat!"

I placed another piece just outside his crate to reinforce he'd done a good thing and then went and stood by the window, only half looking at Sam. After a few seconds I saw movement out of the corner of my eye and when I turned round I saw Sam tentatively venture half a step outside the crate and quickly gobble up the cheese.

"Oh good boy! Right, let's go walking."

I reached in to Sam's crate, clipped the lead on and stood up. Sam stayed put, so I reached in and gently lifted him out. I could feel him trembling.

"I'm sorry Sam but we've got to go outside now. You can't stay in there forever."

I put him down and he immediately lay down and half leopard-crawled behind me to the patio door. Carol had warned me about his leopard-crawling and told me it was a sign of extreme fear, not disobedience. Although I'd been expecting it, it was upsetting to see a dog so scared and to know that I was the immediate cause. But we had to get over this hurdle; Sam couldn't stay inside indefinitely. Due to his extreme reluctance and fear I assumed that our walk would be a short one but I was wrong. As soon as we stepped outside Sam was transformed. He sniffed the air, lifted his face to the weak February sun and his whole body language seemed to change. Never mind the crate, it was the outdoors where Sam felt most at ease.

We walked for a couple of hours – around the fence line, through a small copse that bordered the other side of the housing zone and along the edge of Wild Field that led down to Nallins Pond. It was a revelatory experience and Sam proved he was a completely different dog outside. He was ballsy (despite a recent neuter operation) and confident, walking with a swagger and compulsively sniffing random patches of ground or clumps of grass. We would never walk further than a few steps before his beagle nose picked up another interesting smell that would have to be fully investigated before we could go any further.

The change in Sam was so dramatic that I privately wondered how much Carol had walked him. Surely she would have mentioned the difference between Indoor Sam and Outdoor Sam if she'd known about it? I wondered whether, with the best intentions, she'd been overly cautious about exacerbating his fear and had opted to avoid taking him into the big wide world when actually that was exactly what he needed.

Back home, Sam reverted to the scared little chap I'd collected from the shelter and slunk into his crate as soon as I took his lead off. But I felt elated. I'd seen the dog he could be and being outdoors was the key to unlocking the real Sam.

When Steve arrived home he wisely ignored Sam at first to let him get used to yet another new and frightening person. Sam seemed unsure what to make of this additional human in the house – I suspected he felt outnumbered. That evening he mostly stayed in his crate, only venturing out for a drink of water whilst we were through in the dining room. Steve was horrified at how fearful Sam was; he'd never known a dog like that before.

After dinner we both took Sam out for another walk. I had to put the lead on him when he was still in his crate and lift him out again but as soon as we got outside the confident little beagle persona returned. Steve agreed that the change in him was dramatic. After our walk I sat on the patio with Sam for a while, looking up at the stars and mulling over the events of the day. I gazed at Sam and wondered what he was thinking. In just one day he'd left Carol's house, gone back to the shelter that he hated and then left the shelter with a brand new person. He must have been feeling scared, confused and alone. And underlying that was the abuse and trauma he almost certainly suffered before ending up at the shelter. I was filled with resolve to show Sam that he wasn't alone anymore and ensure he got the life he deserved. But could I, a novice foster carer, really turn him around?

The next day Sam began to venture out of his crate of his own free will and his excursions became more frequent over the following days. In line with the positive reinforcement philosophy, I placed a treat down on the floor whenever Sam ventured out of his crate and then retreated slightly so he was comfortable taking it. Gradually I stayed closer and closer to the treat and then started giving him the treat myself, to show that I was no threat and to establish a positive association to interacting with me. This worked well and after a few days Sam was consistently taking treats from me.

Similarly, Steve and I had decided that the best way to deal with Sam's extreme fearfulness was to ignore it. I knew that Sam wasn't showing fear as an attention seeking-ploy – he genuinely was scared – but as he got more used to me I didn't want to fall into the trap of rewarding his fear. And if we reacted to whatever Sam was scared of then it would also reinforce to Sam that he was right to be afraid.

So for example if one of us dropped a piece of cutlery or knocked a book off the arm of the sofa, Sam would jump up and scurry away from us to the refuge of his crate. Instead of comforting him or talking in a concerned tone or admonishing each other for scaring Sam, we simply acted like nothing had happened. In fact, we made a point of acting relaxed and talking in a cheerful and calm tone of voice to show him that the noise of something landing on the floor or of plates being stacked together was not a precursor to something awful happening; it was just normal life.

And if one of us got too close to Sam and he hunched his shoulders or moved away from us, we wouldn't force him to interact but similarly we wouldn't pander to his fear either. If he ran into his crate I'd respect his decision and his personal space and wouldn't try and pet him. However I might go and sit on the sofa near his crate and read for a few minutes. Then when he seemed calmer I'd place a dog treat or a piece of cheese just outside his crate and pop upstairs for a few minutes, giving him the opportunity to step outside his safe space and literally taste the delights of the big bad world. My theory was this would teach him that I'd never scare him intentionally but equally he wasn't getting rid of me and as I was the source of food that was a good thing.

Sam was still using his crate with his bed inside it that Carol had bought him. However I also bought him another bed which I placed outside his crate as an alternative option. Many dogs love their crate and view it as a safe and cozy den. With Sam, I felt we'd moved beyond that and his crate had become an unhealthy emotional crutch. I wanted Sam to have the option of a bed both inside and outside his personal safe space as I had a theory that his choice of bed would tell me a lot about how he was feeling. And if he picked the bed that was outside his crate then that would tell me he was feeling more confident. At night I purposefully left the door of his crate open so that he could get up and wander around if he wanted. I wanted to get to the point where he viewed our entire house as his safe space and I couldn't achieve that if it was off limits at certain times.

In the first few days Carol had sent me a few emails asking how Sam was getting on. I told about the 'two beds' plan and giving him the freedom of the house and she was sceptical to the point of telling me I was wrong and was going to make things worse. However I was certain this was the right thing to do. I respected Carol's opinion but by her own selfless admission she'd made no progress with Sam and this was my task now.

Gradually my approach started to pay off and within a few days we noticed Sam becoming more confident. He was less hunched over, spent more time in his non-crated bed and his eyes lost their wide-eyed and 'protruding on stalks' look. One morning I came downstairs and for the first time Sam wasn't in his crate; he was in the bed I'd bought him. And what's more, he stayed there and didn't retreat into the crate as I made him his breakfast. I was sure this was a positive sign. It was; Sam used the non-crated bed from then on.

Later that day I had another promising indication that we were making progress. I'd gone upstairs to sort some laundry and when I came out of our en suite bathroom I saw Sam peering round the bedroom door at me. He turned tail and scarpered downstairs immediately but I was overjoyed at this development. Sam actually cared where I was and came to find me.

After that I made sure to go upstairs for the sake of it several times a day, just to see what Sam would do. He started to follow me up every time and began to venture into our bedroom. One afternoon I was lying on the bed reading whilst waiting for Sam to make his appearance. I saw him peer round the bedroom door and then tentatively creep into the room.

"Hi Sam" I said in a soft voice but then ignored him and carried on reading. Sam took a few more steps and then lay down in the middle of our bedroom floor, let out a deep contented sigh and went to sleep. This was huge progress and I was ecstatic for both of us. This was something I'd wanted for as long as I could remember – a dog who would keep me company no matter what I was doing. And it showed that Sam trusted me enough to come and find me and sleep near me.

I was certain that the long walks I took Sam on were a big part of what was making him more confident indoors. And I loved them too. Hank had been injured and Lily had been too young but with Sam I understood the need for twice daily walks and I didn't find it a chore. A shared adventure in the outdoors, even if it was just a walk around the base or Baker Park in downtown Frederick, was the essence of having a dog as far as I was concerned.

At the weekend Steve and I took Sam up to Frederick Municipal Forest, known by everyone as 'the watershed', for a long hike. The watershed comprised 7,000 acres of dense forest and numerous small ponds only about a fifteen minute drive from our house. It was popular with walkers and mountain bikers and hunting was permitted in certain areas. We obviously couldn't take Sam off the lead but we let him decide where we went and so spent three hours at the mercy of a beagle's nose. Sam seemed to have an aversion to the official trails so we dutifully ran through ditches and clambered over fallen down trees, following whatever route he wanted. We had an extremely tired but happy little beagle that evening and his confidence noticeably increased that weekend.

Everything was going so well and I was proud of the progress Sam had made in only a week with me. Which just goes to show that sometimes pride really does come before a literal fall because two nights later disaster struck.

It was about 9:30 p.m. and I was giving Sam a quick walk across Large Field. I'd been wondering if he would make a suitable running buddy so started to jog along to see how he coped and whether he liked it. We were trotting along happily when one of my feet caught the edge of a hole and I tripped and stumbled. To my immediate horror I accidentally kicked Sam in the process who yelped in fear. A human was kicking him, probably not for the first time. I kept stumbling and couldn't recover my balance. It was one of those slow motion falls where you know you're going down but I had long enough to realise I was probably going to fall on Sam who was right underneath me.

I twisted to the side as I fell over and raised my arm so as not to put it down on Sam as I didn't want him to think I was following up the kick by hitting him. Sam was frightened now and understandably bolted away from me whilst I had my arm extended and my fingers splayed out rather than gripping the lead. I landed hard on my shoulder and Sam somehow managed to jerk the loop of the lead from around my wrist. It was one of those freak occurrences that I doubt could be replicated but it happened and Sam was loose.

"Sam!" I yelled in horror as he darted away from me, his instinctive flight response fully activated. I grabbed for the lead but he was too fast and was already out of reach and running away. I'd lost him. As he ran off he looked back at me and barked mournfully as if reproaching me for letting him down, just like every other human in his life.

Ignoring the pain in my shoulder I leapt up, screamed "Sam!" again and took off after him, without doubt the worst thing I could have done but I was panicking. Sam sprinted off into the darkness and I soon lost sight of him. I ran around for a few minutes, calling his name but soon realised it was hopeless. The best thing to do was go home and grab a torch and a husband.

I was in tears as I ran; not only was I desperately worried about Sam but I felt certain that I would be unceremoniously sacked as a foster carer if I didn't manage to get him back. I burst through our front door and Steve looked up in alarm.

"It's Sam, he's run away, hurry!"

"What on earth did you take him off the lead for?" exclaimed Steve, jumping up.

"I didn't, I tripped over and he pulled the lead off my wrist. He's still got it on."

I quickly explained to Steve where I'd lost Sam and the direction he'd run off in, towards the larger housing zone in between Large Field and Wild Field. We agreed that Steve would take up the chase on foot and I'd drive. Steve grabbed his head torch and trainers and took off into the night whilst I jumped in the car in hot pursuit.

I prayed that Sam hadn't run off onto Wild Field as it would be extremely difficult to find him there. Hopefully he was hanging out near the houses and as I drove around I put my headlights on full, crawling along and scouring front yards for a scared little beagle. As I was coming to the end of a street, some movement off to one side caught my eye. In the middle of the grass between two houses, there was Sam. He looked perfectly calm and was just pottering around, sniffing the ground, seemingly quite content. I decided to wait for another pair of hands and feet before I got out of the car, plus I was conscious that only a few minutes ago I'd been the one who'd made Sam run off. Under the circumstances he might be more likely to let Steve approach him instead of me.

I rang Steve and explained where Sam was and warned him to approach quietly. But Sam didn't need his ears – he had a beagle's nose. About a minute later Sam suddenly stopped sniffing the grass and looked up in the direction I knew Steve was approaching from. Sure enough I saw a dark figure creep out from behind a house with what he no doubt thought was catlike stealth. Sam wasn't fooled and took off again, with a now non-stealthy Steve racing after him. This certainly answered the question of whether Sam was a good runner. I hoped that Steve was better.

He wasn't and for the next few hours Sam led me, Steve and the Fort Detrick police force, whom I'd rung in order to enlist more help, on a frantic game of hide and seek around the base. We would get a sighting of Sam and I would drive to the location and poor Steve would run but we never made it in time. We'd frequently catch sight of him in the headlights of my car or a police car, only for our elusive beagle to disappear into the shadows. Sam was adept at choosing a route where cars couldn't follow him and could easily outrun someone on foot. The situation seemed hopeless.

Just before midnight I decided I had no choice but to let Frederick County Animal Control know. Feeling utterly wretched I phoned the main switchboard number and eventually got through to one of the animal control officers who were on duty 24 hours a day. I explained what had happened, confessed that it was all my fault and apologised repeatedly. The officer was far too nice to me considering I'd lost one of their dogs and at no point told me what an irredeemably awful person I was. She said if Sam was still missing in the morning to let them know and they could bring a humane trap on to base.

Shortly after this conversation the Fort Detrick police called me with wonderful news. The officer explained that Sam was effectively trapped by an area of the fence line near the sports centre where for about 60 feet, an old section of fencing (that for some unknown reason had never been removed) ran parallel to the main perimeter fence. The section of double fencing ended on a corner, effectively forming a narrow three-sided cage. The officer had parked his patrol car across the open end and I knew that Sam would avoid going near him so it looked like we had him trapped.

I sped to the location, jubilant at the thought of getting my poor fugitive dog back. My joy was short-lived; it turned out that the old section of fencing didn't quite meet the new section – there was a small gap, just big enough for a determined beagle to squeeze through. And Sam had spotted it before the Fort Detrick police and bounded off like the Scarlet Pimpernel. The lovely police officer who'd called me was almost as crestfallen as I was.

That was unfortunately the last sighting we had that night and at about 2:00 a.m. we had to temporarily admit defeat. Sam had done an excellent job of evading capture and we'd totally lost track of where he was. Steve convinced me that we should go home and get some sleep for a few hours and be up early in the morning to continue the search. I reluctantly agreed.

At the time I was astounded at Sam's endurance and determination to evade capture. He had numerous opportunities to give himself up and return to the warmth of my house and an extra bowl of kibble but he chose to keep running. Only afterwards did I realise how terrified he must have been and how my inadvertent kick as I fell over must have reignited traumatic memories. His past experiences with humans had taught him he was safer without us, even if that meant he was cold, tired and didn't know where his next meal was coming from.

The advantage of Sam being loose on Fort Detrick was that apart from a small number of entrance gates, the entire base was fenced and the integrity of the fencing was regularly checked. He was at least contained, albeit in a very large area. I thought it was unlikely that Sam would approach the one entrance and exit gate that was open 24 hours as there were obviously a number of guards stationed there and vehicles coming and going. Sam would have definitely avoided bright lights and people. My main fear was the risk of him being hit by a car although speed limits were mercifully low on the base.

Steve and I headed home, hoping Sam had at least found somewhere warm to bed down for the night. Steve thought there was a reasonable chance he might come home by himself. I hardly dared hope he was right; I feared I'd traumatised Sam so much that he'd never want to see me again. Nonetheless, we left the garage door open and placed his crate just inside the garage as a beacon to entice him home. Although Sam didn't sleep in the crate anymore, it was something he was familiar with and if he got in it then at least we had the option of sneaking up on him and shutting the door. I also liberally scattered treats around and inside the crate in the hope that they would prove irresistible.

I hardly slept for what was left of the night. I had a permanent sick feeling and it truly felt as if part of me was missing. I set my alarm for every hour on the hour in order to get up and check the crate in the garage, however it remained empty.

At 7:00 a.m. Steve and I both went downstairs and slowly opened the connecting door from the house to the garage. The cage wasn't empty this time – there was a beagle in it! Sam had actually chosen to come home; he'd forgiven me.

I realised that if I crept up on him through the garage it was almost certain that he'd hear or smell me and make a run for it. However if I went out of the front door I could walk up the side of the garage and then appear in front of him which hopefully would make him cower back in his crate and allow me to swiftly shut the door and catch him.

This was obviously a great plan and obviously it didn't work. I eased opened the front door and crept up the path. However Sam's beagle ears were clearly better than my silent creeping skills. As I came round the side of the garage wall, so did Sam. He looked at me startled. His lead was so close, I just needed to dive for it. But he darted away from me, pulling his lead out of my reach and trotted off up the road.

Nevertheless this was progress – Sam wasn't sprinting away from me and he kept stopping and looking back. I followed at a slow walk and at one point he seemed tantalizingly close to letting me approach him but then something made him change his mind and off he went again, disappearing between two houses towards a copse of trees that led towards a children's playground past the far end of First Flight Court.

As tempting as it was to race after him I decided against it. I knew I wouldn't catch him and only risked scaring him further. I was hugely encouraged by the fact that Sam had come home of his own free will. Our house obviously held good connotations for him and if he came back once he could do so again. Alternatively I needed to give him a bit more time to realise I posed no threat and find him again at a point when he would allow me to approach him.

Unfortunately catching runaway beagles isn't part of the army officer job description and Steve had to go to work. I was going to have to continue this operation on my own. As soon as I thought it wasn't too early I rang Penny who'd adopted Hank. I told her everything that had happened and asked her to keep an eye out for Sam when she took Hank for a walk. She was horrified for us but told me not to blame myself and said the blame lay squarely at the feet of the people who'd abused Sam and taught him to be so afraid of people. I appreciated her kindness but I blamed myself nonetheless.

Penny suggested using Hank as a cross between a sniffer dog and bait. She felt sure Hank would smell Sam if he was hiding somewhere and would then lead us to him. Then the presence of Hank might make Sam more likely to approach us. The thought of Hank as some kind of canine sleuth made me smile for the first time since Sam escaped. Surely this had no chance of working. However I didn't have a better idea so agreed gratefully. Penny said she'd be over in half an hour.

Penny duly arrived with Tracker Dog Hank in tow and we decided to check out a landscaped park area beyond the far end and across the road from First Flight Court that separated the residential zone from the start of Fort Detrick's myriad network of laboratories and industrial buildings. Although it was adjacent to the outer fence and the traffic noise of Rosemont Avenue, it was also the closest area to our house that had some decent tree cover and thus places to hide. There was a patch of woodland roughly the size of a couple of American football fields in a corner near the Rosemont Avenue entrance gate and a small rocky hill, known as Colonel's Hill, covered in trees in the other corner. Penny, Hank and I walked around the first wooded area and Hank soon became quite agitated and excited.

"What's there Hank, who can you smell?"

This outpost of Maryland wilderness was pretty dense and overgrown. Penny and I pushed through it for a bit with Hank leading the way, making slow progress and having to retrace our steps several times to avoid large clumps of brambles. However if Hank could smell Sam, Penny and I certainly couldn't see him. We emerged from the tress and made a circuit of Colonel's Hill and climbed up to the top. The tree cover was less dense and we had a clear view of the open grassy area but there was no sign of our quarry. After an hour or so we headed back to my house. I'd left the garage door open and Sam's crate in place but the crate remained Sam-less.

Penny had to go home to wait in for a plumber but offered to leave me Hank in case Sam showed up at the house again. If only to have some canine company I accepted.

Circumstances aside it was lovely to spend time with Hank. I'd seen him a few times since he'd been adopted; Penny had been kind enough to invite me over before Christmas to see how he was settling in and I'd had her and Hank back for coffee since. He'd even escaped from Penny's house one day and made straight for mine. I'd seen a blur flash past my living room windows and then the goofy face of my first dog appeared at the patio door. I'd just let him in and was about to ring Penny when she rang me herself, frantically asking if I could keep an eye out for Hank as she'd seen him sprinting off towards my house. She was equally relieved and amused when I told her he'd already arrived. Hank's surprise visit did at least demonstrate that he didn't hold his eight week incarceration against me and hopefully appreciated that I'd helped him in his hour of need.

Now he was here to possibly return the favour. Hank busied himself with sniffing around his old home, no doubt interested in the scent of another dog. I sat on the sofa looking out of the windows and periodically checking the crate. No luck. The waiting was unbearable.

"Come on Hank, let's try again. You've done so much sniffing of my floor at least you know who you're tracking now."

We repeated the route of our earlier walk. As we neared the first copse of trees where Hank had seemed quite agitated I glanced over to Colonel's Hill. I saw movement; beagle-sized black, brown and white movement. It was Sam, lead still attached. (Incidentally I'm proud that at no point did we break the strict rules on base regarding loose dogs; Sam was technically never off the lead). He was busy sniffing leaves, seemingly without a care in the world.

Hank had seen Sam at the same time I did and stood perfectly still. Hank could be key to getting Sam back and I needed to get this right. This had to be a flawless operation; one mistake and Sam would take off again.

"Please Hank, be less 'you'. Make Sam want to come back to us," I whispered.

Slowly we started to walk towards Sam. It was a bit like a game I'd played as a child called 'What's the Time Mr Wolf?' where you had to creep up on the child acting as the wolf whilst their back was turned. Sam – Mr Wolf – had his back to us, oblivious to the six legs taking careful steps towards him.

We were about 100 feet away when Sam turned around and saw us. I stopped instantly, silently willing Hank not to do anything to startle him. But Hank stopped when I did and was remarkably calm. I would go so far as to describe him as zen-like, not a trait I'd ever seen in him before. Sam looked at us. Slowly, so slowly, I knelt down to show him I wasn't a threat. Sam regarded us for what seemed like ages and then simply lay down and rested his head on his paws.

"Oh Sam, you've had enough haven't you," I said softly. He really looked as though the flight had gone out of him. I stood up gradually and when Sam seemed comfortable with that, Hank and I advanced, a few steps at a time to allow our quarry to get used to our presence. I was ready to stop as soon as Sam showed any sign of wanting to bolt. I tried to exude love, kindness and the promise of endless cheese cubes.

As we got closer, Hank repaid me for caring for him a thousand fold. This normally boisterous foxhound walked serenely and calmly and in doing so, provided me with a canine character reference. Hank felt safe with me and was showing Sam that he should too. Sam had obviously had enough of being on the run and was picking up sufficiently friendly vibes from Hank that he decided his adventure was at an end.

Talking to Sam the whole time, Hank and I got closer and closer. We were twenty feet away, then ten, then five and I knew I was within diving distance of the end of his lead and would do it if I had to. If it meant a broken rib then so be it.

Two feet from the end of the lead now and Hank stopped and I slowly crouched down, talking to Sam, asking him if he'd like to come home. I reached out and grabbed the lead and couldn't quite believe I had him. Overcome with relief, I sat down and started crying. Hank and Sam sniffed each other and ignored me. I put the loop over my wrist and wound the lead around my hand a couple of times for good measure and then reached out and stroked Sam who seemed perfectly content.

"Sam, I'm so sorry. This has all been my fault. Please forgive me."

I gave Sam a cheese cube and rewarded Hank with one too. I was still astonished at his impeccable behaviour and hoped he'd be as cooperative on the walk back to my house. No such luck. Now that the emotional reunion was over, Hank reverted to his usual exuberant self and trying to walk both of them was challenging to say the least. Sam was completely exhausted and didn't want to walk at all and Hank wanted to take off at full pelt. I tried carrying Sam but he was difficult to carry one-armed, as I needed the other for Hank.

I must have looked a ridiculous sight, trying to tenderly cradle a beagle in one arm and wrangling a lanky foxhound with the other. With numerous stops along the way to adjust Sam or plead with Hank to take it easy, we somehow got home.

Once I got them in the house and shut the door I could relax. Hank and I had done it and I still couldn't quite believe it. I broke out more cheese cubes and a bowl of kibble to welcome Sam home and thank my heroic partner. Cometh the hour, cometh the foxhound.

I rang Penny and gave her the great news; she was delighted and said she'd come straight round to collect Hank. But for a wonderful few minutes it was just me, Hank and Sam at home. Sam curled up in his non-crated bed and Hank ran round and round the kitchen island, pausing occasionally to sniff at his new friend.

When Penny arrived I gave her a detailed account of the successful rescue mission. She was amazed at Hank's grace under pressure. Then it was my great pleasure to ring Linda and tell her I'd managed to catch Sam. She was kind enough to say she was so happy for me as she'd known how bad I must have felt. She made no mention of sacking me as a foster carer or having an animal control officer arrest me for stupidity.

Sam got away from me due to a freak accident and he carried on running from me due to his prior experience of people. Neither of those things were my fault. Nonetheless I was his foster carer, his protector. I let him down because I didn't foresee an event like this and plan for it and that was definitely my fault.

The day after Sam's return I went out and bought a second lead, thereafter dubbed the Light Blue Safety Lead. I threaded it through the wrist loop of Sam's normal lead and then threaded its clip end back through its own wrist loop so that it was securely entwined with the other lead. Whenever I took Sam out I'd clip his lead on to his collar as usual but would also wrap the Light Blue Safety Lead around my waist and clip it back on to itself. So if the exact same scenario struck twice and he managed to jerk the lead that was attached to his collar from off my wrist, he would remain attached to me via my waist. Instead of a frantic night pursuing him all over Fort Detrick, or worse – the watershed, he'd be a few feet away.

When I saw Carol at the following Monday's spay and neuter clinic I told her about Sam's escapade. I'd been dreading telling Sam's first foster carer what had happened but she was nothing but sympathetic and congratulated me on my excellent dog handling skills, using Hank to get Sam back. I replied I couldn't really brag about that seeing how it was my clumsy dog handling 'non-skills' that enabled Sam to escape in the first place.

Despite my deserved self-criticism, I was conscious that Sam's return was an endorsement of me. When disaster struck, Sam chose to run away from me, an understandable reaction given his background. What's incredible is that he returned of his own free will. Admittedly he ran off again, but with less certainty, and only a few hours later he allowed me to approach him, catch him and take him home. At some point Sam decided I was different to his previous people and made the choice to trust me. His flight impulse had calmed down and he remembered who I was and how I'd treated him. I started to believe I was good at this fostering business.

Years later, I remain humbled by that incident and see it as a contemporary microcosm of the circumstances that brought about the dog all those millennia ago. The first humans to develop a relationship with the ancestor of the domestic dog forged a mutually beneficial and astonishingly enduring inter-species partnership that changed the course of human history. And they did it without 'how to train your puppy' books, obedience classes, clicker training or TV experts.

The positive reinforcement method of dog training has deservedly become increasingly popular in recent years but it cannot possibly be a new concept. If early humans had been cruel or abusive then those intrepid wolves that tentatively emerged from the darkness and approached a campfire wouldn't have stuck around. We'll never know for sure but I feel certain that those initial interactions between two different species must have been characterised by the most powerful force of all – kindness. And kindness brings exponential rewards.

As a result, and luckily for Sam and for me, the innate bond between dogs and humans is so entrenched that it takes more than one or two vile individuals to destroy it. Sam's ancient instinct had prevailed. He came out of the darkness and found his campfire.

CHAPTER 6

THREE LONG JOURNEYS

SAM'S 'NIGHT OF Adventure' heralded a significant shift in our relationship. He began following me everywhere around the house; if I moved the few feet from the sofa to the kitchen then Sam would come too and if I went upstairs he'd scamper up right behind me. He also started to get up on the sofa and lie down next to us, a show of affection that I never thought I'd see from him. Obviously I didn't mind him being on the sofa; on the contrary I actively encouraged it by rewarding him with a treat or two.

Sam even began sleeping upstairs. In the morning we'd see a shadow in the small gap between the bottom of our bedroom door and the floor and whilst he'd pad noiselessly downstairs as soon as he heard us get up, our suspicions were confirmed by the warm patch on the carpet. I found the fact that Sam slept outside our bedroom incredibly poignant. Only a few weeks previously, Sam was at risk of losing his life due to his fear of people. Now he wanted to sleep as close to me as possible. I wanted to leave our door open so he could come and sleep in our room with us if he chose. However Steve wasn't comfortable with this idea so the bedroom remained off limits at night.

The change in Sam was so dramatic that I began to think that he was ready to be adopted by the right people. I was adamant that being a foster carer wasn't only about the practical day to day task of looking after a dog; I was also the dog's advocate. I had to speak up for my dogs, represent their best interests and never let the fostering be about me. Or in other words, I must never keep a foster dog longer than necessary just because I wasn't ready to say goodbye.

So a week after Sam's impromptu expedition, I had a chat with Linda. I explained that Sam was still a nervous dog but told her about the change in him and that I felt he was adoptable by the right sort of people. I assured Linda that we would foster Sam for as long as necessary but I was convinced it was worth getting his profile on Petfinder and seeing if anyone was interested in him. I didn't say this to Linda but part of my reasoning was that Steve and I had a vacation coming up that we'd booked long before I'd agreed to have Sam. I'd told Linda about our holiday when I took him on and the plan was that Sam would go back to Carol for the week we were away. However I was now worried that returning to someone who he didn't like might set him back and undo some of the progress he'd made.

Linda agreed with me that it was worth putting Sam up for adoption so I immediately wrote a piece for Petfinder and sent Linda some photos. The day after Sam's profile appeared online, Linda called. A man had contacted the shelter expressing interest in Sam and asking if he and his family could come and meet him. Linda told me the man was called Walter Baumann and he had a wife and two young sons.

I was pessimistic about the fact there were two children in the family as I didn't think that would be right for Sam. Nevertheless I rang Walter and we agreed he and his family would come and visit Sam at our house on Saturday afternoon. He explained his wife had some health problems so wasn't able to make the journey but he'd bring the two boys aged seven and ten.

It was early March and the weather that week suddenly turned warm and sunny. I took Sam to Baker Park one afternoon and both of us were full of the joys of spring. The trees were decked with blossom and the park was busy with people enjoying the weather. Sam and I must have been giving off good vibes because we received a lot of smiles from people walking past.

At one point we sauntered past a man sitting by himself in a motorized wheelchair. He pointed at Sam and called out to me, "He's a happy little guy!"

"He certainly is!" I replied. I strolled over to the man, introduced ourselves and told him Sam's story. We chatted for a few minutes and the man told me that Sam and I were the first 'people' he'd spoken to all day. It struck me how the presence of a dog breaks down barriers between people and gives complete strangers a reason to talk to each other. Dogs sometimes expose our humanity in a way nothing else does.

Further down the path, two large dogs were having a loud disagreement. There was a German Shepherd and a Bernese Mountain Dog on opposite sides of the path, snarling and barking aggressively at each other and straining at their leads whilst their people tried to pull them away.

I deliberately didn't react – I maintained my pace and strode on through the middle of it all. Sam did likewise – head held high, he trotted through perfectly confidently without a glance at the two bigger dogs either side of him. There was no danger; the dogs were sufficiently far apart that they couldn't reach us and their people had a firm grip on them, even if they were having trouble moving them on. Nonetheless I was so proud of my little beagle. He had always been so much more confident in the outdoors anyway but the noise and body language from the other two dogs were rather intimidating. Yet Sam acted as though nothing was happening.

A disheveled guy riding past on his equally disheveled bike stopped in amazement.

"Hey," he gestured at me, "How come your dog didn't react to those other dogs?"

"I think it's because I'm calm and he trusts me so he's calm too," I replied.

"Girl, you're like…some kinda dog whisperer!"

I couldn't help but beam at Friendly Bike Man, obviously a wise and perceptive individual. A complete stranger thought I was 'some kinda dog whisperer.' That ranked as one of the best compliments I'd ever received.

Not wanting our Best Walk Ever to end, Sam and I sat under a tree for a while and watched the world go by. Sam had been such a learning curve for me. I'd loved seeing him develop from a terrified dog who'd recoil from human interaction to the cheerful little soul who loved being close to me all the time. I scratched him under his chin and pondered for the umpteenth time how on earth I was going to let him go.

On Saturday morning I was nervous for Sam. I genuinely wanted the visit to go well for his sake. I was also nervous for me. I was conscious that I'd told Linda that in my opinion, Sam had gained sufficient confidence to be marketed for adoption. If this went badly and Sam reverted to his terrified beagle persona then I'd look rather foolish. Having already been responsible for accidentally releasing him into the wild I didn't want to compound that mistake by pushing him into a situation he wasn't ready for.

The Baumanns arrived right on time and Walter introduced his sons Christopher and Cody. My 'Brat Radar' didn't ping; both boys appeared polite and well-behaved and were endearingly excited to meet Sam.

Sam had retreated to his bed when the Baumanns arrived and eyed them warily. However he didn't seem nervous which was encouraging, merely a bit unsure as to why I'd let these people into our house. I suggested we sit down and talk whilst Sam got used to them.

Walter explained that they all fell in love with Sam due to his Petfinder profile, both the photos and the piece I'd written about him. I explained how far Sam had come and regaled them with the cautionary tale of Sam's impromptu Night of Adventure. I told the boys how fast Sam was for a little guy; how Steve running at full speed couldn't get anywhere near him. The boys looked at Sam admiringly.

"Ok", I said to the boys, retrieving a bag of cheese cubes from the fridge, "I'll give Sam a treat first and then we'll see if he'll take one from you guys."

I sat down in front of Sam with Christopher and Cody kneeling behind me. I offered Sam a piece of cheese but to my surprise and disappointment he refused. This was not a good sign; Sam never ever refused a cheese cube. He was obviously far more worried by the presence of the Baumanns than I realised. My heart sank. He wasn't ready; I'd made a huge mistake.

"I'm really sorry, I guess he's still a bit nervous of you all. How about we give him some space and we can try again in a little while?"

Christopher, the older boy, nodded politely and moved away from Sam. Cody smiled at me, grabbed the cheese cube out of my hand and cheerfully shoved it in Sam's face. Sam looked at Cody, then leant forward and took the cheese right out of his hand, gulping it down appreciatively. Cody turned to everyone with a triumphant look on his face.

No one was more surprised than me.

"Er...wow!" I said, taken aback at Sam's acceptance of Cody's rather direct approach.

"He likes me!" announced Cody proudly. Sam certainly did like Cody and that was that. That confident and good-natured proffering of a piece of cheese seemed to seal the deal for Sam. From that moment on Sam didn't want to let Cody out of his sight.

Cody would pet Sam and Sam would let him and then wander off for a bit, all the while looking back at Cody as if inviting him to come along. Cody would oblige enthusiastically at first but then would wander around the house in a different direction and Sam would dutifully go after him. Then they'd switch direction again. Sam even let Cody approach him and stroke him and whilst he didn't look totally relaxed, the fact he let him do it was astonishing.

At one point Cody was sat still watching Sam and I noticed Walter had tears in his eyes. He quietly confided to Steve and I that this was the longest he'd ever seen his youngest son sit still and explained that he and his wife hoped having a dog would prove therapeutic for Cody. Early signs were certainly promising. Sam and Cody were kindred spirits – Sam found it difficult to trust people and Cody found it difficult to focus. But somehow they'd found each other. No wonder Walter was emotional.

I took the boys on a walk with Sam so they could see how confident he was when he was outdoors. They promised they'd give him plenty of exercise and play outside with him regularly.

The Baumanns stayed for well over two hours and I could see they were totally smitten. Walter confirmed they would definitely be putting an application in on Sam first thing on Monday morning. I assured him I'd tell Linda how well the visit had gone and how I was certain that Sam had found his forever family.

I phoned Linda as soon as the Baumanns left and told her all about the visit and how well Sam had taken to the boys. I admitted that I'd been sceptical about whether Sam would feel comfortable around children but I couldn't have been happier when Sam demonstrated that I clearly didn't know what I was talking about. I think Sam chose the Baumanns as much as they chose him.

Two days later Linda told me that Walter had indeed put in an application on Sam and the adoption interview was scheduled for the following Saturday, the day we were going on vacation to Florida. This was great news for Sam and I was both ecstatic and heartbroken.

I'd loved Hank but that had been a completely different experience. And I'd loved Lily but she'd only been with us for a few days. Sam had been with us for three weeks now and we'd been through so much together. I was so proud of him and knew it was going to take me a long time to get over giving him up.

My experience with Sam demonstrated how emotionally difficult it is to foster. Many people have since said to me something along the lines of, "I don't know how you could let them go." The implication is clear, that I obviously wasn't attached to my foster dogs. However nothing could be further from the truth. I considered each and every one of my foster dogs 'my dog'. But you don't 'own' a dog – Sam was one hundred percent part of my family but I couldn't take him back to the UK. Aside from the issues of not being allowed a dog in our apartment and working full-time, Sam was not the kind of dog who could cope with a trans-Atlantic flight. He needed a forever family here in the US and I believed he'd found them.

Fully expecting the Baumanns to pass the adoption interview, I resolved to make the most of Sam's last few days with us. I took him on his favourite walks to Baker

Park and the watershed, fed him his favourite treats and enjoyed plenty of cuddling on the sofa time.

That Friday evening was 'hopefully' our last night with Sam. As Steve and I packed for our vacation, Sam was extremely curious and helped me by sniffing all the clothes I'd laid out in my bag. That night I put my foot down and insisted to Steve that Sam slept in our room. In all the books I'd read as a child where one of the characters had a dog, the dog always slept on their person's bed. As far as I was concerned, that was one of the pillars of having a dog. The two of you had such a close bond that you even slept next to each other.

However Steve had grown up in a house where the dogs, although loved and well cared for, were viewed as, well, dogs. Not friends. And definitely not room mates. But that Friday night I got my way. I carried Sam's bed upstairs and placed it next to my side of our bed. Sam had followed me and took one look at his bed on the floor and then curled up in it as if this was the most normal thing in the world. And as I drifted off to sleep I could hear the comforting sound of my dog breathing next to me.

At some point in the night I was woken up by the bed briefly shaking, something lying down against my legs and sighing contentedly. My childhood dream of having a dog who slept on my bed with me had finally come true. And tomorrow, if I'd done my job right, I'd be giving him up forever.

The next morning I was feeling emotional as we finished packing our car for our vacation; we were starting the long drive down to Florida straight after handing Sam over. I joked with Steve that in the extremely unlikely event that the Baumanns failed their interview then Sam would be coming with us.

When we arrived at the shelter I saw that the Baumanns' car was already there. I went in to let Linda know we'd arrived but agreed with her that as it was nice weather we'd sit outside rather than risk stressing Sam out by taking him in the shelter. So the Williams family of three, soon to be two, sat in the sunshine together for the last time. Sam sat down next to me and seemed to know something was afoot. He didn't seem worried, just alert and expectant. I wondered if he sensed that his new family was nearby.

Linda came and sat outside with us and told me that I'd done a great job. It meant a lot to me that she said that. I wasn't entirely sure how I'd done it but I'd certainly helped Sam become adoptable much quicker than anyone had expected. I reached out and scratched Sam under his chin.

"Not long now Sam, not long and you'll have your forever family."

A few minutes later the Baumanns came out and walked over to us with big smiles on their faces. Unsurprisingly they'd passed the interview, paid the adoption fee and were ready to take Sam home immediately. Sam stood up when he saw Christopher and Cody approach, his nose twitching. I bit my lip, determined not to cry. I gave the lead to Christopher who had the hugest grin on his face.

"Well done guys, he's your dog now," I said, just about managing to hold it together. Sam clearly remembered them and showed no nervousness, no fear. This adoption was going to work.

As the Baumanns made a fuss of their new dog, Steve and I swiftly got Sam's possessions from our car and handed them over – his bed, a few toys and a supply of the food he was used to. Then it was time to say goodbye. I knelt down and petted Sam for the last time.

"I love you Sam, you're such a great dog. Thank you for coming home. Behave yourself now, no more adventures!"

Sam's soulful brown eyes looked into mine. I'd brought him back from the brink and forged a genuine bond with him. I loved him with all my heart and it was time to let him go.

"Happy trails Sam."

We shook hands with Walter and wished the boys lots of fun with their new dog. Walter thanked me again.

"It was my pleasure," I told him truthfully, unable to stop the tears pricking my eyes.

And with that we left Sam with his forever family and headed down to Florida. I think we were almost at Virginia before I stopped crying.

It took a few days to get to the Keys and we enjoyed various stops along the way. The changing scenery as we got further south was fascinating to me and I especially enjoyed the day we spent in the beautiful town of Savannah, Georgia with its antebellum architecture and shady, tree lined streets.

Typically for Steve and I, we loved the long drive. We had a system whereby we took it in turns to drive for two hours then swapped over. The passenger then had a duty to make interesting conversation. This was fine by me as I had something on my mind. I wanted a baby and I wanted one soon.

Historically, I had never wanted children. Not because I didn't like them; I did and they tended to like me. I had a goddaughter and two nephews I loved dearly and enjoyed spending time with. I just didn't want my own child. I thought they required a lot of effort, were too expensive and would restrict my fun and freedom. Steve never disagreed but in hindsight, maybe he never actively agreed either.

About a year before we moved to Frederick, before we knew a trans-Atlantic adventure was a possibility, Steve told me he wanted to discuss having children. This was like a stick of dynamite in the foundations of our relationship and I was quite annoyed at this breach of our unspoken agreement to remain child-free. However Steve explained that he wasn't saying he definitely wanted children, simply that he wanted to talk about it.

I loved Steve, we were perfectly matched in every other way, this was clearly important to him and I did have to acknowledge that we'd never had the discussion. We'd just rumbled along in a blissful state of nights out, expensive holidays and indulgent weekends. Furthermore I knew I wouldn't change my mind. You can't compromise when it comes to having a baby because you can't have half a baby. Someone in the baby-creating gang of two has to concede, one way or another, and I was prepared to lose Steve over this. So there was really no harm in exploring the theoretical possibility of having children, as I knew there was no chance of me changing my mind.

I changed my mind.

The simple act of talking about having a child suddenly made it seem like an attractive proposition. I enjoyed the process of sharing all the experiences we valued from our own childhoods and how we'd replicate them and all the child-rearing tenets that we'd do away with. It demonstrated to me just how compatible Steve and I truly were and raised the possibility of new depths to our relationship. And I couldn't deny that I'd always loved human babies in the way that I love all baby animals.

So we decided that we would have children after all. At some point. Just not now. And we wouldn't complicate matters by actually telling anyone. After all, we had loads of time because we were both only thirty-three so years and years of fertility stretched ahead of us. Decision made, ensuing actions placed firmly on backburner whilst we continued to enjoy zero responsibility, disposable income and the freedom to do whatever we liked, whenever we liked.

We referred to our decision obliquely every now and then but it was still something that we intended to do at some point in our lives without ever pinning down when that was. When we found out we were moving to the US we decided that it would be foolish to have a baby there for reasons we never quite articulated. However this meant we'd both be thirty-seven by the time we were back in the UK.

It was a long drive to the Keys; 1,168 miles from Frederick to Islamorada, the prettiest Key and where we were staying initially. Somewhere in South Carolina, I brought up the subject of children and told Steve that freedom and money and sleep weren't priorities anymore – I wanted a baby sooner rather than later.

There is a tendency, especially apparent on social media, for seeing dogs as quasi-children and particularly in the US they're often referred to as 'fur babies'. Whilst I celebrate the love and devotion that lies behind this trend, it's never resonated with me because I never wanted a dog to be a child substitute – I wanted them to be my friend. 'Dog' is a sufficiently wonderful designation in my view; it doesn't need an anthropomorphic upgrade. Furthermore I'd longed for a dog since I was five; children were a far more recent desire.

Nonetheless my dogs did play a role in making me feel ready to have a baby. Taking responsibility for another life and putting someone else's needs first was surprisingly enjoyable and deeply rewarding. I imagined it could only be more rewarding with my own child. And seeing Steve with Lily the puppy was illuminating and I suspected he was more ready than he realised too.

Yet Steve was reluctant, not because he'd changed his mind but because he questioned whether the timing was right. His fear was that having a baby in tow would restrict our activities in the US. I pointed out that this was March, it would no doubt take a few months and then I'd be pregnant for nine so best case scenario Baby Williams would arrive a few months before we were due to leave. There was still plenty of time for fun. Steve was still unsure.

By the time we reached Islamorada we were at an impasse. I decided to leave the conversation for the time being and focus on having a great holiday.

The Florida Keys is an amazing place. In certain places it feels like the only thing separating your car from the sea is the road. And the reason it feels that way is because it's frequently true. To the east is the Atlantic Ocean and to the west are Florida Bay and the Gulf of Mexico. The fact that you're driving between the two is a testament to the American 'can do' attitude. Want to visit the low-lying islands off the mainland? Sure, we'll just build a highway through the ocean.

We spent our days eating out, going snorkeling at Bahia Honda beach, and generally relaxing and soaking up the Florida sunshine. Sam remained in our thoughts and we talked about him a lot. The Baumanns had been kind enough to email to say that Sam had settled in well and seemed very happy which was wonderful to hear. Amusingly we were often reminded of Sam by the Florida pelicans. They too had a slightly petrified gaze and were often to be seen perched somewhere by themselves looking hunched and tense, just like Sam when he first arrived with us. Sam thus managed to receive a belated nickname and we still call him Sam Pelican to this day.

One hot and sunny afternoon we stopped at a roadside and oceanside market and café complex that also hosted a watersports shack. We noticed that it rented out stand up paddleboards, something we'd been wanting to try since seeing a couple of paddleboarders set out from a waterside bar we'd been drinking at a few evenings prior. We'd commented at the time how romantic it would be watching the sun set whilst stood atop a paddleboard so decided on a spur of the moment adventure.

However as we were filling out the rental paperwork the guy explained we needed to return the boards by 6:00 p.m. As the sun set at about 7:20 p.m. it obviously meant we wouldn't be able to watch the sun go down from out on the sea. We both looked at each other and shrugged; it was a shame but there was nothing we could do about it.

Having lived in the US for a while, we'd grown accustomed to asking for a military discount wherever we went. Americans pride themselves on showing appreciation to their service personnel and many shops and restaurants operated some kind of price reduction to members of the armed forces. As we were about to pay Steve suddenly asked the magic question, "Do you do a military discount?"

"Oh, are you military?"

"Yes, obviously I'm British Army but I'm over here on secondment to the US Army," explained Steve, showing Paddleboard Man his US military ID.

"Ok, we don't do a discount but what we do is trust you to look after yourselves and not steal the boards. So you don't need to be back here by 6:00 p.m., you can return the boards anytime so long as they're here at 9:00 a.m. tomorrow morning. Just stack them up behind the hut. So stay out and have fun! And thank you for your service."

Well that was the best military discount ever. Instead of money off we were getting the perfect view of the sun setting. We spent an amazing afternoon and early evening paddling over to a nearby island and exploring the maze of channels through the mangrove swamps. And we watched the sun set over the sea, sitting on our boards whilst surrounded by a flock of Sam Pelicans. A truly incredible experience and one of those moments in life that you never forget. I remember sitting on my board, looking at my husband, the pelicans and the sunset and thinking how lucky I was. And then I thought about how I wanted to tell my future son or daughter about this experience one day. And I'd tell them that I thought of them whilst the sun slipped beneath the horizon.

We spent most of our evenings in Islamorada at a great outdoor bar and restaurant on Morada Bay. One night Steve turned to me and said he'd been thinking about it and he agreed with me that we should start trying to have a baby.

"Really?" I enquired.

"Really. If you still want to of course."

"I do, very much."

The Keys thus became a rather special holiday.

After a couple more days in paradise, including a hedonistic night in Key West drinking cocktails and dancing until the early hours, we headed back north via the Everglades, Kentucky and North Carolina. Then it was home to Maryland and our new adventure of starting a family, a long journey in more ways than one.

At my first spay and neuter clinic after we got back from the Keys, Linda came to ask me when I was available to foster again. The truth was I needed a break. I was undeniably proud of what I'd achieved with Sam and his story was proof of the power of fostering – it can literally mean the difference between life and death. If Sam had had to stay in the shelter – unhappy, fearful and unwilling to interact with anyone then his chances of adoption would have been slim to non-existent.

Eventually a decision would have had to be made about his future.

Frederick County Animal Control was a low-kill shelter that went to great lengths to give every animal in its care the chance of a new life. But sadly there had to be limits. If the shelter was at capacity then it wasn't fair to euthanise healthy and adoptable dogs because a dog with a low chance of being adopted was taking up a vital space.

Fostering Sam had thus been a huge responsibility and an emotional burden. What if I'd failed? But I hadn't and Sam and I had bonded completely. No sooner had I fallen in love with him than I had to give him up and I didn't think I could go through that again just yet. I explained all this to Linda who completely understood and told me to let her know when I felt ready to foster again.

I didn't want a break from dogs, just fostering, so I threw myself into volunteering at the shelter and popped in most days for a couple of hours. And of course I continued volunteering at the spay and neuter clinic. Carol seemed to have a new found respect for me and praised me to MaryJane and Dr C for my work with Sam which was a much appreciated vote of confidence.

A couple of weeks after we got back from the Keys our friends Amy and Shelley asked if we'd look after their Labrador Sandy for a week whilst they went on an impromptu vacation. Of course we agreed; Sandy was a great dog and I often took her for a walk in Baker Park during the day when I didn't have a foster dog.

Having a much loved dog who'd been with the same family all her life was so easy. Sandy was well trained and had no behavioural issues at all so long as you don't count getting up on the sofa which I don't.

Having Sandy to stay also made Steve temporarily drop his opposition to dogs sleeping in the bedroom.

Sandy always slept in Amy and Shelley's room and I informed Steve that it would be unforgivably cruel to suddenly banish her downstairs. Not only would she be missing her family but she'd be worried and stressed at the change in her sleeping arrangements. Shelley agreed with me and was appalled at the prospect of Sandy sleeping alone. I'm not sure whom Steve was most scared of but the Jenni-Shelley-Sandy 'axis of outrage' won the day and so Sandy duly padded upstairs with us every night and slept by my side of the bed.

It was lovely having her. We went on long walks and I could take Sandy off the lead and play fetch with her in the area around our house. And she actually came back when called and never once ran off and stayed out all night. Sandy and I had a great week together and I missed her when Amy and Shelley picked her up. Shelley later told me that after they got home, Sandy sank into such a sulk that she nearly brought her back.

Sandy was an easy dog to have around because she had been loved and cared for all her life and had no fear that her people might abandon her one day. Every dog deserved a life like that and I was in a position to help. I emailed Linda and told her I was ready to foster again.

CHAPTER 7

DREAM DOG

7ᵀᴴ MAY 2011 is the day I met someone who will forever be one of the most important souls in my life; a dog who worried me, challenged me, confused me and bewitched me more than any other. It was the day I met Jess.

It was Saturday morning and Steve and I were lying in bed wondering whether to go out for breakfast when I heard my phone ring downstairs. I had a missed call from the shelter and a voicemail. The message was garbled and broken up but I recognised Lauren's voice and I caught one marvelous and portentous word – husky.

I rang back immediately. Lauren explained that they had a female husky mix, approximately two years old, who was extremely nervous of people. She would need fostering for an indefinite amount of time; could I help?

I raced back upstairs, all thoughts of lazy lie-ins and a leisurely breakfast forgotten. I didn't bother to ask Steve his opinion.

"Female husky, they don't know how long we'll need to have her but it might be a few months."

"Ok, let's go," replied Steve, almost (but not quite) as excited as I was.

Huskies are my ultimate dream dog. I follow the Iditarod and the Yukon Quest every year and Steve and I went on a fantastic dog sledding holiday in Finland in 2008. When I started fostering for Frederick County

Animal Control, my secret wish list was a puppy and a husky. I'd had Lily, now I'd have the husky.

When we arrived at the shelter Lauren told us the husky was called Jess and explained she was sweet natured but extremely frightened. Lauren thought it would take her a while to trust us. The details of her background were sketchy but the woman who relinquished her to the shelter claimed to have bought her off Craigslist, an American online classified ads website, where she'd been put up for sale by her owners. The woman seemingly knew her owners and knew that they beat her so bought Jess with the best of intentions in order to save her from those abusive people.

However then the woman decided she couldn't keep Jess herself and so surrendered her to FCAC. The shelter environment didn't suit Jess at all. She was refusing to eat and had lost a lot of weight; the fear was that she was going to starve to death. There was no point putting her out on the floor to be viewed by potential adopters because, like Sam, she was so fearful that she just cowered at the back of her enclosure and in any case, she wasn't healthy enough.

Lauren explained that the priority was to get Jess eating and then slowly work on building her trust in people. Lauren's theory was that Jess would start eating if she felt more relaxed and at ease and that was best achieved away from the shelter. Jess was also on antibiotics as she'd tested positive for Lyme's, a nasty tick borne disease.

Lauren said she'd thought of me due to my success with Sam the beagle. She went on to say that she couldn't give us a time frame for fostering Jess, it would all depend on her progress and adoptability. I replied that was fine and of course we'd have her as long as necessary. I suppose I had in mind a few months, possibly less. We'd been told Sam would require months of rehabilitation and actually it had been a few weeks.

"So are you sure you want to take her?" asked Lauren.

"Absolutely!" I replied.

"Ok, I'll go get her."

I loved Jess on sight. She slunk in to the examination room behind Lauren with her head down and a fearful look in her eyes. She was a big dog but was terribly thin and looked scared and defeated. Despite the cowed body language, Jess was stunning. She was mainly black with white legs and a white chest and tummy. She had a typical black and white husky face with a black strip down her muzzle and dark markings like a mask around her deep brown eyes. I thought she was the most beautiful dog I'd ever seen. I still think that.

Jess pressed into the cupboards, trying to keep as much distance as possible between her and these two new people. I was conscious of how frightened she was and how we mustn't overwhelm her. I crouched down slowly but didn't reach my hands out to her yet.

"Hi Jess, I'm Jenni," I said softly. Jess glanced up at me but dropped her gaze almost immediately.

I looked up at Lauren. "Wow, she's very scared."

Lauren nodded. "She really is. Just do your best and if anyone can turn her around you can."

So no pressure then. Lauren handed me the lead.

"Come on Jess", I said, "Let's go home."

Jess didn't so much come willingly as resignedly. Lauren had suggested that we go out the back way of the shelter as it was quieter. I led Jess down the corridor and she crept along the wall, clearly fearful as to what was happening to her now. However as soon as we were outside she started pulling forcefully on the lead and my arm was abruptly yanked forward. Her strength took me by surprise and I nearly fell over.

"She's strong!" I said to Steve, holding the lead with both hands.

"Do you want me to take her?" he asked.

"No, it's ok, I may as well get used to it!"

I had no idea just how much pulling I was going to have to get used to. I managed to hold on to Jess for the short distance from the back door of the shelter to our car. I opened the boot and patted the floor.

"Come on Jess, can you jump up?"

Jess looked at me apprehensively and pulled away in the other direction. I didn't blame her, I wouldn't get into a car with a couple of people I'd only just met either.

"Do you want me to lift her in?" asked Steve

"No, it's ok, I'll do it."

I will admit to being a little nervous. Jess was a fearful dog, who didn't like people, who'd suddenly been thrust from an environment she hated but was at least familiar with into the unknown with two people she'd never met before. She was also a big dog who bore more than a passing resemblance to a wolf. If she'd wanted to maul my face off as I bent down to lift her into the car then she could have done. But as I picked her up I felt her trembling slightly and my heart went out to her.

"Good girl Jess, you're ok," I said softly.

My experience with Sam had taught me a thing or two about scared dogs and I was also aware that huskies are renowned for being escape artists. For a couple of seconds in between me letting go of her lead and shutting the boot, Jess would have the opportunity to jump out of the car and make a break for it. I didn't want to lose her within a few minutes of picking her up. So as a precaution Steve got in the back seat and I passed him the lead to hold whilst I closed the boot. Then I got in the back seat so I could talk to her easily during the short drive home.

"Welcome home Jess," I said as Steve pulled into the driveway. "This is your home too now, you're going to be safe here I promise."

Jess just looked at me impassively. Steve drove into the garage and I waited until the garage door was safely shut behind us before getting Jess out of the car. I took the lead off and she slunk into the house, immediately making for the farthest corner of the living room. She sat down with her back to the wall, eyeing us warily. Remembering our experience with Sam we decided to take things slowly. We had plenty of time to get to know our new dog and it was crucial to make her feel safe and go at her pace.

So after the obligatory trip outside to show her where she could go to the toilet, Steve and I carried on with normal Saturday morning tasks and let Jess sit in the living room and decompress from the shelter. It was a beautiful day so we spent a lot of time sitting outside on the patio; Jess could see us easily through the window but also had space to get used to her new surroundings.

After lunch I drove down to PetValu to stock up on treats and dog food. Jess hadn't been eating properly in the shelter and was extremely thin. She only weighed 52 lbs and you could see the outline of her ribs through her fur. She looked horribly malnourished. I was therefore on a mission to buy her the tastiest, most delicious and most nutritious dog food that money could buy.

Part of the foster care agreement was that the foster carer was responsible for providing food for their dog. However the shelter regularly received donations of dog food and so helped its foster carers out whenever possible. When I'd fostered Hank and Lily, Linda had given me bags of donated food and when I fostered Sam, Carol had sent a whole bag of food that she'd bought him and had generously refused my offer to reimburse her.

However the shelter didn't have any reserve stocks of food to send with Jess and I'd have refused it now anyway. I'd recently taken an interest in dog nutrition and wanted to buy Jess food that I chose.

As I browsed the numerous options a brand called 'Taste of the Wild' caught my eye. It was grain free, which I'd recently learned was considered the best quality food, and this particular flavor contained roasted bison and wild venison. Not only was it reassuringly expensive but it seemed appropriate for Jess who looked rather wolf-like. I heaved a large bag into the trolley.

Jess's coat was also in poor condition; it was dull and felt course to the touch and showed how badly nourished she was. Browsing the aisles I saw bottles of salmon oil, high in omega fatty acids and good for a dog's skin, coat and joints. You drizzled the oil over the dog's regular food and the label promised that the salmon oil would help encourage fussy eaters too. So that went in the trolley too. And just for good measure I picked up some canine vitamin tablets. I was determined that Jess was going to be a picture of robust health within a couple of weeks. I also bought a large dog bed so Jess had a space that was purely hers.

I hurried back home, anxious to see how Jess was. Steve reported that she'd remained lying in the corner of the living room the whole time I'd been gone. He looked at the big bag of Taste of the Wild, the salmon oil and the vitamin tables and raised an eyebrow at me in mock exasperation.

"That all looks expensive! Just how much have you spent Mrs Williams?"

"Er...a bit! We eat well and so should Jess!"

I decided to feed Jess right away. The shelter fed their dogs at 7:00 a.m. and 1:00 p.m. I planned to gradually move the 1:00 p.m. meal back to 5:00 p.m. but it was already early afternoon and Jess was hopefully hungry now.

I prepared a bowl of the Taste of the Wild, drizzled with salmon oil, and with a vitamin tablet and her antibiotic mixed in. I put her bowl down for her and then Steve and I went and sat outside on the patio. I wanted Jess to have some space whilst she was eating so she had nothing to feel nervous about.

After a while I went back in. Jess was lying in the middle of the living room. I looked over at her bowl; to my delight it was empty. That was a great start.

"Good girl Jess! Brilliant, well done!"

I was ecstatic, as I knew this was more than she'd eaten in a long time. I showed Steve the empty bowl through the window and he grinned back at me. I had a good feeling about this latest fostering assignment.

"We can do this Jess," I smiled at her. "I'll buy you all the expensive food you like, you just have to eat it for me. And you have to let me show you that some people can be trusted."

Jess looked at me. She already had a slightly different look in her eyes to the fearful expression she'd worn in the shelter that morning.

Our next task was a walk. Jess had been in the shelter for a while which meant she'd been walked on one small field only and I suspected her previous people had never given her much exercise. That was about to change.

I grabbed Sam's old lead and the Light Blue Safety Lead, threaded them together by the wrist loops and then clipped the faithful Light Blue Safety Lead around my waist. Jess was much bigger and stronger than Sam and I didn't fancy seeing how fast she could run if she got away from me. Jess looked nervous as I approached her to clip the other lead on to her collar and looked away from me as if hoping I'd change my mind if she didn't make eye contact.

"It's ok Jess, we're just going for a walk. You're ok."

As soon as Steve opened the patio door, Jess made a beeline for it and I again felt how strong she was.

"I'll be getting some decent arm muscles!" I said to Steve, hanging on to the lead with both hands and attempting to restrain her as best I could.

As we made our way towards the fence line path from our house, it was obvious that Jess loved being outside. Much like Sam, her demeanor seemed to change and she seemed more confident once she was outdoors. However Jess's walking style couldn't have been more different to Sam's. She didn't show any inclination to stop and sniff every few yards and instead was on a mission to cover as much ground as possible. If that meant removing my shoulder from its socket then so be it. This really was a case of the dog walking the person and I realised within a few minutes that we'd need to work on this. But not now on this first walk.

We headed over to the path that followed the Fort Detrick fence line and strode at a brisk pace all the way to Nallins Pond and back. When I used to do that walk with Sam, we'd rarely make it to the pond as Sam spent so much time sniffing around. With Jess we made it in extra quick time as she barely stopped pulling the entire time. Steve took her on the way back and agreed she was incredibly strong. We did gently pull her back when the pulling got too bad but the purpose of this walk was mainly to get her used to us and show her that we'd always give her plenty of exercise so I didn't want to curb her enthusiasm too much.

This excursion showed us how Jess blossomed in the outdoors so once we got home I drove back to PetValu for the second time that day and picked up a

'Dog Tie Out' so that Jess could sit outside with us at every opportunity. This useful dog gadget was a large metal corkscrew that you screwed into the ground to provide a firm anchor point. It came with a sixteen-foot wire lead attached to give your dog plenty of freedom whilst keeping them safe. Jess seemed to enjoy being outside with us and the cable meant she could keep her distance and yet be close enough to hopefully form the view that Steve and I were nothing like her previous humans.

That night we barbecued a couple of ribeye steaks for dinner. As I hoped, Jess's nose began twitching appreciatively when the aroma of juicy steak wafted in her direction and she took a few brave steps towards the barbecue. When the steaks were finished I took her several choice pieces and she approached me, emboldened by the promise of grilled meat. If the way to Jess's heart was through her stomach then I felt sure we could make some progress.

That night I placed her new bed in the middle of the living room and patted it encouragingly.

"You can sleep on this Jess, bit more comfortable than the floor."

Jess just looked at me, not unhappily, but it was clear she had no intention of lying on the bed whilst I was there. What was she thinking? This was her first night in her new home. Would she settle down and sleep comfortably? Or would she be on edge, not knowing what to think about the direction her life had taken today? I fully expected to come downstairs to some kind of stress-induced destruction in the morning but that was a risk we'd have to take.

"Night night Jess, sleep well."

And with that I turned the living room light off and followed Steve upstairs to bed.

The next morning I woke up early and remembered with a rush of excitement that we had a new foster dog who was waiting for me downstairs. Jess was lying on the living room floor, next to but not on her bed, looking at me expectantly. She stretched her long legs and stood up, cautiously keeping a slight distance from me whilst I prepared her breakfast. She then ate it with what seemed a lot like enthusiasm. I was hugely relieved that she seemed to be eating now and it showed that she was significantly more relaxed in our house than at the shelter, despite having been here less than 24 hours.

I watched her as she ate, still overwhelmed with how beautiful she was. In terms of looks, she really was the dog of my dreams. Lauren had described Jess as a husky mix, a Siberian Husky crossed with another breed of dog. However there is another husky which is characterised as a type rather than a breed and that's the Alaskan Husky. They're bred for a purpose – pulling sleds – rather than to a breed standard and therefore don't have a typical colour or markings. It is these dogs that prevail in dog sledding races such as the Iditarod and the Yukon Quest. I decided that with her inclination to pull at all costs and her long, lanky legs, Jess was clearly a fine example of an Alaskan Husky. And an Alaskan Husky just so happened to be my favourite dog. I already had a thought forming in my mind but I pushed it away – I needed to get to know Jess better before I shared my thought with Steve.

We decided to take Jess to Gambrill State Park, about fifteen minutes from us, for her morning walk. Gambrill made up the southern section of the watershed forest that Sam had loved so much and it was indistinguishable in terms of scenery and terrain. I never understood why one section of forest was designated a state park and one section was a municipal forest – the trees all looked the same to me.

Jess was in her element and pulled me along enthusiastically. I didn't enjoy our walk at all however, and felt on the verge of being dragged over the entire time. Many of the trails at Gambrill were quite rocky underfoot and so I had to keep my eyes glued to the ground in order to keep from tripping up.

I tried standing still whenever Jess pulled which is how you're meant to teach a dog to walk respectably on the lead. However it was clear Jess had never read a dog training book and was so strong it didn't matter – she pulled me anyway. If this didn't settle down then we had a bigger problem on our hands than just her fearfulness. Steve had a turn of walking with her and even he struggled to hold her sometimes. Of course I couldn't really blame Jess – it was her husky genes making her want to pull. If I'd been stood behind a dog sled, headed towards the finish line at Nome, then Jess's pulling would have been a virtue. However I was a foster carer in Maryland, not a musher in Alaska, and this was definitely going to be something we needed to work on.

That afternoon and evening Steve and I sat outside with Jess clipped to the ground stake. This first couple of days had been promising. Although Jess still seemed a little unsure of her new people and her new environment, she didn't seem actively scared of us. The fearful expression and hunched demeanour she displayed at the shelter had largely gone and had been replaced by an expectant expression on her face, as if she was prepared to believe that her life had taken a turn for the better. She watched us with interest, as if appraising us carefully and forming an opinion as to whether she could trust us. Despite her size and slightly wolf-like physical appearance, Jess seemed incredibly vulnerable. She carried the weight of being let down once too often and I believe that by the time she'd entered the shelter she'd virtually given up. Now there was a glimmer of hope in her eyes again and it was up to me to be worthy of that.

The next day was Monday and Steve was back at work after the weekend. It was the first day when it would be just me and Jess. I decided to introduce her to the watershed as Sam had loved it so much up there.

I loved it up there too but hadn't been for a while. I'd been for a run up there by myself a couple of times before deciding that I felt slightly uneasy going on my own. It was bigger and more remote than Gambrill State Park and I was still learning my way around the trails. The forest was dense and there was hardly anyone around, plus the mobile phone reception was extremely patchy. If I'd met any crazed axe murderers then I'd have been at a distinct disadvantage. With Jess by my side I felt no such fear. She looked fierce and intimidating enough to deter anyone with malign intent.

Unsurprisingly Jess loved the watershed too. She seemed to sense its remoteness and was getting excited on the drive up as the houses became scarcer and the tree cover became denser. By the time I parked and got her out she was impatient to explore this new area and took off at husky pace. I loved her urge to explore but became increasingly frustrated at having to pull back on the lead constantly and there were times when I had to hold the lead with both hands and use all my strength just to slow her down. It wasn't much fun, not least because I started to worry about the effect on her neck.

For reasons of self-preservation I didn't have a choice but to restrain her as much as I could although the trails at the watershed were less rocky than at Gambrill so it was easier stumbling after her. I managed about 45 minutes before I'd had enough and turned my four-legged cruise missile around and headed back to the car.

That afternoon I took Jess to Baker Park and resolved to make a concerted effort with the 'stop walking every time the dog pulls' method. After half an hour my resolve crumbled and I realised that if I kept this method up then we'd never get anywhere. Quite simply Jess's determination to pull beat my patience with standing still; I actually wanted to walk too. This is why I was a good foster carer and would be a terrible dog trainer – I have far more patience with the undesirable behaviour than I do with the corrective training. However more importantly, Jess was becoming increasingly confused as to why I kept stopping. At the point at which she started to look nervous I made the decision to knock this particular training technique on the head. I didn't want to stress Jess out or damage our emerging bond.

I felt certain that, just as with Sam, regular walks were helping Jess's confidence and I didn't want to hinder that. On the other hand, her pulling would be detrimental to her chances of adoption if it continued. I'd just have to hope that it settled down or come up with another method of training her to walk nicely.

The next morning I decided to take Jess for a run around the base. I was an enthusiastic rather than gifted runner – my style could best be described as a 'determined plodder'. But I enjoyed it nonetheless and thought it was a safe bet that an Alaskan Husky would enjoy going for a run too. I also hoped that the fact we'd be moving slightly faster would mean she didn't pull quite so much. I was right on both counts. And when she did pull, it was much less frustrating for me because the effect of her pulling was mitigated by the fact that I was moving faster.

The Light Blue Safety Lead system also meant I could run 'hands free'. Jess was attached around my waist so I didn't need to hang on to the lead the whole time. I did still have to be careful and occasionally had to grab the lead to slow her down but it was a definite improvement on our frustrating walks. Of course this wasn't a solution – there was no way I could run with her twice a day, and I needed to prepare Jess to be adopted by someone who wasn't a runner at all. However our successful run gave me the germ of an idea to try in a few days if necessary.

It was lovely having Jess all to myself when Steve was at work. I was utterly captivated by her and after only a few days I couldn't imagine life without her. She was my dream dog – beautiful, athletic, wolf-like but also undeniably good natured. She embodied all my childhood reasons for wanting a dog and I couldn't believe how lucky I was to be fostering her.

Jess was still an enigma to me though; she was clearly on her guard which was unsurprising given her history and there was so much about her that I didn't know. But I had faith that we'd get there. I loved her presence, loved just looking up from whatever I was doing and seeing her there. She seemed to complete me; she was the dog I'd always wanted.

One afternoon in Jess's first week with us, I was reading on the sofa and Jess was lying down on the floor a few feet away. She had her back to me and there was just something so inherently vulnerable about the way her shoulders were hunched up and the rise and fall of her body as she breathed. I was suddenly overwhelmed with love for her. I'd heard mothers talk about the rush of love they experienced when they held their newborn baby for the first time. This moment was similar for me.

That evening I told Steve I wanted to keep Jess; that she was the dog I'd always dreamed of and I didn't think I could give her up. It had been traumatic enough to give Sam up and I loved Jess more already. Steve was sympathetic but asked me how it would work with our life back home. I didn't have an answer. I didn't want to think about going home, I just wanted Jess to be my dog forever. We agreed there was no rush and this was something we could think about in slow time. But I didn't see how I could possibly let Jess go.

Five days after we got Jess, it was Frederick's first 'Alive@Five' of the summer. Alive@Five was a weekly, outdoor, dog-friendly concert and beer fest with various local bands playing and naturally it was extremely popular. It seemed like a great socialisation opportunity for Jess as we'd be surrounded by dog-friendly people and other dogs so we decided to take her with us.

Alive@Five was held just off Frederick's historic Market Street, next to the more urban stretch of Carrol Creek, which wound through downtown Frederick from Baker Park. The city authorities had poured a lot of money into downtown Frederick in recent years, adding a spruced up pedestrianised area along both sides of the creek that played host to a variety of outdoor events. Alive@Five was held at the grass-covered Carroll Creek amphitheatre and was already busy when we arrived. A band was playing, the beer and food tents were clearly popular and plenty of people were enjoying the warm evening, many of them with a beer in one hand and their dog's lead in the other.

I sat down on one of the terraced steps and Jess immediately pushed herself behind my legs and lay down. She didn't move for the rest of the night. She didn't seem scared, just determined to keep my legs between her and the rest of the world.

We were meeting Amy, Shelley and Sandy the Labrador there and there were also a number of other people we knew. Everyone wanted to meet Jess and thought she was gorgeous, however Jess stayed resolutely behind my legs and make it clear she wasn't in the mood to make new friends. She wasn't aggressive in any way, just anti-social, although she tolerated a friendly sniff from Sandy, the dog who made me decide to foster again after the emotional rollercoaster of Sam.

I knew this must have been an ordeal for Jess but we needed to show her that normal life was nothing to be scared of. She was safe and no one was going to hurt her. Considering the upheaval of the last few days, she did brilliantly. It was also nice that though she'd only known me for five days, my legs were considered a safe refuge. It was a great evening and I hoped we'd be able to take Jess to future Alive@Fives.

The next morning brought another frustrating and potentially neck-breaking speed-hike up at the watershed. We'd had Jess almost a week now and her pulling hadn't settled down at all. I decided to try the idea I'd thought of after our run – a retractable lead. My theory was that maybe Jess wouldn't pull so hard if she had a little more freedom and a retractable lead would give her that. Retractable leads are controversial for good reason and Steve was thoroughly opposed and thought it would make her worse. As the person who walked her the most, I didn't think it could possibly make her worse and would give me the opportunity to instill in her that walking nicely earned her the reward of having a longer lead as I'd only press the button to extend it when she wasn't pulling. Hopefully this positive reinforcement would encourage her to stop yanking my arm off.

I'd also been concerned for Jess's neck and the effect that Jess pulling one way and me pulling another must have had on it. So I decided we needed a harness as well as a new lead. Back I went to PetValu.

"Back again?" smiled the sales assistant.

"Should have bought shares!" I replied.

I picked up a sixteen-foot retractable lead which would give Jess a lot of freedom if she deserved it and then browsed the vast array of harnesses on offer. Some were advertised as 'no pull' or 'correctional' but they either looked too flimsy or were the type that attached around her muzzle. I guessed that Jess would be horribly stressed by that kind of constraint.

I decided that a step in harness would be the best option. This was a type of harness that essentially looked like a diamond with a sternum strap dissecting the harness across the middle. Her legs went either side of the sternum strap and the two sides were then pulled over the top of her back and clipped together with a robust plastic clip. The harness was fully adjustable for a snug fit. The shelter used these harnesses with certain dogs so I was reassured that they were suitable. I parted with yet more money and returned home to my favourite reason to spend it.

Against all the odds, the retractable lead proved marginally successful. And I stress 'marginally' – Jess still pulled and the lead was by no means a miracle cure. But by being strict about when I put the lead in 'free run' mode and when I locked it, I was able to reward Jess for not pulling and reel her back in when she did. Over the next week I sensed that she was beginning to learn that walking agreeably got her more independence and freedom and pulling meant she had to walk next to me for a while. I have since become vehemently opposed to retractable leads, not least because they can be dangerous to people, but it definitely helped with Jess.

One issue I had to be aware of with the retractable lead was the need to be constantly aware of our surroundings. If Jess spied a ground hog or squirrel with the lead in 'free run' mode then she potentially had sixteen feet to accelerate to full pursuit speed before reaching the end of the lead and her forward momentum at that point could easily pull me over. It was therefore vital to remain alert at all times so I could brace for impact if necessary. There was an abundance of ground hogs on Fort Detrick and a similarly healthy population of squirrels at Baker Park so digging my heels in and tensing my upper body to check Jess's crazed pursuit of small prey was a fairly regular occurrence. Fort Detrick also lay underneath the flight path from the White House to Camp David and we often had helicopters flying low overhead. I discovered, to my astonishment and exasperation, that Jess had a prey drive for helicopters as well as small furry animals.

The harness eased my concern over the effect that Jess's pulling was having on her neck. However after a couple of days I noticed that the adjustable buckles had moved by a couple of inches, no doubt from Jess's pulling, and the harness was now hanging rather loosely on her. I didn't see how she could possibly escape but nonetheless, I didn't want to underestimate a husky. So I reset the buckles and wound some gaffer tape around them to stop them slipping in future.

"There! Nice try Jessica but you'll have to try harder to escape from me!" I grinned.

Jess grinned back at me and did just that.

A few days later, I took Jess for a walk up at Gambrill. We'd been hiking at a fairly brisk pace for well over an hour and Jess had begun to tire and so was behaving quite well. We were walking along a rocky and quite narrow section of footpath with trees on either side so I had the retractable lead locked at about half its length.

Then Jess veered slightly off the footpath and passed a small tree on the opposite side to me. The lead caught around the trunk and stopped Jess in her tracks.

"Come on Jess, back this way," I said to her, giving the lead a gentle tug to encourage her to go back on herself and walk the correct way around the tree.

Jess looked at me, obviously confused as to what was preventing her from moving when I was stood right next to her. She turned around to face the source of the problem and pulled again, except she was now essentially pulling backwards in the harness instead of forward in it.

I would never have believed that what happened next was possible if I hadn't seen it happen right in front of me. In one smooth movement that looked like she'd practised it, Jess simply reversed out of the harness by pulling back sharply, ducking her head under the plastic clip in the middle of her back and stepping out backwards. She was loose and had bounded a few feet away before I had a chance to grab her. My heart lurched and my first instinct was to run after her. Thankfully my head remembered what had happened with Sam so I stayed rooted to the spot.

"Clever girl Jess," I said calmly, not making any move towards her.

Jess was staring at me, seemingly a bit confused by what had just happened. I was certain she hadn't meant to escape; she had simply tried to dislodge whatever was holding her back. But escape she had. Jess turned and trotted a few feet away and then stopped and turned towards me again. She was free and now she knew it. I'd only had her for ten days and her experiences prior to being fostered were still fresh in her head. And now she had a choice – to choose life with me or to run away.

I sat down, doing my best not to show how scared I was.

"That was awesome Jess, I didn't know you could do that. I don't think you knew you could do that either! Clever girl!"

Jess looked at me hesitantly for a moment and I could almost see the thought process playing out in her head. Then she sat down too but her body language was tense and I knew I had no hope of lunging for her. I stayed sitting for a while longer, trying to project an air of calm confidence that I certainly wasn't feeling. I avoided looking at her for too long, casually letting my gaze wander as if admiring the forest scenery. I told Jess what a great walk we'd had and how much I'd enjoyed it. After an interminably long couple of minutes, Jess sighed, lay down and rested her head on her front paws.

"Good girl Jess."

I smiled at Jess and slowly stood up. Jess stayed lying down. Then pretending that we were simply in the living room I strolled over to her, stroked her head, gently took hold of her collar and clipped the lead on. The fear of the last few minutes flooded through me and I felt wobbly. That could have been disastrous. I sat down with Jess and petted her, shaking from the shock of nearly losing another dog and losing her where I had next to no chance of finding her again.

I looked at Jess with heartfelt gratitude. Jess chose not to run away from me. She had plenty of opportunity and I'd have never caught her. But she didn't run off, she lay down and she let me approach her. Despite what had happened it was amazing to know that Jess trusted me. Given the choice, she chose to stay with me. It was a huge vote of confidence.

Back home I threw the useless step in harness away immediately and Googled 'escape proof dog harnesses'. I found a robust looking one from Ruffwear that had been specifically designed for search and rescue dogs. Made from strong nylon, it had five points of adjustment for a snug and secure fit, a padded chest strap and a tummy strap for added security. You attached the lead to a solid looking aluminum ring that had been sewn into the harness with reinforced stitching. It was bright red, reassuringly expensive and I ordered it right there and then and paid extra for speedy delivery so we'd have it in a couple of days. I didn't want any more votes of confidence from Jess quite like that one.

Jess's decision to not run away from me showed me that the burgeoning bond we had wasn't a figment of my imagination. From the day we brought her home she had seemed content to be in the same room as us although she remained on her guard initially. Gradually the wariness subsided and she seemed increasingly relaxed. She'd let us pet her for short periods and after the harness incident started to come over and nuzzle affectionately in to me every morning when I came downstairs.

Then we had another significant breakthrough – Jess decided to join me on the three-seater sofa. I'd been priming her for a few days by putting treats on the sofa for her, to show her it wasn't out of bounds and there would be no punishment. The first few times she took a treat off the sofa I then gave her another treat as a reward.

Then one afternoon I was surfing on the laptop and Jess crept over and stood at the other end of the sofa, looking slightly pensive. She slowly raised a long foreleg and tentatively placed her paw on the seat cushion. When I didn't react she climbed up and lay down, suddenly looking wary as if she wasn't at all confident that this incursion into an elevated human space was allowed.

"Good girl Jess," I said encouragingly, shooting her an approving smile. Joining me on the sofa was an important indicator of her burgeoning confidence and trust in me and I had to reassure her that she'd done nothing wrong. Back when I'd fostered Sam, I realised that his desire to get on the sofa – to be close to me at my level – signaled a huge improvement in his confidence and it was the same with Jess. She felt accepted in the family and wasn't nervous of being told off. From that day on, that was Jess's end of the sofa.

A few days later I was having an afternoon snooze on the sofa and Jess was curled up at her end doing the same. I didn't hear Steve arrive home so he was able to take an amusingly incriminating photo of me fast asleep next to a guilty looking Jess. But the great thing was, Jess woke up when Steve walked in the house but stayed on the sofa whilst Steve was silently laughing at us and taking his sneaky photo. This was another important indicator in that she knew she had nothing to fear from Steve either.

Another measure of her confidence was how comfortable she felt in our house. For the first week or so, Jess stayed downstairs. Then, just like Sam had done, Jess started to follow me upstairs. I'd be in our en suite bathroom and I'd see the tip of her nose poking round our bedroom door, just sniffing to check where I was. She never let me catch her; as soon as I made towards the door she'd be off, slinking silently down the stairs seemingly unaware that I was watching her over the banister. I started calling her my Ghost Dog as she seemed to be in possession of supernatural stealth powers.

In fact Jess soon had quite a few affectionate nicknames; Ghost Dog, Crazy Wolf or simply Jessica as a more formal name for telling her off when she pulled too much. "Take it easy Jessica, your Jenni's on the other end of this lead," I'd remind her and she gradually, slightly, almost imperceptibly started to take notice.

Crazy Wolf was the nickname we used most often due to her close resemblance to her wilder cousin. She did have long legs and remarkably big teeth and she seemed to exude a wild and independent spirit. I was never really sure that she was meant to be tamed. One night Steve was remarking on how wolf-like she was and on a whim threw his head back and howled. Jess looked at him quizzically, her head cocked to one side.

"Come on Jess," he said, "Howl with me!"

Jess looked at me with an amused expression on her face and so I howled too. Steve joined in and then an amazing thing happened – Jess howled with us. It was an incredible moment hearing her 'voice' and feeling like the three of us had become a quasi-pack, which of course we were.

Despite the tenets of 'pack theory', a thoroughly discredited view of dog behaviour still espoused by certain celebrity dog trainers, a wild wolf pack is simply a family group. It is not a collection of individuals vying for power and supremacy like a canine version of a medieval royal dynasty. Steve, Jess and I were family, a pack, and this howling became a regular bonding ritual. Fortunately our house was detached although I dread to think what anyone walking past must have thought.

We'd now had Jess for nearly three weeks. She was eating brilliantly, so well that it was easy to forget that this had been one of the original reasons for Jess going in to foster care. She'd put on 8 lbs, a healthy amount of weight, her eyes were bright, her coat shone and you could no longer see her ribs. The expensive food and salmon oil had been worth the money. She was definitely more confident, more affectionate and the pulling had improved by about ten percent. I'd even trained her to 'sit' for a treat, about the only thing I ever managed to train Jess to do. Everything seemed to be going well. Then another issue started and this was potentially extremely serious.

One morning I was walking Jess on Fort Detrick. She was pulling as usual – it tended to be worse at the start of a walk – and I was following my usual positive reinforcement policy of ignoring the pulling as best I could and then praising her for any brief period when the pulling stopped and rewarding her with a longer lead. At one point Jess had been walking next to me for a few seconds when I suddenly felt a searing pain in my ankle. I actually cried out in pain and in shock – Jess had bitten me. I looked down and Jess was grinning up at me in a perfectly friendly fashion and wagging her tail, whereas I had a large graze oozing blood on my right ankle.

I was horrified and upset and didn't understand what had just happened. I was momentarily fearful that Jess was about to attack me but the happy tail wagging and tongue lolling continued and I realised that she wasn't being aggressive; she was being playful.

It's perfectly normal for puppies to nip as a precursor to playing. They naturally grow out of it – as puppy siblings nip each other they begin to understand that it hurts. Humans can reinforce this with the 'yelp and shun' technique that I'd used when I fostered Lily. I hadn't needed to consciously 'yelp' when Jess bit me however, I had yelped out of genuine pain. I hoped my anguished reaction would teach Jess a swift lesson in dog-human etiquette and the bite would be a one off.

But it wasn't a one off. Unfortunately it was the beginning of a long phase which in terms of Jess's adoptability was a huge setback. Whilst Jess never again drew blood and she never bit me as hard as that first time (I think my yelp of pain taught her what my threshold was and she wasn't trying to hurt me), every walk would start with her mouthing me a few times. I understood that she wasn't being aggressive – to her this was akin to a good-natured slap on the back or a playful punch on the arm – but the first ten minutes of every excursion were not at all enjoyable for me. She was trying to initiate a bout of rough and tumble the way that puppies do. Except Jess wasn't a puppy, she was a large adult dog with big teeth and if she went too far one day she could do some serious damage.

On one walk the mouthing was so unrelenting that the thought entered my head that I might need to return her to the shelter. I immediately dismissed this option. I never asked but I suspected I had been Jess's last chance so there was no way I could let her down. A foster dog who'd been on the brink of being euthanised and who was then given up by her foster carer for continued nipping probably wouldn't have a long life expectancy.

I continued to yelp and shun whenever Jess's canines made contact with my skin and this quickly reduced the force of her mouthing so if she got me on the arm or calf then it didn't really hurt. However being nipped in a sensitive place like an ankle or on my waist was more painful. She even managed to jump up and get me on the shoulder once. I tried turning my back on her, to really press the point that this was not the way to get my attention. If Jess had read any dog training manuals she would have known that she was supposed to stop the behaviour that caused me to ignore her. Instead she deduced that she needed to make her point more forcefully; she bit me on the bottom instead.

Jess's behaviour obviously left me extremely worried for her adoption prospects. As soon as I had realised that Jess's mouthing was an ongoing issue I had discussed it with Didi, a dog behaviourist who'd recently joined Frederick County Animal Control as the education officer. Didi assured me that I was doing everything right – yelping and shunning and praising her when she stopped – and assured me that by all the rules of dog training, things would start to improve. They didn't.

Obviously this new behaviour meant that we now had another challenge to contend with before Jess could be adopted. Not only did we have to work on her confidence but we had to stop this mouthing.

I noticed that Jess hardly ever mouthed me if we were running and I guessed that running gave her something else to focus on. So I tried giving her a tennis ball at the start of a walk, to distract her and give her something to chew on. She took it from me, looked confused for a second and then dropped it and started mouthing me. So much for that theory. There was nothing for it but to hope this was a phase and continue yelping, shunning, and crossing my fingers.

Thankfully, despite all this challenging behaviour going on outdoors, Jess remained a dream dog indoors. She never ever nipped when she was inside and was becoming more confident and affectionate by the day. Our morning greeting entailed a few minutes of nuzzling and cuddling and her trips upstairs were no longer stealthy ones. And just as Sam had done, Jess started sleeping outside our bedroom door. Steve usually got up before me and would open the door and let her in, whereupon she'd wake me up with a 'kiss' by gently touching my face with her nose. It was the best possible way to start the day.

Jess began coming upstairs with me quite openly and went through a phase of not wanting to let me out of her sight. If I went up to collect some laundry or have a shower then she'd come into the bedroom and lie down and wait patiently for me. This habit of following me upstairs soon morphed into a game.

One day I was running late to meet a friend for lunch and realised I'd left my car keys on my bedside table. So I ran back up to fetch them. For reasons known only to herself, Jess decided this was terribly exciting and so bounded up after me. This became a ritual – whenever I need to go upstairs I'd run up so that Jess would chase me, boisterously pushing past my legs and always beating me to the top. Then she'd grin at me as if to say, "Nice try Jenni but you know I'm faster!"

Then one afternoon, Jess was snoozing on the sofa in a warm pool of sunshine and I decided to take advantage. I ran up the stairs two at a time and my crazy wolf's reaction was a little slower than normal. I'd almost made it to the top of the stairs before I heard Jess leap off the sofa and chase after me. Our bedroom was opposite the top of the stairs and I decided it would be funny to hide behind our bedroom door and jump out at her. She hadn't turned the corner of the stairs yet and hadn't seen me duck behind the door. Sure enough Jess raced into our room and then stopped abruptly, no doubt wondering where her Jenni had gone.

"Raaahhhhhh', I cried, leaping out at her from behind the door. As I did so I remembered how handy Jess was with her teeth and realised I'd just done an incredibly stupid thing. But Jess spun around, the surprised look on her face turning to playful delight as she knocked into my legs and let me pet her all over.

So 'Find Jenni' became a welcome addition to the 'Chase Jenni up the Stairs' game. Jess soon got wise to my hiding place behind the door so sometimes I'd crouch behind one side of the chest of drawers or the bed, or behind the door of our en suite bathroom, to keep her on her toes. We played 'Chase Jenni up the Stairs' and 'Find Jenni' several times a day, each game ending in us 'laughing' together and having a conciliatory half-cuddle, half-wrestle to show there were no hard feelings. And to think some people worried that being unable to work would leave me bored and unfulfilled.

Now that Jess was becoming so much more confident with me and Steve, I decided to start working on building her confidence around other people. I was still torn between wanting to keep her and admitting to myself what a significant challenge that would be in a flat in England with (hopefully) a new baby. My strategy was two-fold – pray for some kind of miracle that meant we could keep Jess whilst simultaneously working on making her as adoptable as possible. Ultimately what I wanted was much less important than what was right for Jess.

We took her back to Alive@Five a couple of times and she seemed to tolerate it but never actively enjoyed it. I also took her to Baker Park regularly although we kept our distance from all the other people who inconsiderately insisted on using it too.

A few weeks before we started fostering Jess, Steve had signed up to do a mile-long swim in Maryland's beautiful Chesapeake Bay. I had always planned to go and watch him but now that we had Jess I was concerned about taking her. The race started and finished at a waterside restaurant and there would be hundreds of people there. We'd never been to this place before so didn't know the layout; however I felt certain it wouldn't be a Jess-friendly environment.

We'd be gone far too long to leave her however and Steve looked disappointed when I mentioned I was having second thoughts about going to watch so I decided we would just have to make it work. Worst case scenario, Jess and I would find a quiet stretch of beach somewhere.

In actual fact our Chesapeake outing proved to be a valuable experience for Jess. We arrived at the race venue early having scouted out a couple of places where I could take Jess for a walk if necessary. Interestingly I noticed that on the walk from the car to the restaurant, through the car park thronged with other people, she didn't mouth me once. I suspected she wasn't feeling playful because she was in a strange environment with lots of people around and so was nervous and on edge. This confirmed my theory that the mouthing was Jess's way of being playful and when she wasn't feeling playful then the mouthing stopped.

We explained to the restaurant host that we had a nervous foster dog and he thoughtfully showed us to the perfect table in the far corner of the outdoor seating area, with a stretch of lawn and then the beach in front of us. It also offered a good view of where Steve would start and finish his swim. As Steve went off to register and get changed, Jess and I deposited ourselves at the table and the waiter brought her a bowl of water. To my relief Jess lay down in the shade and was as good as gold.

The start and finish point for the race was on the beach adjacent to the other end of the restaurant so we were well out of the throng of people but still with a great view of Steve. I watched him start out and then almost immediately lost sight of him amongst all the other bobbing swim hats. So I read my book and sipped my Coke and enjoyed sitting in the sun with my unusually well-behaved dog. I knew Steve was expecting to complete the mile swim in about thirty minutes so started watching out for him a few minutes before. I was fairly sure I recognised him from his swimming style when he was a few hundred feet out and sure enough, when the figure emerged from the water it was my husband.

Steve was elated from his swim and as he came over Jess realised who it was and scrambled out from under the table to greet him. It was nice to note that she'd realised Steve was missing and was pleased to see him again. Then we celebrated his achievement with cheeseburgers and fries. It was a lovely afternoon that gave us a glimpse of what life could be like with an easy-going and non-nervous Jess.

Afterwards we took Jess to a nearby nature reserve for a walk. The trail was reasonably short and ended at a secluded sandy beach. Best of all, there wasn't anyone else there. The retractable lead came into its own here, allowing Jess to run in and out of the surf and leap over the waves as they rolled in. She was having a wonderful time and her happiness was contagious. Steve and I took our shoes off and paddled in the sea with her.

This successful outing gave me hope that Jess was turning a corner. So after our next walk in Baker Park I decided to walk her into town in order to get her used to people and traffic in close proximity. However it proved to be a disaster. Jess clearly wasn't comfortable and whereas she could cope with strangers in a large open expanse like Baker Park, provided they didn't get to close, she couldn't cope with new people within a few feet of us on the sidewalk. As someone approached, Jess would flatten herself against the nearest shop front and cower in fear. Frederick was a dog-friendly town and a few well-meaning people attempted to pet her and reassure her. Unfortunately this just made her worse. Jess didn't want to be reassured, she wanted to be left alone, and I had to politely ask people not to approach her.

Rather than retrace our steps I decided to walk back to the car along Carroll Creek's pedestrianised zone where there would be no cars and more space. I hoped this might calm Jess down a bit. However something clearly triggered her and she suddenly became extremely upset, pulling wildly and bucking around and scrambling up on a raised flowerbed in order to escape a man who made the mistake of walking too close to us. I ended up having to pick her up and carry her until we could make our way back to the car via a couple of quieter side streets.

I told Didi about what happened and we agreed to hold off on making Jess walk through town for the time being. She was nowhere near ready for adoption due to the mouthing and pulling so her unhappiness in a busy environment wasn't the most urgent issue. I decided to continue our regular trips to Baker Park and work on her fear of strangers by inviting more people round to meet her at our house, somewhere where we knew she felt safe and comfortable.

Amy and Shelley had come round one weekend soon after we'd started fostering Jess and she had clearly been nervous. She actually growled at them but it was definitely fear, not aggression, as she was backing away the whole time and retreated to her 'safe space' on the sofa. Amy and Shelley were experienced dog people and completely unfazed by Jess's attitude. They stayed for coffee and Jess settled down but we agreed not to push things. A few nights later they came for dinner and Jess was much calmer and laid down next to the table as we ate. This showed me that Jess could get used to other people; we were just going to have to persevere.

The pleasantly warm weather of May had given way to a June heat wave. Not only was it hot but it was humid too. I had to stop running with Jess due to the heat and we started going for our morning walk by 9:00 a.m. Even so, we'd get home and Jess would flop down on the floor directly in the cold blast of the air conditioning unit. By midday the temperature would frequently reach 100 degrees Fahrenheit on base. The watershed became our preferred walking location as it was significantly cooler due to its elevation and the cover of thousands upon thousands of trees.

I'd always driven to the same parking area at the top of the watershed. There was a well-maintained network of trails up there that offered extensive hiking through beautiful forest, plus a couple of ponds that Jess could cool off in. Then one day on the drive up, just after the houses gave way to forest, I noticed a truck parked on a patch of cleared ground just off the road that I now realised was a small layby.

"Hmm," I pondered to Jess, "Is this a trailhead for a trail we haven't discovered yet? Fancy investigating?"

Jess grinned back at me, her pink tongue lolling out and her eyes bright with anticipation. Clearly I was giving off 'exploring' vibes. I pulled in and parked next to the truck and got out. However we'd only walked 50 feet back from the road when I decided this couldn't be a trailhead as there was a stream running parallel to the road which was also fed by another stream coming down the hill. Whilst the stream was extremely shallow and easily crossable there didn't seem to be a trail leading away from it. I let Jess have a paddle which was fortuitous as then a guy and his dog appeared from around some rocks and I realised there was a trail if you knew where to look.

And thus Jess and I discovered our favourite hike in the whole of Maryland. This trail was a great find and perfect for our needs that summer. It was a brisk 45 minute walk up to the top, the trail crisscrossing the stream the whole way and with ample spots where Jess could get in the water and cool down. A couple of the water holes were nice and deep and came up to her shoulders. It was also rare to ever see anyone else. If we did see anyone, Jess would turn to me in surprise, looking rather annoyed that other people had gatecrashed our own private hiking trail. I agreed with her. I began to realise that Jess and I were extremely similar – we were both expected to be friendly and sociable yet we both liked a bit of space and our own company. We didn't want to be 'socialised' – we were quite happy to be sociable so long as it was on our own terms.

In the slightly cooler evenings, Jess and I often walked the fence line or across Wild Field down to Nallins Pond and back. One night we were walking back from Wild Field, past a rectangular copse of trees just before the housing began, when I noticed the whole of this small patch of woodland was sparkling. There must have been a huge swarm of fireflies because I could see numerous pinpricks of light flickering on and off in the darkness like a canopy of twinkling stars. It was beautiful. I sat down next to Jess and we watched the display for ages.

The night was perfectly still and quiet and we could have been a woman and her dog from another age, witnessing the magic of nature in silent companionship. I felt blissfully complete. I was privileged to have a dog like Jess who was everything I'd ever dreamed of and more. The Jenni with Jess by her side was the Jenni I was meant to be and I believed we'd been destined to meet. Yet again I asked myself why I simply didn't throw caution to the wind and adopt her.

However no matter how much I loved Jess, there was no getting away from the fact that whilst she was perfect for our life in Maryland, she wasn't perfect for our life in England. The thought did cross my mind that something was wrong here. If my perfect dog wasn't the right fit for my 'normal' life then maybe the problem wasn't with the dog – it was with the life. And maybe that life needed changing.

Living in the US had transformed me. I was bowled over by the space, the opportunities, the sense of being much closer to nature and the wild. I didn't want that feeling to end and I knew Steve felt the same. Steve and I had decided that we craved wilder wilderness and greater adventures than the UK could provide and were seriously considering the prospect of Steve transferring to the Canadian army to enable us to emigrate.

Our dream was to end up living somewhere remote, with as many dogs as we felt appropriate. But we did have to go home first – Steve couldn't just leave the army as that was our route into Canada and so returning to the UK for a certain period of time was non-negotiable. And I couldn't simply put Jess in storage for a few years.

Jess was the dog I always dreamed of having. I felt a deep bond with her that I hadn't felt with any of my other dogs, that I actually hadn't felt with anyone before. We seemed to fit together and I knew I never wanted to be apart from her. Yet reluctantly I had to face the fact that her behaviour meant we couldn't adopt her, not least because it wouldn't be fair on her.

We were going home to our two-bedroom apartment. Jess barked and growled whenever someone came near our front door or perfectly legitimately walked past the back of our house across the communal lawn. Imagine her frenzied reaction to someone walking up or down the communal stairs in a block of flats and passing right next to our door. We weren't allowed a dog in our apartment anyway and couldn't risk a noise complaint, a council official coming to investigate and Jess growling at the official and being designated a dangerous dog under Britain's draconian Dangerous Dogs Act. That would have meant Jess could have been seized by the police and destroyed and it was unthinkable that we would risk that.

In addition Steve and I were trying to start a family. I tried to imagine wrangling Jess along our town's narrow pavements or crossing the road with her whilst pushing a pushchair. I now boasted fairly impressive muscle definition on my right arm from the constant effort of hanging on to Jess whenever we went for a walk and it was frequently a two-handed job anyway. Quite simply pushchairs and Jess were not a safe combination.

And this was without considering the mouthing. I could put up with it and I understood that Jess wasn't being malicious. But whatever her motivation, she had the ability to seriously injure a baby or toddler. And that would certainly have dented my love for her.

Whichever way we looked at it, Jess simply wasn't compatible with our life in the next few years. Our worlds had collided but not melded. We were soul mates destined to be apart. It broke my heart but I had to accept that for Jess's sake, for our sake and for the sake of a future baby, we simply couldn't adopt her.

CHAPTER 8

THE MAGNIFICENT SEVEN

ON THE MORNING of Thursday 23rd June, the population of the Williams's house stood at three with an ethnic makeup of two-thirds human and one-third dog. By that evening the population had swelled to ten and the human race was outnumbered eight to two.

It was another blazing hot day and Jess and I had hiked for an hour at the watershed that morning and were settling down to a pleasant air-conditioned afternoon of snoozing and watching a movie, followed by a walk in Baker Park when it was cooler. That evening Steve and I were going out to our favourite pizza restaurant. All in all, life was pretty good.

Then my phone rang; it was Didi. She told me she had a litter of seven Labrador / German Shepherd cross puppies that needed fostering for a couple of weeks; was I interested? I certainly was. I'd adored having Lily, the Belgian Malinois puppy, and I'd always hoped I'd have the opportunity to foster another pup. Fostering one for two whole weeks would be wonderful.

"Of course Didi, I'll definitely take one of them for you," I said, over the moon at the thought.

"Oh no, I'm sorry Jenni, to be clear I need someone to take all of them. They're so young that it's best for them to stay together at the moment."

Well obviously I couldn't take the whole litter. That would be utter madness, especially as I had Jess as well.

Only a delusional, Crazy Dog Lady would agree to foster seven puppies when they already had their work cut out with a high-maintenance husky.

"I'm really sorry Didi but I just can't take them all, what with Jess..."

"Actually it would be great for them to be around Jess, she'd be a kind of surrogate mom to them."

That actually made a lot of sense. But the answer was still no. Even if I thought I could cope with seven puppies, there was another insurmountable problem – the housing rules on Fort Detrick stipulated that the maximum number of dogs you could have in your house was two. The litter of puppies plus Jess would make eight. There's bending the rules and then there's brazenly trampling all over them. I explained this to Didi and said I didn't want to get thrown out of Fort Detrick and cause a diplomatic incident.

"I wouldn't worry about that," said Didi brightly. "The thing is they'd report you to Frederick County Animal Control and I'm pretty sure we'd go easy on you!"

I hesitated. Didi sensed my weakness and went for the knock out blow.

"How about you just come down and meet them? No pressure. See if you like them."

See if I like them? As opposed to the distinct possibility that I might meet a puppy I didn't like? Didi knew what she was doing.

On the short drive to the shelter I kept telling myself that I was only going to look, that I really couldn't take in seven puppies. It was a lovely thought but completely unrealistic. I'd meet the puppies and then tell Didi that I was terribly sorry but she would need to find another foster carer on this occasion.

Didi greeted me in reception and led me down to the quarantine room.

"You're going to love them, they're adorable," she told me.

Well that's as may be but I still wasn't going to foster them. I was just there to look, out of professional foster carer interest. And then I was going to make my excuses and head home to Jess and my otherwise uncomplicated life.

I followed Didi into the quarantine room and there in one of the pens were seven balls of absolute cuteness. "Ooh", I think I exclaimed.

"Here, get in with them," said Didi, carefully opening the door of their pen so I could squeeze in.

"Yay, MOMMY!" cried seven puppies as they launched themselves at me en masse.

I sat down with the puppies and was swamped. They all wanted a cuddle and they all wanted to lick my face and eat my hair and chew my shoelaces at the same time. They smelt of puppy breath and wee and I was in heaven. All rational thoughts went out of my head; the puppies and I had bonded.

"Oh my goodness, you're all lovely. Would you like to come home and live with me? Yes? You would? Alright then, it's a deal!"

I turned to a grinning Didi.

"Er, well I should probably check with Steve but obviously I'm going to take them," I said, trying to stifle a grin of my own.

"Thought you'd say that."

Two of the puppies were black but one had a white chest so it was easy to tell them apart. The other five were all predominantly tan coloured but had slightly different markings. There were two boys, the black puppy with the white chest and the largest tan puppy. The rest were girls.

Didi told me that the puppies were five and a half weeks old, which meant I'd need to have them for two and a half weeks. Under Maryland law puppies couldn't be sold or given up for adoption until they were eight weeks old. After a few more minutes of getting acquainted, I delicately extricated myself from the cage whilst promising my new friends I'd be back soon.

"Ok, let's go and sign the paperwork," smiled Didi with a self-congratulatory twinkle in her eye which I graciously chose to ignore.

In all honesty, as much as I was excited at the thought of having seven puppies in the house, I was also apprehensive. Although I'd fostered Lily for three days, she was one puppy. This was seven puppies for two and a half weeks and I also had Jess. How was I going to manage this?

Didi appeared to have infinite faith in me however. She told me she'd got me a puppy play pen and large crate from the storeroom so I could set up a safe and secure puppy area at home. Obviously I couldn't just bundle up seven puppies in my arms and drive back by myself and having them loose in the car was out of the question. Didi and I agreed I'd take the crate and pen first and set everything up so the house was ready for them. Then I'd drive back with Steve later that afternoon and we'd bring a large dog travel crate I'd impulsively bought for Jess recently in anticipation of a possible camping trip one day. (It was on offer, I hadn't bought a dog 'gadget' for a while and I figured Jess could sleep in the crate in the car if she was too scared to get in a tent). Although we'd never used it, I knew it fitted nicely in the back of our car if you put the seats down. We could then safely transport the puppies home in that.

I drove home with the pen and crate, two packs of puppy pads, a large bag of puppy food, a load of towels and a few food and water bowls. I set up the pen and crate so that the puppies could have the run of the open plan entrance hall that led from our front door and garage door through to our dining area and living room. The hallway floor was all tiled which would make mopping up the inevitable accidents a lot easier.

I made a padded sleeping area in their crate with a couple of folded over towels and left a bit of space at the end for a puppy pad and a water bowl. I also rolled up a couple of towels and lay them along the edge of the crate to act as a draught excluder or a pillow if the puppies needed one. All I needed to do now was confess what I'd done to Steve. I phoned him at work.

"Hi babe," I said. "I have something to ask you. It's something I really want to do but you need to agree. How do you feel about fostering a litter of seven puppies?"

Steve laughed nervously, "Er, what? What have you agreed to now Crazy Dog Lady?"

I explained the situation, how these poor puppies were desperate for a loving foster home and we were their only chance. I explained how having Jess as well was a real positive and would actually make our life easier, not harder. I almost convinced myself.

It's fair to say that Steve had a few reservations so I went on to tell him that we – by which I meant 'I' – would be unlikely to ever have a litter of puppies otherwise. One of his family's black Labradors had had a litter when Steve was a child and he often talked fondly about it. I reminded him of this and how it was abundantly unfair that he'd had such a lovely experience and I hadn't.

My husband knew when he was beaten. Steve duly agreed to our new houseguests and assured me he'd be home on time so we could go and collect them together. I still had a couple of hours to kill so I took Jess for her afternoon walk, rightly assuming that the rest of the day would be rather busy.

By the time Steve arrived home he'd had a while to get used to the idea and was as excited as I was. We jumped in the car and headed down to the shelter, both of us eager to bring our new family members home. And as soon as he saw the puppies he was smitten; Steve isn't as tough as he likes to think.

Together with Lauren and Didi we gathered up all seven pups and carried them out to our car and placed them in the travel crate for the short drive home.

"Good luck!" smiled Didi.

"Anything you need let us know," said Lauren, "And have fun!"

"Thanks so much!" I laughed.

Then we took our precious cargo back to their new home. We carefully lifted the travel crate out of the car and carried it into the living room. Before we left the house I'd put Jess up in our bedroom. I was sure she'd accept the puppies but deemed it best to control the introduction. If Jess was up in our bedroom then we could get the pups settled before letting her come downstairs to meet her new playmates.

We set the crate down in the middle of our living room, unzipped the mesh opening and six little puppies came tumbling out, eager to explore their new environment. Incredibly one of the pups remained asleep in the crate.

We immediately discovered that a litter of free range puppies is utter chaos. Within thirty seconds there were three wees on the floor and the rest of the pups had run through the puddles so we had wee footprints all over the place.

The black boy with the white chest instantly bounded off into the living room, making straight for the far corner where the laptop was kept. And naturally the laptop cable needed chewing. I lifted him away and he headed straight for the kitchen and interesting objects like the bin. He was the first puppy to get a name – Lewis after Merriweather Lewis, the famous American explorer. I could hear Jess running around our bedroom. She knew that something exciting was happening downstairs but we couldn't add her to the mix just yet.

The biggest puppy, the tan coloured boy, had remained asleep during the initial chaos. Then he suddenly woke up, stretched and went tearing off around the living room.

"He's just had his Scooby snack!" I remarked to Steve. So we named him Scooby. Right after getting his new name, Scooby added to the collection of puddles on the floor.

"We need to get them outside or there's going to be more wees on the floor," said Steve, scooping up a couple of wriggling pups.

"Ok but we can only take two each so let's put the other three in the pen and then we can swap them."

So we deposited three puppies in the pen and took the other four outside.

"Ok gang, this is where you all 'go potty', anywhere you like out here", I informed them, using the American terminology and setting my two squirming pups down.

The four ran around in a little gang and we immediately realised that letting them out to poop and wee all together was asking for trouble. Not only was it difficult to keep an eye on four puppies but as one puppy would be pooping, one of its siblings would invariably run up and playfully knock the still-pooping puppy over into its own poo.

Steve went in and brought out the travel crate so that we could contain those four puppies, at least two of whom now needed a bath due to inadvertent poo rolling.

Then we brought out the remaining three and the same thing happened. This 'going potty' en masse approach was creating more work. We decided in future that we'd take out one puppy at a time per person and take each one far enough away from each other so that we had time to pick up each poo before they got a chance to roll in it. At some point that night this routine got christened the 'puppy poo shuttle'.

After they'd all been to the toilet we filled one of our plastic crates with warm water and gave them all a bath. This was easier said than done – puppies are nothing if not squirmy. But there was no way they were going back in the house until they were clean and sweet smelling.

When they were all presentable again we brought them back inside and placed them in their pristine, towel-lined crate. They'd had a lot of excitement and unsurprisingly were beginning to get tired. One by one the pups began to fall asleep, all curled up together.

"Aaah, look at them!" I whispered to Steve, "So cute! This was definitely the right decision!"

Steve laughed at me. "It's only the first evening, say that in a few days time!"

I suddenly remembered we had another dog upstairs. Poor Jess who was being ever so patient. I ran up to our bedroom and was greeted very enthusiastically.

"I'm so sorry Jess, you've been such a good girl! Come down and see what I've got for you!"

Jess bounded downstairs and made straight for the crate. She regarded the seven little balls of fur with nervous interest bordering on trepidation and then looked at me as if to say, "Er… what have you done Jenni?"

"I'm really not sure Jess! But don't worry, you're still my best dog."

"Hey, we haven't finished naming them yet," said Steve.

The smallest puppy, a tan girl, we named Tanny after Steve's dog who had been the runt of the litter. It also suited her colour. We therefore called the black girl Kim, after Steve's other family Labrador who I'd known and loved.

That left three fawn girls. We named the most golden one Honey and the prettiest one Mollie after my grandmother who had died a few years previously. That left the most confident and self-assured girl, the one I had already decided would be the one I'd keep if that were remotely possible. I named her Scout after the little girl in "To Kill A Mockingbird", Harper Lee's classic book set in the Deep South. Scout was my favourite literary character and ages ago I'd decided that would be what I'd call my first dog.

Thankfully it was easy to tell the puppies apart. Kim and Lewis were both predominantly black but Lewis had a white chest and white paws. Scooby and Scout both had dark ears and a dark muzzle but Scooby was bigger and a boy. Tanny was the smallest puppy and tan all over. Honey had darker colouring around the side of her face but was lighter otherwise and Mollie had a slightly dark muzzle, which wasn't as dark as Scout's. I never got them mixed up.

We had a couple of hours of respite whilst the puppies slept, during which time we managed a peaceful dinner. Then one of the puppies started to stir and they all woke up within seconds of each other. The puppy poo shuttle got repeated, this time with Steve and I each taking one at a time which proved far more conducive to a clean and efficient toilet experience. We put the pups who'd been outside loose in the pen so they could have a run around and a play and so we didn't get mixed up with the puppies who were still in the crate and hadn't been outside yet. Once they were all done, Steve and I got in the pen and just enjoyed playing with them.

I also let Scooby and Mollie out of the pen in to the living room to see what Jess made of them. She looked appalled for a few minutes and then sensibly retreated to the sofa and regarded them with a mixture of curiosity and mild alarm. I suspected that instead of being a surrogate mom, she'd be more of a reluctant big sister who longed for the days when she was an only child.

The rest of the evening involved two more puppy poo shuttles, more playing and a lot more wees on the floor. But as I watched the puppies fall asleep in their crate for the night, I had a warm glow of satisfaction that my seven new fosters were clean, fed, and cared for.

The next morning I woke up just before Steve's alarm went off at 7:00 a.m. Despite my drowsy state I was aware that something was happening today, something important. Then it all came flooding back – there were seven puppies downstairs and they all needed to go outside right now. And so the whole relentless puppy poo shuttle routine began again, a veritable conveyer belt of pup wrangling and poop-scooping.

That first morning established a pattern that remained unchanged for the entire two and a half weeks. My day would start before 7:00 a.m. when I'd give Jess her breakfast and then take her outside. Then the puppies would start waking up and the race would be on to get all of them outside before one of the remainder decided I was taking too long and pooped in the crate. And then of course, they'd all walk through it and there would be poo paw prints all over the towels. Steve usually left for work by 7:30 a.m. so I was on my own which increased the pressure.

Then it was breakfast time and I had about 60 seconds to bundle up the wet and soiled puppy pads and put them in the bin and then bundle up the wet and soiled towels, invariably with little paw prints of poo now adorning them, and shove them in the washing machine.

Then I'd turn my attention back to the puppies who'd finished their breakfast. There was always at least one wee on the floor whilst my back was turned which signaled it was time to take them all outside again. The digestive systems of puppies are a closed system. They need to go first thing in the morning but once you've introduced another tummy load of food, they need to go again. So the same ritual was repeated and each puppy went out individually.

It was another race against time that I never seemed to win. There was always one who pooped in the house whilst I was outside with one of his or her siblings. The strange thing is they would all have a second poo outside so at least one of them was having three.

Eventually it was playtime for them and 'clean out the crate' time for me. I'd wash up their water bowl and put fresh water in, spray the floor of the crate with 'Pee Off' dog disinfectant and put fresh puppy pads in one half and clean towels in the other. Then I'd join them in the puppy run for cuddles and play time. However it wouldn't be long before they'd start to drop off and I'd place them back in the crate so they could go to sleep.

As I watched them snuggle into each other, the overriding thought that went though my head was 'thank goodness for that.' Then it was time for my breakfast.

Then I had to shower and dress and take Jess for her walk which got shortened to 45 minutes because I had to get back for Puppy Poo Shuttle No 3. By the time we got back, invariably one or two of the puppies were beginning to stir and there was always at least one wee patch on the pads.

After Poo Shuttle Number 3 it was outdoor playtime when I took them outside in pairs for 10-15 minutes of running around and chasing each other. If I was feeling particularly organised then I'd make the effort to take the puppy pen outside so those not running around could at least still be outside with us. The houses on Fort Detrick didn't have fenced yards and whilst I could keep tabs on two puppies at a time I didn't fancy my chances with seven.

In addition I was trying to be discreet and not advertise the fact that I was a secret puppy hoarder, albeit one with the best of intentions. Whilst I knew FCAC would let me off, I didn't fancy getting into trouble with the Fort Detrick housing office.

My main aim during this fostering assignment was survival, theirs and mine, and puppy training was not my priority. However I did start them on the basics such as housetraining, recall and bite inhibition. This was especially important as they had sharp little teeth and being nipped by one was not fun, especially as a few others then invariably joined in.

During puppy playtime I'd call them over to me and then make a big fuss of them and give them a piece of kibble as a treat. This sowed the seed in their minds that coming when your human calls means good things like a treat and a tummy rub. After puppy playtime I'd bring them back in the house and sometimes gave them the run of the living room whilst I cleaned out their crate again. Jess would usually retreat to the safety of the sofa during what I termed 'puppy break out time'. Then when they were all safely back in the crate for their afternoon snooze, this was my opportunity to have my lunch and do a bare minimum of household chores.

After a few days I started to give each puppy one on one time with Jess. She much preferred dealing with one puppy at a time and would allow them to climb all over her and playfully bite at her ears and legs. Her patience with them astonished me. If one got a little too boisterous she simply pinned it to the floor with one of her front legs for a swift 'time out'.

Steve and I were fully in the throes of trying to conceive and I couldn't help but view my seven puppies as practice babies. I don't believe you should ever use a dog as a child substitute but those puppies definitely kick-started some maternal feelings. Didi had talked about Jess being their surrogate mom but in reality I was. I was the one who fed them, cleaned them up, gave them cuddles, and finally 'tucked' them in their crate at night. And when they were lying in their crate, small and helpless, I felt enormously protective of them.

The two and a half weeks with the puppies was hard work, huge fun, and complete and utter chaos. And as a measure of the nitty gritty of what having seven puppies means, Steve and I worked out that we picked up over 1,000 puppy poos in those two and a half weeks.

I found it fascinating that despite the fact that they were so young, all of the puppies had distinct personalities. Scooby was easy going, fun loving and confident, the consummate all-rounder. Kim was quiet and was the pup who most often took herself away from the melee to lie by herself. Lewis was affectionate and sweet and was particularly attached to Steve. Honey was calm and always amongst the first to fall asleep, Mollie was hyperactive, and Tanny was feisty and quick to snap at one of her siblings if they took advantage of her small stature. Scout was intelligent, independent and slightly stubborn. She was the pup least likely to be enticed away from exploring outside by the promise of a treat. She remained my favourite although I tried not to let it show.

The only downside of fostering as far as the dogs were concerned is that they weren't physically in the shelter and therefore weren't visible to prospective adopters. To mitigate this disadvantage, Didi had encouraged me to let our friends and acquaintances know that we had seven puppies who would soon need forever homes.

We'd only had the pups a few days when Steve's colleague and our friend Amy asked if she could come round to meet them. Other friends, Jan and Dick, who also worked with Amy and Steve, asked to come too.

They were all immediately smitten and the puppies loved having more people to play with. Although Amy made it clear that she wasn't in the market for a second dog, Jan and Dick kept looking at each other knowingly. Jan was particularly taken with Tanny.

To our delight, Jan and Dick decided they wanted to adopt Tanny and planned to go into the shelter the following day to fill in the paperwork. I emailed Didi to let her know the good news.

"Congratulations Jenni, you already set a new record for fastest foster pick up and now you've got fastest foster adoption!"

So that was one down, six to go. About a week before the puppies were due to go back to the shelter, we started to think about marketing them on Petfinder. One sunny evening we held a photo shoot and spent an enjoyable hour taking photos of each puppy. Steve got a particularly great action shot of Scooby leaping up on his back legs with his two front paws out in front of him. I emailed the photos to Didi along with a short profile that I'd written about each puppy.

Didi published the photos and profiles to Petfinder with an explanation that the puppies were still in foster care but would be available for adoption within a week. The photos proved to be a masterstroke. Didi told me that they'd never had so much interest with loads of people ringing up and asking how to apply. One caller even demanded to know how we'd photo-shopped the aforementioned photo of Scooby and didn't believe Didi that all the photos were genuine.

I had given Didi my phone number and told her to feel free to give it out to prospective adopters who had questions about the puppies. So I was pleasantly unsurprised when my phone rang the next day and the caller introduced himself as one Peter Murray. Peter explained that he and his wife had been struck by a photo of Lewis strutting around our patio and had put an application in on him.

Peter sounded like a suitable recipient of one of my pups and asked lots of questions about Lewis and the fostering programme. Then he put his wife Sandee on and she sounded lovely too. She mentioned they'd only been married for a few months and they wanted a dog before they had children. I approved of Sandee's order of priorities.

I also had a phone call from Lauren. Friends of hers had seen photos of the puppies and had fallen in love with Scooby. She asked if they could come and meet him on Saturday morning. I agreed immediately. Lauren's friends turned out to be the perfect family for Scoobs. Mom, Dad and three kids, they lived in rural Carroll County and had been missing a dog in their life since their Rottweiler had died the year before. Meeting Scooby in person convinced them he was the dog for them and the feeling was clearly mutual. Scoobs had definitely found his people and they left ours to go straight to FCAC and put in an application.

So three of my seven puppies had definite applications on them before they'd even gone back to the shelter and there was considerable interest in the others. I felt proud that we'd done our best to ensure that the puppies could go to their forever families as swiftly as possible.

Our last weekend with the pups was bittersweet. It was extremely hot and I was nervous about exposing them to the intense July sunlight; I didn't want them getting heatstroke on their last weekend. So we pulled our car out of the garage and opened the main door and side door for ventilation and set the puppy pen up in there. It was in fact now two foldable puppy pens clipped together to make one big pen – the puppies were considerably bigger than they had been and wouldn't all fit comfortably in one pen anymore

When it was cooler in the evening, Steve and I enacted a routine we'd started the week before of taking two puppies at a time to run to the summerhouse on the communal lawn in the middle of First Flight Court and back again. As there were seven of them, Scooby got to go twice as he had the most energy to burn off.

Then the Monday morning came when it was time to say goodbye. I had mixed feelings that morning and intense relief was one of them. It had been hard work and I was looking forward to a slightly emptier and easier nest. On the other hand, I'd loved having them and I knew I'd look back on the experience entirely fondly. I also think Jess benefited, both the socialisation with the puppies and Jan's regular visits to Tanny. Jess had become increasingly relaxed in Jan's presence which was encouraging progress.

Steve got up with me and we undertook our last puppy poo shuttle and breakfast routine. I put the travel crate in the back of the car and one by one we loaded all the pups inside; they took up considerably more of the crate than they had two and a half weeks ago and there was a lot of treading on each other's paws.

Due to having seven puppies to deal with, I'd agreed with Carol that I'd be justifiably late for the spay and neuter clinic. Lauren was already at work when I arrived and said the pups could go straight into the puppy room, which was separate to the main adoption floor, and they'd be assessed and processed before the shelter opened. They were too big to all occupy the same cage so we put Scooby, Mollie and Kim in one and Lewis, Tanny, Honey and Scout in the cage next door. I realised that the car journey from my house to the shelter was the last time that all the siblings would be together in one place.

After the spay and neuter clinic I went to check on them. It had been a few hours and I was worried about whether they were settling in to their new surroundings. I needn't have worried. It was mid July and schools had already closed for the summer, hence the shelter was busier than normal in the middle of the day.

Both cages were surrounded by people, including a number of children, all cooing at the puppies. There was also a volunteer sat in with Scooby, Mollie and Kim, stroking them and letting them climb all over him. The pups were loving the attention and didn't notice their erstwhile foster mom who was craning her neck trying to get a better look at them. I wanted to shout "Stand back, I'm their foster mom, let me through!" but I managed to hold it together. There was no rush, they wouldn't be going anywhere for a couple of days.

When I got home after the spay and neuter clinic it truly hit me that they'd gone. The house was incredibly quiet without them and Jess seemed slightly thrown. I had a peaceful lunch and then Jess and I went for an extra long walk at the watershed to reward her for her incredible patience and understanding. It was lovely to be out with her and not have to think about getting back.

Later that afternoon I headed back to the shelter to drop off the crate and puppy pens as there hadn't been room for them in the car when I'd transported the pups back that morning. As I was passing reception, I noticed a young couple filling in some paperwork.

"Hey Jenni, this is the Murrays," said the receptionist. "They're here for their adoption interview for Lewis. And this is Jenni Williams, Lewis's foster mom."

Peter and Sandee were as great in person as they seemed on the phone. We swapped emails and they promised to stay in touch and let us know how Lewis was getting on. Sandee rather nervously asked if I'd mind if they changed Lewis's name. I assured her that would be fine!

By Monday evening I was missing the puppies unbearably. I had nothing to do. Steve decided we were going out to celebrate getting our life back and I was forced to admit that it was nice to be out without a care in the world. Steve told me it was nice to be out with a wife who didn't smell of puppy wee. I had a few beers and a huge burger and enjoyed the fact that I could eat slowly and savour each bite and didn't have to keep an eye out to check whether someone was pooping whilst I ate.

The way we'd promoted the puppies meant we were able to keep in touch with three of them straightaway. Scooby was adopted by Lauren's friends and they kept the name because their kids didn't want to change it. I went to visit him several months later and he was exactly the same easy going and affectionate boy except he was huge. He was clearly doted on and loved being a family dog. Melissa the mom was planning to attend therapy dog training with him as he had such a calm and steady temperament.

Lewis was adopted by Peter and Sandee and became Patrick. Peter and Sandee were kind enough to send photos and let us know how Patrick was settling in. We started meeting up for walks in Baker Park and then the humans started meeting up for beers and meals. We remain good friends to this day. Patrick now has two little Murrays to take care of, Winnie and Benjamin. He is a certified therapy dog and has his own Instagram account. He certainly found the perfect family for him.

Jan and Dick had their interview on the Wednesday and were unsurprisingly approved. They took Tanny, now Cali, off to her forever home a couple of days later. Jan and Dick both retired a few years ago and Cali now leads a life that most humans would envy. Not only are Jan and Dick extremely active people who love the outdoors but they have a luxury camper van and take off for months at a time, chauffeuring Cali all over the USA. We regularly see envy-inducing photos on Facebook of Cali leading Jan and Dick on a hike in some amazing location, usually with a lake somewhere in the photo. That dog certainly landed on her paws.

At the time, I didn't know who adopted the remaining four puppies but I was assured that they all went to great homes. Sadly that wasn't the case, as we would soon discover.

CHAPTER 9

DOG DAYS OF SUMMER

THE NEXT DAY was the first full day without either the puppies or spay and neuter clinic commitments. I decided to devote the day to Jess to thank her for her patience during the last two and a half weeks. Despite the chaos and the numerous puppy break out sessions and the fact that all of a sudden she didn't have her Jenni's undivided attention, Jess had been amazing.

Furthermore I'd inevitably had less time to walk her. I usually gave Jess two hours of walking a day but that had reduced to about one and a half hours during the puppies' stay with us and I felt bad about that.

So on Tuesday morning Jess and I set out early for an extended walk at the watershed. We hiked our favourite trail following the stream uphill and then continued even further in to Gambrill State Park before turning back on ourselves and heading back down. We hiked for over two hours in total. Then that afternoon we went to Baker Park and paddled in the creek and sat under the trees and watched the world go by. I told Jess how much I enjoyed being just 'Jenni and Jess' once more and promised not to bring home an entire litter of puppies again.

Although having the puppies had been a magical experience, it had naturally restricted what we'd been able to do and Steve and I both had a touch of cabin fever. We decided to take off on a camping trip to New

Germany State Park in Western Maryland that weekend. We'd been thinking about taking Jess camping for a while although I was slightly nervous that she might tear through the tent and escape. We decided that worse case scenario, if it looked as though she was stressed in our fairly snug tent, then she could sleep in the travel crate in the back of the car and one of us would sleep in there with her. Not even Jess could tear her way out of a 4 x 4.

On Saturday morning we packed up our car and set out on the scenic drive west. New Germany State Park is situated in Western Maryland, about an hour and forty-five minutes from Frederick. It borders the Savage River State Forest and boasts five hundred acres of forest, hiking trails, a campsite and small lake. It sounded idyllic and just what the three of us needed.

When we arrived I was pleased to see that the campsite wasn't busy and we had a secluded pitch with no one else near us, which boded well for Jess's state of mind.

"I think you're going to enjoy this," I told her, scratching her head. "It's just you, me, Steve and the outdoors. Your favourite things!"

Camping with Jess was always going to be a logistical challenge. She wasn't the kind of dog who would potter around reliably close by whilst you set up camp. We'd brought the ground stake and long wire lead to clip her to but Jess was so excited watching us unpack the car and begin to lay out the tent that she was constantly jumping around and getting herself tangled up. So Steve sent me and Jess on a walk around the lake to get her out of the way. By the time we returned, Steve had done a great job. There were logs in the fire pit all ready for later and the tent was up with our mattresses and sleeping bags laid out inside.

Eager to explore and give Jess some proper exercise we set out on a hike for the rest of the afternoon. Jess was excited to be having another walk immediately after the first one and pulled us along enthusiastically. We followed the stream that ran past the campsite and then the trail took us up into the forest. It was a sunny day and the sun streamed through breaks in the tree cover, illuminating the sea of green that encircled us. After a while Jess settled down and walked well, leaving Steve and I free to immerse ourselves in an enjoyable conversation about our fantasy ideal log cabin in the woods that we would definitely build one day.

Naturally we started to pay slightly less attention to our surroundings. We'd visited various national parks in Canada and the western US before and were therefore well versed in bear etiquette – stay alert, talk loudly, clap your hands regularly, and carry bear spray. However maybe we'd become complacent about bears because this was only Maryland and felt safe and homely. So we hadn't brought our bear spray with us and were talking fairly quietly as we walked through an area of quite dense forest. And neither of us noticed a rather large furry mass off to our right.

As Jess had been walking reasonably well, I'd allowed her the full length of the retractable lead. She suddenly jerked forward off the trail, her hackles shot up and she started barking furiously. I looked off to my right – about 100 feet away a black bear was thankfully running away from us, its bulky hindquarters moving surprisingly athletically.

I reached behind me and grabbed Steve. "Bear!" I gasped.

"Whoa, good girl Jess," exclaimed Steve.

"Well done Jess," I said, "At least one of us is paying attention!"

It was a great sighting, not least because the bear decided to leave us alone. It was also a bit nerve wracking and we made sure to make more noise after that. But most of all, it was humbling to note Jess's reaction – she instinctively knew to warn us of danger and even though she was an incredibly nervous dog, at the point she saw the bear she leapt forward rather than slunk back. She chose to put herself in the way of something that could kill me and I was deeply touched. What a comfort dogs must have been to those early humans who faced this kind of peril on a daily basis. The wild must have seemed a lot less threatening with a dog by your side.

When we got back to the campsite we clipped Jess to the wire on the stake and made sure she had her water bowl within reach. She flopped down contentedly, although clearly still intrigued as to what was going on. Steve busied himself with the fire and camp cooking and I busied myself with a beer. We had a great evening around the campfire, chatting and periodically gazing up at the twinkling ceiling of stars. It was a timeless scene – humans, a fire and a dog.

Eventually it was time for bed. I was still uncertain as to how Jess would react to this new sleeping arrangement but I needn't have worried. I unzipped the tent and crawled in first and then Steve handed me Jess's lead. She didn't hesitate but followed me in enthusiastically, went straight to the end of our camping mattresses and flopped down, grinning at me.

"She looks happy!" remarked Steve.

"Good girl Jess, do you like camping then?"

Jess looked totally relaxed and I felt confident there was no way she'd try and escape now. Sleeping in a tent with her two favourite people appeared to be her idea of heaven. So the three of us settled down and went to sleep, that particularly satisfying form of sleep that seems synonymous with the great outdoors.

I woke up once in the night, perhaps sub-consciously feeling the need to check Jess was still there.

She was fast asleep at the end of my mattress. I lay awake for a while, listening to the deep breathing of my dog and my husband. I felt safe in a fundamental way. My dog, an animal whose ancestor had formed a relationship with humans tens of thousands of years ago based on mutual trust and companionship, was lying at my feet. Her nose and her ears would pick up approaching danger long before mine would. And her teeth were quite a lot bigger than mine and I knew the pain she could inflict with them when she was merely being playful. Goodness only knows what damage she could do if she used them to protect someone she loved.

This feeling of sleeping with my dog was an experience I'd always wanted. There is no more tangible an example of trust between two different species – dog and human trusting each other enough to completely let their guard down with each other. One has big teeth and one can use tools. Each could kill the other in its sleep. But not only does that not happen but each trusts that it won't. This was one of those moments in life you remember forever; camping under the stars with the two most important people in my life. As I succumbed to sleep once more I was about as content as it's possible to be.

Back at the shelter on Monday, I told Didi about our camping trip and how much Jess had enjoyed it. She was impressed that we'd taken Jess with us and said how positive it was that we did activities like that with her. Didi felt sure the camping trip would have been a formative experience for our nervous foster dog.

Whether our mini adventure had indeed had some kind of effect or whether Jess just appreciated having me to herself again, our bond went from strength to strength. Her behaviour on walks was still terrible but we seemed to reach a new level of closeness. Ironically the closer Jess and I got, the more ready for adoption she was because my initial task had been to get her to trust people again. But I tried not to think about that. She was still sufficiently unhinged that I felt sure that we had plenty more time together.

I had adopted a new strategy to deal with Jess's mouthing because ignoring the behaviour wasn't working – if she nipped me then we went straight back inside the house. I'd make her sit down, tell her how disappointed I was in her and then I'd wait a minute or so before going out again. I hoped the message was getting through – bite your Jenni and your walk is delayed. This strategy started to pay off and gradually Jess's mouthing improved. The irony was that I trusted her implicitly inside and never once felt threatened by her. She just had an inappropriate way of asking me to play with her.

Jess's pulling on the lead had also slightly improved in recent weeks, however one painful and probably inevitable incident demonstrated her capacity to cause serious harm to anyone walking her. I'd taken her to Baker Park, home to countless grey squirrels, for a stroll along the creek. A short distance from the car, Jess squatted down for a wee. I had the retractable lead in free mode yet it was fully wound in because Jess was right next to me. This meant that at the precise moment of disaster, the lead had a long way to unwind and Jess had optimum acceleration opportunity.

Whilst Jess was relieving her bladder, my attention was diverted from her and what was happening around us by a classic old Cadillac cruising down the street adjacent to Baker Park. So I didn't notice the squirrel that scurried temptingly down a tree only a few feet away from Jess and didn't notice her dart off in pursuit. My brain registered the whirring of the retractable lead too late, just as Jess reached the end at full speed. Suddenly my right arm was yanked forward, I felt myself pulled through the air and then I hit the ground heavily. The lead's plastic handset was pulled up into the bottom of my jaw and rattled my entire head.

I did actually see stars and was dragged along the ground for a couple of feet by Jess before she stopped. I was dazed, in pain and furious with myself. Jess wasn't exactly my favourite individual on the planet at that moment but all she'd done was chase a squirrel. I was the idiot who'd given her the wherewithal to hurt me whilst doing so. And she had hurt me – my jaw throbbed, I had a big cut on my elbow and the hand that wasn't holding the lead was horribly grazed.

I got to my feet, staggered unsteadily the short distance back to the car, got Jess and myself in and then burst in to tears. Partly it was shock, partly it was actual physical pain and partly it was frustration and concern for Jess's future. Normal dogs didn't do this. Normal dogs walked nicely on a single lead that didn't need to be attached to another one around the person's waist. People with normal dogs didn't risk serious physical injury every time they went for a walk. Why couldn't Jess be a normal dog?

Back home I examined my wounds. My hand and elbow were bloodied and stung as I cleaned them up. I had a bruise coming up across my jawline and another one coming up on my right eye. I vaguely remembered the handset making contact further up my head after initially hitting my jaw. But at least all bones were intact. I spent the rest of the day lying on the sofa and feeling sorry for myself. The perpetrator of my injuries did at least keep me company and kept coming over to bestow husky nose kisses as a mark of her concern.

When Steve got home he was horrified and tried to convince me to throw away the retractable lead. Despite what had happened I didn't want to do that as I felt that would have undone some of the progress I'd made with

Jess. The broader rights and wrongs of retractable leads aside, I remained convinced that it was helping her walking. I assured Steve I'd learnt my lesson and wasn't about to make the same mistake again no matter how many classic old cars drove past. However this incident did at least make me resolve to do whatever it took to make Jess more desirable to walk.

Earlier on that summer I'd met a woman I'll call Jane at a friend's BBQ. Jane and I started talking and quickly got on to the subject of dogs. Jane had two red setters and I told her all about my fostering experiences and mentioned the problems I was having with Jess and her pulling. Jane said she'd had similar problems with her male setter who I'll call Rusty. I asked her how she'd dealt with it and she launched into a long explanation about how she practiced a form of yoga with him and had learnt how to hold him and transfer her calm energy to him. The upshot was that he now walked beautifully on the lead and she was always receiving compliments about how well trained he was. Jane offered to come for a walk with me and Jess and demonstrate the whole 'calm energy' method.

At the time that had sounded somewhat far-fetched for my liking but after the squirrel incident I was willing to try anything and there was no harm in simply going for a walk together. I texted Jane to tell her briefly what had happened and how I was at my wit's end. We agreed to meet in Baker Park so I could learn how to transmit serene vibes to Jess and miraculously turn her into a paragon of walking virtue.

Yet when I met Jane, she seemed reluctant to elaborate on her 'dog yoga' technique. When I pressed her for details she was rather vague and said it was difficult to explain. I asked her if she could demonstrate with Rusty but she just told me it was all about your inner attitude as opposed to any tangible dog-calming methods. I began to feel like I might have a bit of an attitude coming on myself but not necessarily the one Jane meant.

Despite my growing cynicism, I did have to admit that Rusty walked nicely on the lead, in marked contrast to Jess who was up to her usual tricks. Then I noticed a flash of silver metal around Rusty's neck. At one point when Jane's attention was diverted by her female setter, I surreptitiously ran my hand through the long fur on his neck and felt metal. A quick look confirmed it – Rusty was wearing a prong collar. A prong collar is an unpleasant device, essentially a choke chain with elongated 'U' shaped links. When the dog pulled, the open ends of the 'U' would dig in to the dog's neck.

I suddenly saw Jane in a different light. All this lofty talk about using the power of her mind and thinking tranquil thoughts and she was in fact, using a device to inflict pain on Rusty to punish him for pulling. I suppose that's one way to get a dog to stroll sedately by your side but I'd rather have my arms ripped from their sockets than resort to that. We didn't walk with Jane again.

As if the pulling and the mouthing weren't enough to be dealing with, Jess was becoming increasingly adept at escaping from us, albeit temporarily. One evening I'd pan fried some sea bass fillets for dinner. They were delicious but the whole house smelt of fried fish. To get rid of the smell I opened all the downstairs windows which was perfectly safe as they had built in insect screens so Jess couldn't use a window as an escape route. Otherwise I had no doubt we'd be treated to a demonstration of her hurdling skills.

A summer storm was forecast that night and it was an overcast and extremely blustery evening, the wind making a dramatic whistling sound as it gusted through the house. The action of opening the windows must have created a wind tunnel because we suddenly heard the sound of the front door blowing open and banging against the wall in the hallway.

The houses on Fort Detrick had not been built to the highest specification. The front door was essentially no different to an internal door in that it didn't self-lock when closed, had a handle on both sides and could be opened from outside if the door was unlocked – which it was. Fort Detrick didn't exactly have a high crime rate and we only locked up when we went up to bed for the night. The bolt itself was small and as it turned out, ineffectual in high winds. It had always performed the job of holding the door shut before but clearly wasn't big enough to withstand the force of differing wind pressure swirling inside and outside the house.

The noise of the door had startled Jess and she jumped up and went to investigate, me right behind her but not close enough. The open doorway was too tempting for Jess and she bounded out excitedly and started doing laps of the large communal lawn in the middle of First Flight Court, a big grin on her face and her long legs reveling in the freedom to run at husky pace instead of mine. There was obviously no point chasing her so I darted back inside and grabbed the Ruffwear harness and lead.

"Come on Jess, let's go for a walk," I yelled, waving the harness in the air. We were due our evening excursion anyway and Jess always associated the harness with an outing. To my relief she completed a final loping circuit of the lawn just to show she was a free spirit who didn't take orders from anyone and then bounded up to me and allowed me to put the harness on and take her for some more sedate exercise. Crisis averted. We kept the front door locked at all times after that.

Only about a week later we were all sat outside one weekend afternoon and Jess was attached to the ground stake. She was wearing the harness with a bungee dog-lead extension that attached in between the wire cable and the harness. I'd bought it a few weeks before to alleviate Jess's tugging on my arms. We also used it when she was on the ground stake in order to help her judge the length of the cable and give her a gentler tug back if she reached the end. Mostly however, she ran round and round in circles or lay happily on the ground near us, enjoying her relative independence.

I went inside to replenish our drinks whilst Steve lit the barbecue. Retrieving a couple of cold beers I looked up and saw Jess running past the window. I smiled as she looked so ecstatic, a vision of freedom with her tongue lolling out in sheer bliss. Then I realised that if she was running past the window she was no longer attached to the ground stake.

"STEVE!" I yelled, running outside, "Jess is loose!"

Steve looked up from the barbecue in surprise, immediately taking in the fact that Jess was no longer lying where she should be. We ran round the back of the house to see that Jess had sprinted all the way along the line of the houses, about 100 yards, but was now sprinting back towards us.

She still had her harness on – which meant I couldn't use the 'wave the harness at her' method on this occasion – and I couldn't work out what had happened. There was no wire or metal corkscrew trailing behind her – not even Jess had managed to pull the stake out of the ground.

Steve and I both stayed calm and called out "Good girl Jess, come here", as she bounded back towards us. However as she got closer she flashed us one of her kooky grins as if to say, "Isn't this just the best fun?" then turned and raced off again. Despite the worry that she was loose, the sight of Jess at full speed was an awe-inspiring sight. She was an impressive athlete and the speed and fluidity of her running was beautiful.

She turned and sprinted back towards us for a second time and as she pulled up just short of us, then turned and dashed away again, it was clear that she was much faster than us, was having a blast and had no intention of stopping. Steve and I stood still where we were. There was no point chasing her and we didn't want to scare her and send her off into the wilds of Fort Detrick. I hoped she might get tired at some point and would come over to us when she'd had enough.

Jess ran back and forth a couple more times and then I had an idea. She loved going out in our car because it always signified a walk somewhere interesting. I'd always slap the floor of the boot and she'd leap in obediently, excited at the prospect of an adventure in the outdoors.

"Steve, quick, go and reverse the car out onto the driveway and open the boot, she'll jump in."

I gave Steve a couple of minutes to do just that, then as Jess was tearing towards me again I jumped up and down, waving and calling to her and then ran round the side of the house to the driveway. Just as I'd hoped, she followed me, probably assuming this was a variation on our 'Chase Jenni up the Stairs' game.

Steve had opened the boot as planned and as Jess and I ran towards the car he banged the floor of the boot. I ran up to it and did the same and Jess dutifully leapt in with an excited expression on her face. I immediately jumped in after her and held her whilst Steve shut the boot and drove the car the few yards back into the garage. We shut the garage door and then let our escape artist out, giving her lots of praise for being such a good girl for getting in the car and ignoring the circumstances that led up to it.

We soon solved the mystery of how Jess escaped – she had bitten clean through the bungee cord and she must have done it in one single, effective snap of her jaws as Steve was within a few feet of her and hadn't noticed her gnawing at it. Examining the bungee lead more closely I discovered that underneath the fabric covering the essential part of the bungee was just a bundle of thin lengths of rubber. They looked easy to cut through and I kicked myself for not thinking several steps ahead of Jess. We'd had that bungee cord for weeks and I don't know why Jess chose that particular moment to bite through it but at least she did it next to our house and not up at the watershed.

This incident heralded a new problem – biting the lead. The yelping, shunning and returning to the house for a 'time out' was gradually doing the trick and Jess had been nipping me less and less. Instead she turned her attention to the appendage that was keeping her safely attached to me. For the first ten or so minutes of every walk, Jess would now grab the lead in her mouth and try and maul it to death, all whilst leaping around like a beast possessed. This was a slight improvement on her nipping at me but still didn't look good. We must have looked an absurd sight – me doing my level best to ignore the deranged dog cavorting in front of me and Jess looking for all the world as if she was resisting being dognapped by a real life Cruella de Ville.

I continued to ignore the behaviour, praise her when it stopped and try and distract her. I updated Didi with this latest issue and as always, she assured me that I was doing everything right. She did suggest trying the tennis ball again as Jess clearly wanted something to chew but she still showed no interest in it. She would eventually release the lead in order to then focus on her usual irritating pulling, which was enough of an issue in itself.

Given Jess's track record with the bungee I was concerned that she would inevitably try to bite through the retractable lead. The first section of the retractable lead was a 50 cm length of tightly woven fabric about 1.5 cm in width that looked pretty robust. This part of the lead didn't retract into the handset due to a rubber stopper that held it in place. The rest of the lead was a thin woven cord although it did look a lot tougher than the rubber threads that made up the bungee extension. Nevertheless, I bought some anti-chew spray from the pet store which tasted of bitter apple and promised to deter chewing instantly. Unsurprisingly, despite me dousing the lead in this stuff, it didn't bother Jess in the slightest.

Just to be on the safe side I decided it would be sensible to reinforce the material strength of the lead. Our garden hose was one of those ones inlaid with wire to stop kinking – I judged it would also hinder lunatic wolves. I cut a length off with my Leatherman, which I was confident was considerably sharper than Jess's teeth, slit it up the middle and then wrapped it around the lead and secured it with a generous amount of gaffer tape.

My 'gaffer taped garden hose' contraption didn't stop Jess biting the lead but I was at least reassured that she couldn't bite through it. I checked the gaffer tape after each walk but aside from some chafing caused by Jess's teeth, it remained intact and dutifully held the wire-reinforced hose in place. Even so, I replaced the gaffer tape every couple of days. Surely this was sufficient and I congratulated myself on having devised a Jess-proof lead system and tried not to think about how we must have looked with the Light Blue Safety Lead round my waist and a lead reinforced with hosepipe and gaffer tape.

My ingenious solution worked perfectly for about a week. Then one morning Jess and I were going for one of our usual walks on base. We'd crossed Large Field behind our house and Jess was bucking and pulling and lead-biting as usual. I was doing exactly what I was supposed to do – ignoring the bad behaviour. This meant not looking at her either as eye contact counted as attention and was therefore rewarding her for what she was doing.

We crossed the road and got onto the track that lead to Wild Field, Jess still pulling and biting, me resolutely refusing to look at her in order to deny her the attention she was so shamelessly seeking. Suddenly I heard a brief whirring noise and my right arm felt slack at the same time. I looked down at the plastic handle of the retractable lead – the cord had disappeared and a short length of the fabric section hung forlornly from the handset. I looked at Jess. The remainder of the first stretch of lead was still attached to Jess's harness but that's all it was attached to. Half of the makeshift hosepipe reinforcer was lying on the ground between Jess and me and the other half was still in Jess's mouth, protruding like a celebratory cigar. She had bitten clean through the gaffer tape, the wire reinforced hose and the strong fabric lead.

I stared in disbelief at Jess who was looking up at me contritely. She had a look in her eyes that just said, "Oops!"

My brain suddenly realised that the wanton destruction of my foolproof system meant that Jess was no longer attached to me and I instantly reached out and grabbed her harness so she couldn't run off. However I don't believe that was ever her intention. In the couple of seconds that it took my confused brain to take in what had happened, Jess could have easily escaped from me if she wanted to. But as soon as I heard the whirring of the chewed retractable lead retracting, she'd stayed totally still and now looked rather apologetic.

Thankfully I had a spare lead with me, the Light Blue Safety Lead that was looped around the handle of the retractable one and clipped around my waist. I simply took it off and used that instead although we had to go straight home as obviously Jess could have easily bitten through that one too if she wanted. However, Jess behaved impeccably on that walk home. She trotted meekly at my side, made no attempt to bite the lead and didn't pull in the slightest; not a single time. Despite what happened I was heartened that Jess clearly didn't want to run away from me but I was utterly confounded by her. She had just shown me that she could walk perfectly to heel like a 'Best in Show' winner when she wanted to so why oh why did she choose to act like a deranged, rabid wolf the rest of the time?

I deposited Jess at home and went straight out to PetValu and bought one of those awful looking chain leads, not a choke chain, simply a chain lead with a normal spring clip at the end. I didn't want to as I think they make you look as if you're trying to be intimidating but frankly it was a last resort as there was now no fabric lead that I trusted to secure Jess. I took the destroyed retractable lead and the remnants of my hosepipe contraption with me and on the way home went via the shelter to tell them what had happened, show them the evidence and ask for advice.

Didi was in her office with Lauren when I knocked at the door. I simply held up the lead and the bits of reinforced hosepipe and said, "Now don't worry, she's safe because she didn't actually run away from me but look what Jess did!"

"No way!" exclaimed Lauren.

"Whoa," said Didi. "Did Jess do that? What happened?"

I told them the story and how Jess could have run away from me if she wanted to but didn't and then walked back beautifully. Didi complimented me on the Light Blue Safety Lead system around my waist as it meant I had a spare lead to be able to get her home. I reminded her that I'd started that system after losing Sam so didn't deserve any plaudits.

"Ok, what you need to do is get down to the pet store and buy a chain lead. It's the only option now," said Didi.

"Already been to get one, it's in the car."

Didi, Lauren and I were stumped. The fact that Jess didn't run away when she had the chance and then walked home like a pedigree show dog, strongly suggested that she wasn't trying to escape from me. She was a mystery and my only consolation was that the professionals were as mystified as I was.

I got home with the chain lead, attached the Light Blue Safety Lead and took Jess out for another walk as our first attempt that day had been curtailed. Jess started to bite the chain lead which I was fully expecting but I did assume she'd stop when she realised it was a hard substance. But no, she carried on as enthusiastically as ever. I couldn't believe it and now I was worried that she might crack a tooth. But there was nothing I could do about it other than hope it would stop.

Jess continued to chew on the solid metal lead for the next few days so I again consulted Didi. She'd been thinking about Jess's lead biting and had an idea. Her husband used to work for a telecoms company and developed a foul tasting gel to discourage groundhogs and squirrels from chewing through the telecoms cables. Apparently one taste of the gel was all it took and the animal concerned would hurriedly slink off to find a more appetising snack.

I popped in the next day and Didi handed over a small tube of the gel. She warned me to be sure to wash my hands after handling it, as it was so potent that if I inadvertently transferred it to some food I was eating I'd taste it for days.

Back home I smeared the chain lead with the gel, making sure there were some generous globules between the links and immediately washed my hands. Surely this would work and in one swoop we'd save Jess's teeth and make her look less deranged and thus more adoptable.

Yet not only was Jess completely unbothered by the gel but she seemed to like it and carried on biting the lead and licking the gel until there were no remnants left on the chain. Didi was astonished when I told her and admitted defeat. We agreed we'd tried everything and there was nothing more we could do other than be prepared to treat a cracked or broken tooth if necessary. Jess wasn't following the rulebook, her behaviour had stumped a professional behaviourist and I was more concerned than ever about her adoption prospects.

The urgency was real – Steve and I were going on vacation for two and a half weeks at the beginning of September and I'd agreed with Didi that as Jess would be going back to the shelter whilst we were away anyway, it made sense to put her on the adoption floor and see if there was any interest.

I was always conscious that my foster dogs were with me temporarily and it was my job to ensure they were adopted as soon they were ready. Fostering must never become my de facto way of having a dog – I was there for the benefit of the dogs, not the other way round.

Jess had a long way to go in terms of her behaviour and her new family would need to be experienced with dogs and willing to invest a lot of time and patience in her. I suspected she would never be comfortable with strangers or in crowded places. That didn't mean she wasn't adoptable – she just needed to be adopted by a person or people whose lifestyle was a good fit. If our circumstances and life plans had been different then Steve and I would have adopted her without hesitation.

On the upside, she was a lot more confident than she had been and had shown that she could develop a strong and loving bond with someone she trusted. She just needed a strong-armed, literally thick-skinned, unfailingly patient, quick-thinking, outdoorsy, active person with liberal views about dogs on sofas to fall in love with her and give her the forever home she so deserved. It still stung that that person couldn't be me but I loved Jess and would do anything for her – including letting her go.

CHAPTER 10

SCOUT RETURNS

IT IS TEMPTING to view shelters like FCAC, independent rescue organisations and initiatives such as fostering as a panacea for humankind's inhumanity to dogs. Yet this is naive; sometimes an ostensible happy ending is just another false start for a dog who has done nothing wrong.

One Monday morning, six weeks after the Magnificent Seven puppies had gone to their forever homes, Lauren came to see me in the spay and neuter clinic. She looked uncharacteristically serious.

"Hey Jenni, don't leave today without coming to see me first, okay?"

"Sure." I was intrigued and slightly worried. What had I done wrong?

A couple of hours later I went to find Lauren in the kennel tech room.

"I'm so sorry to have to tell you this but one of your puppies has been returned to us and she has a broken foot."

This was horrible news. "Who is it?"

"It's one of the girls," said Lauren, checking the paperwork. "She's called Bella now but it's the one you called Scout."

Scout, the one I would have kept if I could.

"What happened?"

"So the story is she bit their two year old, they left the kid and Bel...sorry, Scout, jumping on the bed alone together and Scout bit him."

I was absolutely furious. What kind of an idiot leaves a two year old and a puppy jumping on a bed together? Clearly the child had jumped on Scout, broken her foot and Scout bit him out of shock and pain; awful for the child but completely understandable from Scout's point of view and not her fault. I said as much to Lauren who agreed with me.

"Yeah I know. But now they've surrendered her. And the thing is, because they're saying the bite broke the skin then she needs to be quarantined for ten days because of rabies."

"What? That's stupid!"

"I know, I know. Now normally we wouldn't put her out to foster care and she'd have to spend the quarantine period here. But if we had an experienced foster carer who knew Scout and who we trusted to abide by the quarantine rules then she could spend the quarantine period with them."

I immediately understood what Lauren was alluding to.

"Of course I'll take her, I'll take her for as long as necessary. Where is she?"

Lauren led me into the quarantine room and a loud cacophony of barking started up when we entered. All the pens were occupied by dogs of various sizes, all desperate for our attention. Scout wasn't in any of the pens but I could see a small crate down on the floor.

"She's in this crate." said Lauren, "She's pretty scared and subdued. It may take her a while to remember you."

This upset me more than the broken foot. Scout wasn't the subdued type; along with Scooby she was the most confident and sociable of all the puppies. Just what exactly had she been through?

Lauren and I sat down in front of Scout's crate. I could see a timid little face peering out at the room where I'd collected her and her siblings less than two months before. Lauren opened the wire door and gently lifted Scout out. My former foster puppy took one look at me and scrambled out of Lauren's embrace, on to my lap, up into my arms and nuzzled in to my chest.

"Oh my goodness, look at that," cried Lauren, clearly moved.

I held her tight.

"Alright Scout, you're safe now. Jenni's here. You're coming home with me, it's all going to be okay."

Lauren explained that Scout had an appointment at Kingsbrook Animal Hospital that afternoon. We decided that I'd go home and walk Jess and set up a crate for Scout, then come back to take her to her appointment at Kingsbrook and take her straight home from there.

Firstly I needed a briefing from one of the animal control officers about quarantine procedures. The officer explained that because she had bitten someone and broken the skin, she needed to be isolated and observed for ten days. She'd been surrendered on the Saturday afternoon so had already completed two days of the quarantine; that left eight days to go. Scout could be in the same room as Jess so long as she remained in her crate at all times. She was allowed out if Jess was securely shut away in another room. Obviously these strict conditions were for Jess's benefit – in the unlikely event that Scout bit Jess then Jess would need to be quarantined too.

Nobody seriously thought that Scout had rabies. She was a three month old puppy with no fresh bite wounds on her and no scars indicating a historic bite. She had gone to FCAC when she was five weeks old and then to me, then back to FCAC and then to her adoptive home. There was no sign that she'd ever been bitten by another animal and therefore she'd never been exposed to rabies for her to then pose a danger to anyone else. However the rules were the rules – a child had been bitten and Scout needed to be observed. FCAC trusted me to follow the rules and I had no intention of betraying their trust.

I picked up a large crate from the storeroom, a couple of metal bowls (as obviously Jess and Scout wouldn't be able to share food and water) and some towels to make my jailbird as comfy as possible. Then I drove home to walk Jess and prepare for Scout.

"Guess who's coming back to live with us!" I announced to Jess when I got home. She grinned at me expectantly, picking up on my excitement. It would be interesting to see how Jess behaved with a single puppy, once they were allowed to interact. The quarantine period would end the following Tuesday so they'd have a few days together before both would need to go back to the shelter when Steve and I went on vacation.

After walking Jess I headed back to FCAC to take Scout to Kingsbrook. It turned out that 'Bella' had been registered at Kingsbrook by the people who adopted her so the staff knew her well. And therefore it was Kingsbrook where she'd been taken when her foot was broken.

Everyone at Kingsbrook made a point of telling me how pleased they were that Scout was being fostered by me again. I sensed there was something going on that I was unaware of and soon found out the full story when one of the vets checked Scout over and showed me her original x-ray.

"Lauren told me that the two year old jumped on her and broke her foot," I commented as I looked at the X-ray.

The vet replied in a deliberately measured tone, "Actually no, that kind of break is consistent with being hit with something."

I felt sick. Scout had come to live with me and Steve and Jess when she was only five and a half weeks old. I had loved her and cared for her as if she was my own puppy and been the best non-canine surrogate mum I could be. And then poor Scout had ended up with people who'd hit her with something and broken her foot. I immediately doubted the story of the bitten child and guessed this was a convenient way of getting rid of Scout without having to answer any awkward questions about how she received her injury.

"You know she's already a different dog," said the vet, "She was really timid before, she seems much more confident already."

I explained that Scout was coming back to be fostered by me during the rabies quarantine period. The vet asked why she was being quarantined and I said because she bit the child and broke his skin.

The vet looked surprised and showed me the form that the parents had filled in at Kingsbrook – they had explicitly stated to Kingsbrook that the bite hadn't broken the skin. They had obviously embellished the story to FCAC to justify why they were giving Scout up and in doing so had condemned Scout to ten days of confinement. The vet explained that the break was healing well but Scout still needed her foot strapped up and would need considerable crate rest. Quarantine rules aside, Scout would need to be mainly confined to a crate for the next week or so anyway. This did at least sweeten the punishment.

After our consultation with the vet, a couple of the veterinary technicians came in to change Scout's bandages; whilst they were tending to her they kept calling her 'Bella' until I said, "Actually we're calling her Scout again which was her name when I first fostered her."

"Oh, it's just she's Bella on all her records here," replied one of the vet techs.

"Well I didn't break her foot so I think my name wins!"

The vet tech smiled at me. "That's a fair point!" she replied and promised me she'd change Scout's records.

I wasn't simply being difficult. I was obviously going to be calling Scout 'Scout' again and furthermore, it was likely that 'Bella' would have negative connotations for her as it would remind her of a less than happy time in her life. It was a name that was best consigned to history.

I thanked the Kingsbrook team and Scout and I headed home. I left Scout in the car briefly whilst I went inside and greeted Jess and then took her upstairs to my room.

"Just stay in here for a couple of minutes Jess and then I've got a great surprise for you!"

I went back down to Scout, let her go to the toilet outside first and then carried her over the threshold of our house once again. She seemed to recognise where she was which was lovely. I let her have a thorough sniff for a few minutes but then it was time for her to go in her crate. I'd made it cozy with a couple of soft towels and she had a bowl of water and a couple of toys from the shelter in there.

"There you go, settle down. Good girl Scout."

Then I phoned Lauren and told her what I'd learned at Kingsbrook about the fake bite story and asked if the quarantine restrictions could be lifted. Lauren was sympathetic and agreed with me and said she'd go and speak to someone and call me back.

However when she did, it wasn't the news I wanted. Understandably FCAC had to comply what the parents had told them and there was unfortunately no getting around the quarantine period. Poor Scout. I had no choice; I had to abide by the rules. To do otherwise would only have betrayed Scout and Jess and FCAC.

I was at least pacified by the fact that the quarantine rules didn't actually make that much difference to Scout – she needed plenty of crate rest anyway. She could still spend time outside the crate with me and she could still go outside on the lead. All it really meant was that she couldn't physically interact with Jess – and the last thing her foot needed was leaping around with Jess anyway. So my query on her behalf was really a point of principle rather than a point of practicality.

With Scout safely in the crate I went to get Jess who was waiting impatiently in my bedroom. She was pacing back and forth in anticipation, just like that afternoon two months ago when Scout and her siblings first arrived in the Williams household.

Jess bounded down the stairs and her and Scout sniffed each other with interest through the bars of Scout's crate, tails wagging happily. I'm sure they recognised each other although it was easier for Scout – Jess hadn't changed whereas Scout was rather bigger and didn't have her six sidekicks with her.

"Look who's back!" I said to Jess. "And don't worry, it's just her. The rest of the gang aren't about to show up I promise. Well at least I hope not."

Having just one puppy who needed a lot of crate rest was a whole lot easier than having seven. Thankfully Jess seemed to readily accept Scout's presence and also accepted that the new member of the family had to stay behind bars. She seemed to regard Scout with keen interest, bordering on affection, and was surprisingly cooperative about the quarantine procedures that I had to implement.

Scout got a few short walks outside every day to go to the toilet and whenever I took her out Jess would have to go up to the bedroom and be shut away. I also gave Scout time outside her crate so she could potter around freely or cuddle up to me on the sofa and again, Jess would be banished upstairs, safe from the rabid puppy.

One afternoon I was lying on the sofa watching a movie; Scout was curled up asleep next to me. Then I suddenly heard and felt what I assumed was Jess jumping on and off our bed. The noise got louder and the vibration increased and I realised with a stab of fear that the walls of the house were shaking. Scout startled awake and I heard Jess barking frantically.

Was this an earthquake? I grabbed Scout and was just debating how I was going to deal with an earthquake, Jess and a quarantined dog when the shaking stopped. It had only lasted about ten seconds.

I put Scout in her crate and ran upstairs to check on Jess. She barreled in to my legs, both excited and nervous. I still wasn't sure exactly what just happened so I did what everyone does in the event of some kind of civil emergency in the 21st century – I went on Facebook.

"I think I was just in an earthquake. Did anyone else in Frederick feel that? Dogs and I ok," I wrote. As my post flashed up I saw another post by a Frederick friend – it simply said, "QUAAAAAAAAAAAAKE!"

It turned out that it really was an earthquake. The magnitude was 5.8 on the Richter scale and the epicentre was in Virginia. In seismic terms, this was a minor event. However at the time I didn't know it was going to be minor and of such short duration. I realised hours later that in the seconds when the house started to shake, my overriding emotion was fear for Jess and Scout. My instinct to protect them prevailed over any feelings of self-preservation.

The days passed and being able to tick off Scout's sentence in quarantine was bittersweet as I was also counting down to having to say goodbye to her again. Back when we'd fostered Scout's litter, she had been my favourite. 'Scout' was always going to be the name of my first dog and I'd named her Scout on the off chance we could figure out a way to keep her. Despite the awful circumstances, it seemed like fate that she'd come back to me.

But nothing about my life had changed. In terms of dogs who needed fostering, my situation was perfect. But our life 'back home' wasn't. There was no realistic alternative - I knew I would have to say goodbye to Scout for a second time.

The day before Scout's quarantine period was up, I took her back to Kingsbrook to have her foot assessed. The vet was satisfied with how it was healing and said that she could spend more time out of the crate and could play with Jess inside the house. He specified gradually diminishing crate rest and some guidelines for building her walks up slowly over the next month.

I noted the guidelines down carefully because Steve and I were going on our vacation that Friday and Scout and Jess would both be going back to the shelter the day before. Scout would have to continue her recovery there. However that afternoon I had a welcome phone call from Didi.

"Jenni, one of the vet techs at Kingsbrook would like to adopt Scout."

The vet tech in question was called Nikki and she'd looked after Scout when she was first treated at Kingsbrook. She and her husband were thinking about getting a dog anyway and when she heard that Scout would be going up for adoption when she was fully recovered, they decided the time was right and Scout was the dog. Nikki had rung the shelter to find out when they were accepting applications.

Didi had previously mentioned to me that the shelter wouldn't put Scout up for adoption until her foot was fully healed. However we both agreed that an application from a veterinary professional who could be trusted to follow the vet's instructions on walks and crate rest – especially when that vet was her boss – was a wholly different matter.

Obviously Nikki already knew Scout but I sent her Scout's original profile that I'd written for Petfinder, together with a few early puppy photos. Nikki was delighted with the photos and told me her and her husband were head over heels in love with Scout. Her effusive email assured me that Scout was going to a great home.

The following day was the end of the quarantine period and at long last I was able to let Scout out of her crate in the morning with Jess right there. They seemed overjoyed to be allowed to interact at last; Scout's confinement had given Jess ample time to get used to her. They both seemed smitten and a beautiful, albeit short-lived, friendship ensued.

Jess took on the role of a good natured and unfailingly patient big sister who Scout adored and followed everywhere. Scout still needed periods of crate rest but Scout and Jess were now allowed to play together so long as they didn't tear around the house. Thankfully they seemed to enjoy gently wrestling each other on the floor or on the sofa, which was perfect.

Jess was in her element with Scout around and I saw a sociable side of her that I hadn't seen before. Funnily enough she was much happier with just one puppy in the house as opposed to seven. Two dogs was an entertaining dynamic and I noticed how they competed for my attention, good-naturedly shoulder barging each other out of the way to get to me. If the love of one dog boosts your self-esteem then two dogs is exponentially better.

I was painfully aware that my time with Scout and Jess was running out. Not only would I definitely be saying goodbye to Scout but the time when I was possibly saying goodbye to Jess was fast approaching. We all thought it would be miraculous if Jess did get adopted and if she didn't then we would of course be taking her back upon our return. But it would be wrong to waste the opportunity whilst she was sat in the shelter anyway. I'd written a glowing but truthful piece about her for Petfinder and Didi had published it with a selection of photos that showed her at her best.

I needed to prepare myself for the possibility that Jess would be adopted and I had mixed emotions – genuine hope that someone would see her the way I did and snap her up and a secret wish that she'd be waiting for me when I got back so we could have longer together. I wasn't ready to lose my dream dog yet; I never would be.

For the best of reasons, I knew I wouldn't be fostering Scout again as Nikki and her husband had been swiftly interviewed and approved. So the day before our vacation I took Scout back to FCAC first thing in the morning and said goodbye for a second time. I was as confident as I could be that this was finally the happy ending that Scout deserved and she wouldn't be coming back again. Nikki was going to pick her up at lunchtime and take her back to Kingsbrook for the afternoon before taking her to her forever home.

"Bye Scout," I said to her as she nuzzled in to me. "Nikki is going to pick you up later and you're going to have an amazing life now. Thanks for coming back to see me. Happy trails."

Of course I could have taken Jess at the same time but I was acutely conscious that this might be our last day together and I wanted to have some one-on-one time with her. I'd arranged to drop her off later on in the afternoon instead. That morning we hiked our trail at the watershed, the one we'd discovered at the height of a hot summer, where we'd rarely seen another person. It had been our refuge and thanks to Jess's constant pulling I felt like I knew every protruding tree root or uneven patch of rock on the ground; I had to constantly be aware of my footing due to Jess's ability to disrupt my balance. I'd never known the actual terrain of a trail so well.

It was a beautiful day, with the sun doing its best to break through the mesmerising canopy above our heads. The leaves variously shone bright green or were dappled with the silhouettes of the leaves above them. I could have walked that trail forever without getting bored. Jess was in high spirits as always, jumping in the stream at every opportunity. I wished I could be as carefree but I carried the secret of what would happen later that day. Jess was oblivious to the fact that her life was about to change again. I looked at her and fervently wished there was someone out there who could make her that happy forever. I had a heavy heart and wondered if I'd ever walk this trail again – I wasn't sure I could bring myself to do it without her.

Back home we played a rambunctious game of hide and seek. After a few rounds of this Jess flopped down panting on the bedroom floor. I lay down too and rolled over on to my stomach and just looked at her, wanting to remember every single detail about her. I'd wanted a dog from the age of five and always knew I'd love having one but never in my wildest dreams did I ever think I'd experience the bond that I had with Jess. We understood each other without speaking and that understanding transcended minor issues such as her maddening inability to walk calmly on the lead or her proficiency at escaping from me.

Jess gazed back at me. Despite our close bond and the affection she showed towards me, Jess had always liked her own space after a while. But I felt something had changed today. I slowly reached out and stroked her muzzle, giving it a nice slow scratch. Jess had never let me do that before. We lay there for ages, me scratching her muzzle and stroking her head. She had come so far and I felt she trusted me like never before.

I wondered if she'd soon be lying on a different bedroom floor, playing hide and seek with a different person and chasing them up a different set of stairs. Her big wolf-like grin would light up someone else's day and all I'd have left would be memories like this one.

All too soon it was time. I loaded Jess in the car together with a supply of her food and drove the short distance to the shelter. Lauren had thoughtfully reserved her a kennel on the end of a row where it would be slightly quieter. We hoped this would help Jess to settle in as well as possible and enable her to give a good impression to prospective adopters.

Everyone at the shelter knew about Jess's lead biting and escapology skills. I'd strongly suggested, and Didi had immediately agreed, that volunteers should not be allowed to walk Jess. She was too strong, too clever and too unpredictable. I'd also said the shelter could use our chain lead and harness whilst she was with them and if she did get adopted, we would donate them to her new person as I considered them essential to keeping her safe. I was therefore relieved to see that the chain link door of her kennel was decorated with two large signs stating "Kennel tech ONLY to walk" and "Escape Artist!!! Use own Ruffwear harness and chain lead only and clip blue lead around your waist." It couldn't have been clearer.

I walked Jess into her kennel, unclipped the Light Blue Safety Lead, took off her harness and chain lead and clipped the entire ensemble to the door. Jess was looking at me, a guilt-inducing look of nervousness in her eyes. However awful this goodbye was for me, it was far worse for Jess who didn't understand what was happening to her. I knelt down and hugged her and told her how much I loved her.

"I love you Crazy Wolf. Be good. Show everyone what a great dog you are. Happy trails Jess," I whispered.

I didn't want to let go; I couldn't bear to think this was the last time I'd see her, the last time I'd have my face buried in her neck. I genuinely wanted Jess to be adopted by the perfect people in my fantasy – the child-free couple who worked from home and spent all their free time running and hiking or cross-country skiing in the winter. But if they failed to materialise, I knew I'd be over the moon to have her back when we returned from vacation.

It was difficult extracting myself from her cage, as Jess couldn't understand why I was leaving her there and had no intention of making this easy. Lauren held the door as firmly closed as possible whilst leaving a small gap for me to squeeze out of. Even then Jess was jumping up at me, pushing against me as I backed out. I had to keep one hand gripped around her collar so I could gently push her away until it was just my arm between the wall of the pen and the cage door. I pulled my arm away and Lauren swiftly slid the door shut and padlocked the catch mechanism.

"Bye Jess," I whispered, and turned and walked away. I looked back and saw Jess frantically jumping up at the cage door, barking and yelping, clearly unable to understand why the person she trusted most in the world was abandoning her. It was heart-wrenching but I had to smile too; I had a funny feeling I'd be seeing her when we got back. I doubted that anyone would adopt that crazy dog.

Lauren gave me a hug and assured me they'd look after her. I believed her. As soon I got in the car I burst into tears. I felt utterly wretched.

That evening, the house felt awfully strange with just Steve and I in it. Dogs bring a different energy to a house and there'd been at least one in ours since the beginning of May, almost four months ago. Just a few hours without a dog was enough to convince me that this was not a state of being that I wanted to replicate too often. I hoped that on our return from vacation there would be a dog in need of fostering waiting for me, and selfishly, I secretly hoped that dog would be Jess.

CHAPTER 11

ESCAPE AND EVASION

THE NEXT DAY we flew from Baltimore to Reno, Nevada and then drove straight to Tahoe City on the north western shore of beautiful Lake Tahoe. Lake Tahoe is North America's largest alpine lake and lies within the Sierra Nevada mountain range, with California to the west and Nevada to the east. Tahoe City has an incredibly misleading name; it's a small town bounded by alpine meadows, forest and mountains on one side and the lake on the other.

Our motel was only one block from the lake and after checking in we strolled across the street to a perfectly situated waterside bar and ordered a couple of beers. The view, the company and the pale ales were perfect and just what I needed. I felt more relaxed than I'd been in a long time.

The last four months since Jess entered our lives had been wonderful but demanding; we'd had Jess, the puppies and then Scout back in quick succession. Although it had been great fun, it had also been hard work and new emotional territory for me. I'd been responsible for eight lives, one of them twice, where previously I'd only ever had to look after myself. Dealing with Jess's behaviour and the impact on her adoption prospects had been a constant source of worry and I'd lived with the fear that she was unadoptable every single day. Every walk served only to reinforce the concern I felt for her future. And now she was sat in a cage at Frederick County Animal Control on the off chance that someone was going to see her and fall in love with her despite her frustrating quirks.

Sitting next to the lake and gazing at the incredible view whilst working our way through a couple of beers and then a bottle of excellent Californian wine was cathartic. We didn't have to worry about getting back to let someone out for a wee or Jess's utter disinterest in turning herself into a respectable, easy-going, family dog.

The following day we fueled up with breakfast at a classic American diner – eggs, bacon, hash browns and endless coffee. Then we spent the day hiking in the stunning alpine meadows above the town and then rafting down the Truckee River, which ran from Lake Tahoe to Pyramid Lake in Nevada, 121 miles away. Dinner was burgers and more craft beer in a riverside bar. It was almost my idea of a perfect day. I say almost because we were missing a certain four-legged accessory.

The next day we left Tahoe City and drove south along the impossibly scenic Lake Tahoe road. Our destination was Yosemite, one of the USA's most revered national parks. We'd been there on vacation a few years before and had immediately decided it was one of those 'once in a lifetime' destinations that deserved more than one visit.

Yosemite's stunning Tuolumne Meadows sit at 8,600 feet above sea level in the eastern section of the park. A sub-alpine paradise of seemingly endless meadows with views of the Sierra Nevada mountains, the area boasts incredible hiking and the most stunning scenery I've ever seen. Even the air smells wild and bewitching.

Our accommodation was the forested Tuolumne Meadows campsite, rustic and basic but a picture perfect location. We were allocated one of the best pitches, right next to the Tuolumne River and with an immaculate view of Lembert Dome, an imposing 800 feet high granite dome rock. We spent our first evening drinking beer by the river and talking until the dome was bathed in moonlight.

The next day we hiked from our campsite across the main meadow, up into the pine forest to the promisingly named Dog Lake. Sadly there were no dogs there but it was spectacular nonetheless, a pristine expanse of crystal clear water surrounded by pine trees. I thought how much Jess would have loved running in and out of the water and racing through the trees, if we lived in a parallel universe where letting her off the lead was even remotely possible.

"Do you think if I let Jess off the lead here she'd come back?" I asked Steve jokingly.

Steve laughed. "Er, definitely not!" he replied. "Not for a few weeks anyway!" That light-hearted comment was sadly prophetic.

We spent five days in Yosemite – hiking, bathing in the Tuolumne River, gazing at the views and exploring trails that weren't on the map. It was idyllic and in hindsight, the calm before a husky-shaped storm. I had no phone reception in Tuolumne Meadows and was therefore oblivious to whatever was happening with Jess. I purposefully tried my best not to think about her too much and mostly succeeded; I had to trust that all was well.

All too soon it was time to leave the sanctuary of Yosemite. I could have stayed much longer but we had an ambitious itinerary and our next stop was the town of Bishop, about halfway between Yosemite and Death Valley National Park. Steve was driving and as we left

Yosemite and descended from the heavens towards civilisation, I remembered I might have an email about Jess waiting for me. I was eager to hear how she was getting on and whether there'd been any interest in her now she was physically in the shelter. As soon as I had reception on the iPhone I checked my emails and one popped up from Didi entitled, 'Jess'. It had been sent the previous afternoon.

"I've got an email about Jess, what if she's been adopted?" My heart sank. What if I was never going to see her again?

"Of course I hope she has been adopted," I corrected myself as I waited for the email to load.

But unfortunately Jess hadn't been adopted – she'd escaped. A volunteer had taken her for a walk and somehow she got loose from him. She was hanging out in the field behind FCAC but wasn't letting anyone near her.

I couldn't believe it and was furious at everyone involved. How could they have let her escape? Why was a volunteer walking her when they weren't allowed to? And why weren't they using the escape proof Ruffwear harness I'd bought her? Something had gone seriously wrong and as a result, Jess was running around a field next to a busy four-lane road.

Didi's email went on to tell me that there was a humane dog trap out for Jess, basically a large crate with a spring-loaded door that would shut behind her if she entered. Didi concluded, "Please remember...we are expert at reclaiming dogs from this type of event."

"Not Jess you're not," I said out loud. There was no way Jess would enter a dog trap, no way at all. I knew then that if Jess was going to come back it would be to me and me only.

I rang Didi immediately and got the full story; the volunteer, Joe, had applied to adopt Jess and as a result, opted to ignore the 'Kennel Tech ONLY' sign on her kennel and walk her himself. They didn't get far. Once they were on the field behind the shelter Jess had done her usual deranged leaping about and had somehow wriggled out of her escape-proof harness. Joe had tried to grab her but she ran away from him. She obviously didn't like her prospective adopter and had voted with her paws.

I swallowed my anger and concentrated on giving Didi ideas for getting Jess back such as driving a 4 x 4 onto the field and opening the boot in the hope she'd think it was our car and jump in. Capitalising on her recent friendship with Scout, I also suggested they use a puppy as bait. I thought she might just allow someone to approach her if they had a playful pup with them. Steve suggested they barbecue a steak out on the field as she'd find the smell irresistible and would also hopefully associate it with us. We'd barbecued a lot of steaks that summer.

Didi assured me she would pass our suggestions along to the animal control officers and keep me informed. She said she was confident they would have Jess back in the next few hours. Despite the veracity of my Jess-catching advice, I wasn't so optimistic.

I felt utterly sick with worry. I also felt guilty; I should never have left Jess. She must have thought I'd abandoned her. The thought crossed my mind that she was trying to find me. Steve stopped the car and gave me a hug. He was as worried and as angry as I was.

It was a two-hour drive to Bishop through beautiful scenery that I barely noticed. I checked my emails constantly the whole way but there was no news from Didi. California was three hours behind Maryland and so by 2:00 p.m. our time I knew the shelter would have closed and I wouldn't hear anything until tomorrow. However the animal control officers were on duty 24/7 and I hoped and prayed they'd manage to catch her and she wouldn't be spending another night outside.

On arrival in Bishop we quickly found a motel and headed out for ice cream to cheer ourselves up. It didn't work. Neither of us thought that Jess would simply walk obligingly into a dog trap; she was far too smart for that. In addition the thought of how close she was to that busy road was hugely worrying. I doubted that Jess had any road sense although I did suspect that she had a pretty good sense of direction. And Fort Detrick and our house were the other side of that road. What if she realised and decided to head for home?

Ice cream time merged into beer o'clock and we decided to stay out for dinner. We found a bar and restaurant that had our favourite Sierra Nevada Pale Ale on tap. After a couple of beers we managed to find a funny side to this horrible situation, that Jess had evidently decided she didn't like the shelter or Joe, the guy who wanted to adopt her, and had taken the first opportunity to make a break for it. Maybe she was already running west to find us and we'd see her sat by the side of the road in Nowheresville, Nevada, her head cocked to one side as she waited for us to show up.

"There you both are! I ran all the way from Frederick to find you!"

It helped to make light of the situation, to think that maybe Jess knew what she was doing and would return when she was ready.

The next morning when I woke up, I experienced that momentary confusion when you know something awful has happened but can't remember what. Then it all came flooding back and I felt that sick, sinking feeling all over again. I checked my emails immediately but unsurprisingly there was no news. This was unbearable.

Before heading south to Death Valley National Park, we wanted to visit the gallery of the world-renowned adventure photographer, Galen Rowell, which was situated a few blocks from our motel. The Mountain Light Gallery is a fantastic showcase of the late photographer's work in the Sierra Nevada and around the world and a suitably calm space in which to appreciate the majesty of the natural environment. Nonetheless I was impatient for news about Jess, checking my iPhone for an email every few minutes.

Finally I couldn't stand the lack of information any longer and rang Didi for an update. I wished I hadn't because all she was able to tell me was that Jess had disappeared from the field at some point during the night and they now had no idea where she was. Suddenly our joke from the previous evening about Jess going on the run to find us wasn't funny anymore.

I could tell Didi was embarrassed. Not only had the professionals lost Jess but they'd also failed to get her back. Joe was apparently feeling dreadful and had been left in no doubt what the staff at the shelter thought about his reckless disregard for the rules.

In a fleeting moment of forgiveness I told Didi to tell him not to feel too bad. Although I still couldn't imagine how Jess had managed to get out of the harness and felt sure he must have put it on wrong, I knew what she was like better than anyone and she had escaped from me a few times. The difference was that she loved me and always came back to me after a few minutes.

Didi told me that the animal control officers were going to start patrolling Fort Detrick to see if Jess had headed back there. I explained the route along the fence line that we often walked and how there were ample places for a dog to hide out on Wild Field. I also suggested patrolling Gambrill State Park and the watershed forest as we went walking in one of those places pretty much every day. Didi thanked me and rang off, promising to let me know as soon as she heard anything.

I went to tell Steve the bad news that Jess had disappeared and then went and sat down on one of the gallery's sofas to email Didi. I wanted to give her directions to our favourite hiking route at the watershed as the trailhead wasn't obvious and would be easy to miss. Whilst I was sat down, a man entered the gallery accompanied by his dog who wasn't on a lead. She was an older mutt of some kind, possibly a collie mix, but she looked a bit like Jess, predominantly black with a white chest.

The man struck up a conversation with the sales assistant behind the counter and seemed oblivious to his dog who looked around as if she was searching for someone. Her gaze fixed on me and she walked straight over. I knelt down and she put her nose to my forehead, just like Jess did, and tenderly licked my face.

"Are you telling me Jess is okay?" I asked, stroking her under the chin. Her soft brown eyes stared into mine.

"Thank you," I said. "Please tell Jess to come home, her Jenni loves her very much."

The man finished his conversation with the sales assistant and called to his dog who turned away from me and followed him out of the gallery.

It was a strange encounter, which probably lasted less than ten seconds, but it brought me great comfort. Was Jess trying to get a message to me? Had the 'twilight bark' gone out to the dogs of the USA to be on the look out for Jess's person, a brown haired woman with a distinctive accent? Many would call me delusional but nevertheless that incident gave me hope that the dog world somehow had the situation under control and from that moment on I never doubted that I'd see Jess again.

After Bishop we drove through Death Valley (or Deathly Boring Valley as we subsequently dubbed it) and on to Arizona and Utah. Over the next week we visited the Grand Canyon, Zion National Park, Bryce Canyon, Arches National Park and Moab. It was an amazing vacation but Jess was constantly on my mind.

I kept in regular touch with Didi, checking my emails whenever I could but there was no news of Jess's whereabouts until a couple of days before we were due to fly home. A stray dog matching Jess's description was hanging around on a farm a few miles from FCAC. The farmer was putting food out for the dog but it appeared too nervous to approach him or his wife. That certainly sounded like Jess. We were flying home on Sunday 18th September and it was agreed that I'd go into FCAC first thing on Monday morning to get directions out to the farm and go straight there. I was filled with hope.

"Just hang in there Jess," I thought, "Your Jenni's coming to get you."

We arrived home late on Sunday evening and for the first time in my life I was pleased a vacation had come to an end. Before I went to bed I prepared my 'Jess Catching Kit'; a selection of her favourite treats, a handful of kibble, a spare Ruffwear harness that I'd had the foresight to buy a few weeks before in case it was ever necessary and one of my unwashed T-shirts to hang in the humane dog trap that had been placed near the entrance to the farm. Her usual harness that she'd been wearing when she escaped was already in the trap in the hope she might recognise it but it predominantly smelled like her. I hoped the scent of me on a t-shirt might be more tempting.

Of course a major piece of Jess catching equipment was my car. If I saw Jess at the farm I intended to wave the spare harness at her to show her we were going for a walk. Then I'd slap the floor of the boot as I always did in the hope she'd remember all the good times we'd had together and come running back. I also intended to liberally scatter kibble and treats in the boot for good measure as I guessed she'd be hungry.

At 7:00 a.m. the next morning I arrived at the shelter to meet one of the animal control officers. Normally I'd be assisting in the spay and neuter clinic but all the team understood how I needed to get out to that farm as soon as possible. Carol was hugely supportive and told me how her heart sank when she'd heard the news. She also told me that Joe hadn't done anything to help catch Jess and since she'd absconded from the field, hadn't even contacted the shelter to ask for news. My previous forgiveness evaporated. Jess was right; he didn't deserve her.

Officer Mike, one of the animal control officers, gave me the address of the farm and explained where it was.

"If you're driving up the driveway and find yourself thinking, 'Hang on, I think I'm in a horror movie' then you're at the right place!"

That turned out to be an all too accurate description. The farm was only a fifteen minute drive away, where the city of Frederick gives way to rural Maryland, and was easy enough to find. I turned off the road and up the rutted driveway, which was bounded on both sides by cornfields. Those tall rows of corn were a great hiding place; Jess could be anywhere in there.

I came to the end of the drive and pulled into the yard in front of the dilapidated looking farmhouse. A pack of small dogs, mainly pugs and Chihuahuas, came running out to the car, yapping ferociously. I got out of the car, the pack of dogs snapping at my ankles. The yard was filled with rusting bits of machinery, a couple of ancient looking farm vehicles, a pungent smelling compost heap and the odd pile of non-descript rubbish.

There was also a couple of large German Shepherds who were chained up and barking at me. Officer Mike was right, I did feel as if I was entering some kind of horror movie.

"Thanks a lot Jess, of all the farms in all the world you had to pick this one," I muttered.

I felt a bit apprehensive about approaching the farmhouse, not least because it resembled the infamous Amityville 'horror house' that gained notoriety in the 1970s. Just as I was wondering what to do, the front door opened and a woman emerged, waved and walked over to me. Yelling at the dogs to quit bothering me, she introduced herself as Phyllis, the farmer's wife.

I explained who I was and thanked her profusely for reporting the stray dog to FCAC and for letting me visit. Phyllis said the stray dog seemed really sweet but just wouldn't approach her. The dog was comfortable around her dogs although they'd started to tie the German Shepherds up at night as she was worried they'd go for her as she was taking their food. Phyllis told me I was welcome to wander all over the farm as much as I liked and wished me luck.

The farm consisted of the two huge cornfields either side of the driveway, some derelict looking barns and outbuildings up near the house and beyond them a large field containing a herd of fairly scrawny cows. Phyllis had explained that this field extended a fairly long way and backed on to the Interstate 70, a major highway. I wandered around, calling Jess's name, scanning the terrain for any sign of her.

A small creek, shrouded by trees, ran along the western boundary of the farm. This meant that the stray dog had a constant source of water. Up near the outbuildings, I discovered a track that led over a culvert in the creek and up into a scrubby field that ran adjacent to Phyllis's property. On the left hand edge of the field, back towards the road, I could see a trailer park. Down to the right would be the I-70, but along the far length of that field were yet more fields. Essentially the elusive stray dog had an easy route in and out of the farm and could come and go as it pleased which would make finding it a lot more difficult.

Officer Mike had explained that the animal control officers had placed the humane dog trap all the way back down the drive near the road, just on the edge of one of the cornfields. I found it easily enough and wasn't in the slightest bit surprised that it was empty, save for a bowl of water, a bowl of cat food which smelt like it had seen better days, and Jess's now infamous escape-proof harness. I added my unwashed T-shirt and a few pieces of kibble. However I still doubted that Jess would ever willingly enter a crate, even if it did smell of her Jenni.

After a couple of hours of searching I gave up. I'd walked round the whole farm, including through some of the rows of corn, calling Jess's name. I was convinced she would come to me if she heard my voice and therefore felt certain she wasn't there. Before I left I went and thanked Phyllis once more and gave her my number in case the dog showed up again. Phyllis promised she'd call if she saw her and told me I was welcome to come and wander round the farm anytime, day or night, and didn't need to ask permission first. She told me she'd described me to her husband so he wouldn't shoot at me; I'd lived in the US long enough by now to know she wasn't joking. I suspected Phyllis and her husband were people who didn't trust the authorities or the outside world so I was doubly grateful to them for giving me free rein to wander around their property whenever I wanted. A shared love of dogs can bring very different people together.

Over the following week I went looking for Jess every single day. I'd go out to the farm most days to check the trap and just have a walk around. And I never once got shot at which was a bonus. I'd also just drive around the local rural area, hoping to get a glimpse of my elusive ghost dog raiding a bin or drinking from a stream. However I was conscious of the fact that we weren't 100% certain that the stray dog on the farm was Jess and so on days I didn't go out to the farm I went up to Gambrill or the watershed forest in case she'd headed for one of our regular haunts.

I also varied the time I went to the farm, going at all times of the day and night, hoping I'd get lucky and my search would coincide with one of the dog's visits. Sometimes I parked near the road, other times I parked up near the house and braved the pack of miniature guard dogs. On Saturday evening Steve and I went to the Frederick beer festival at the showground on the outskirts of town. I wasn't drinking anyway due to our efforts to conceive so we decided to swing by the farm on the way home. We got to the farm after midnight and spent about an hour traipsing around in the pitch dark, pleading with Jess to step out from behind a barn or emerge from a row of corn. She didn't.

It was now late September, Jess had been on the run for two and a half weeks and Phyllis hadn't reported any new sightings of the stray dog we suspected was her. Both Steve and I missed Jess dreadfully but I felt her absence especially keenly. My life just wasn't the same without her. For the four months I'd had her, Jess and I were inseparable; her presence in my life was a joy and a privilege that had changed me at a deep and fundamental level. I knew how much Jess distrusted other people and the fact she had decided to trust me, and had forged the bond with me that I felt we had, was incredibly affirming. I felt truly loved. As anyone who has ever had that kind of bond with an intelligent animal knows, it's completely different to loving human relationships. In some senses Jess was the most important relationship I'd ever had and the loss of it was a constant source of pain.

The length of time that Jess had been missing was significant in other ways. During the Monday morning spay and neuter clinic, Mr Domer came to see me and told me he would soon make the decision to end the search for Jess and recover the dog trap.

I wasn't stupid; I knew that everyone thought Jess was probably dead. I didn't though. I had an unshakeable conviction that she was still alive and would come back to me. I'd even placed her bed back in its usual place in the living room, my version of a yellow ribbon tied around a tree. The prospect of FCAC ending the official search didn't worry me however as I wasn't planning on ending my search and I'd always thought that Jess was more likely to come to me anyway.

A few nights later, Steve and I were getting ready for bed when my phone rang. It was Phyllis – the dog was at the farm. We were in the car within sixty seconds and at the farm ten minutes later, which was strange considering it was a good fifteen minute drive away. We walked around in the pitch dark, calling Jess's name, for about an hour and a half before giving up and going home, in equal parts elated that the mysterious dog was still around and totally frustrated that we hadn't seen her.

I went to see the animal control officers the next morning to let them know the stray dog was back. We guessed that the dog was hanging out somewhere else but kept returning to a reliable source of food. Didi later told me that as a result of this most recent sighting Mr Domer had agreed to keep the trap out for a while longer, in a new location nearer the farm.

However after another unsuccessful week of searching and no further sightings at the farm, I began to sense everyone's renewed optimism ebbing away again. Jess had now been missing for four weeks. My rational head knew full well that the odds were against her. And yet despite that, I couldn't shake my gut feeling that Jess and Jenni were destined to see each other again.

CHAPTER 12

REUNITED

ON THE MORNING of Saturday 8th October, Steve and I were just waking up when the phone rang. It was Lauren.

"Hey, I have two miniature Pinscher-Cairn terrier puppies who need fostering for two weeks. Are you interested?"

"Of course, we'll be right down!" I replied. A mixture of relief and joy flooded through me; I needed dogs in the house and in my life again. As I was getting dressed I joked to Steve that we'd be sure to get Jess back now.

The two puppies were named Duke and Lightning. Duke was the larger of the two and had clearly got the bulk of the Cairn terrier genes. He was fawn coloured and stocky with a confident demeanor and large, bat-like ears. Lightning was darker and quite a bit smaller. He looked like a mini Pinscher although his coat was more brindle coloured.

In all honesty Steve and I had never really been fans of small dogs. However Duke and Lightning managed to change our minds within a few minutes of getting them home. Duke was the big brother who instantly decided he was the head of the household and swaggered around like John Wayne. I wondered if that was why he'd been called Duke. Lightning was tiny but this didn't stop him giving as good as he got during bouts of puppy rough and tumble. He also lived up to his name and tore around the living room in a blur of dark fur.

Lightning swiftly discovered that his diminutive size enabled him to get under our sofas and stay there until he decided it was time to come out. Lightning thought this was great fun – Duke, Steve and I didn't, for different reasons.

It was an absolute joy to have dogs in the house once more and Duke and Lightning proved an extremely entertaining distraction that weekend. We set their crate and pen up in the living area and quickly adapted to the demands of having puppies again. Although compared to our recent experience with our Magnificent Seven litter, two puppies seemed pretty easy.

The next day was warm and sunny so we spent a lot of time outside watching them chase around after each other. By the early afternoon they were both shattered so we settled them down for a sleep in their crate and took the opportunity to drive up to Gambrill State Park for a walk and a Jess patrol. We took one of our usual trails that I'd taken with Jess many times, periodically calling her name in case she just happened to be nearby. We also let out a few howls in the hope we might hear her howl back at us but our call of the wild went unanswered. Nevertheless I had to believe that even if Jess couldn't hear us she'd somehow sense that her Jenni and Steve were still looking for her.

On Monday morning I got up at 5:30 a.m. as usual for the spay and neuter clinic. It was 10th October, Columbus Day, and although not a universal public holiday, the military had the day off. Steve couldn't enjoy a lie in though; he was on early morning puppy duty and then had a physiotherapy appointment on the other side of Frederick and needed the car so dropped me off at FCAC at 6:30 a.m. As I arrived, Mr Domer and

Officer Deb Norris, one of the animal control officers, were outside having a cigarette.

"Any word on Jess?" asked Officer Norris.

"No unfortunately. But we got two new foster puppies on Saturday so she'll show up now just to inconvenience me!"

Mr Domer and Officer Norris both laughed. Less than two hours later, Didi appeared at the door of the operating room.

"Jenni, a guy who lives up on Gambrill Park Road has reported a stray dog on his property and he's emailed a couple of photos. I think it's Jess but will you come and see what you think?"

A wave of intuition flooded through me; it was as if I recognised this moment. We had a dog on the table but Carol and MaryJane were there. "Dr C, could I..."

"Go!" urged Dr C.

"Yes, for goodness sake go," said Carol, "I so hope it's her!"

I followed Didi to her office where she had the photos open on the computer. They were grainy and poor quality but I only needed one look.

"That's her! That's definitely her!" Jess was alive and she was hanging out near Gambrill State Park where Steve and I had gone looking for her the previous afternoon. Had she heard us howling for her?

Didi grinned. "I thought so too but I wanted you to see her. She looks really good! Right, let's get you up there with Officer Norris."

I practically skipped back to the operating room and told Dr C, Carol and MaryJane the wonderful news. They were overjoyed that we now at least had a confirmed sighting and Carol asked me if I had a plan to catch her. In actual fact I was a bit worried. My Jess catching plan had always centred on our car. I felt sure she'd recognise it, associate it with going on a walk and happily jump in like she always did when I slapped the floor of the boot. But very unusually I didn't have my car today – Steve did. Furthermore my 'Jess Catching Kit' of her favourite food and the spare harness was in the car.

I rang Steve but he was already at his physiotherapy appointment and wasn't answering. I left a message telling him what was happening and asking him to come to the shelter as soon as he was finished.

Didi had given me a wire lead that not even Jess would be able to bite through. It had a clip at each end so I could loop one end around my waist and clip it back on itself and still have one end I could clip to Jess's collar, assuming she still had it on. I also took two additional leads, one normal lead with a clip at one end and one slip lead. As with the chain lead and Light Blue Safety Lead, I looped the normal one round my waist and clipped it to itself, then threaded the slip lead through the wrist loop, leaving the noose end free. That way I had two leads to secure Jess with and both were secured round my waist. If Jess ran off again she'd be dragging me behind her.

Officer Norris appeared at the door and smiled at the complicated set up around my waist.

"You ready to go catch a dog?"

"Let's go!"

Officer Norris was a tough-looking and experienced animal control officer, about fifteen years older than me. I hadn't spoken to her much before but she had always seemed friendly enough if ever so slightly intimidating. She had a commanding presence and I suspected she had no trouble dealing with pesky stray animals or less-than-wholesome members of the public. On the drive up to Gambrill, she assured me that she had a tried and tested technique for catching dogs.

"I think it's highly unlikely she'll remember you," she said, firmly but not unkindly. "So I need you to stay in the van and I'll only use you if I need you."

I promised to do as I was told but although I knew Officer Norris had Jess's best interests at heart, I was a bit annoyed that she thought Jess wouldn't remember me. I also doubted that the tried and tested dog catching technique would work on Jess. Officer Norris's method involved attracting the dog with balls of tinned cat food that she would throw to the dog and gradually entice it towards her. Dogs find cat food irresistible as it's so rich. This may have worked beautifully on normal dogs but Jess wasn't a normal dog.

Officer Norris must have sensed my scepticism. She grinned at me.

"Don't worry, I've never failed to catch a dog yet and we're not coming back without her!"

I immediately felt reassured. I could tell Officer Norris was a woman of her word and her no nonsense approach did at least inspire confidence in her intentions. She may not know Jess like I did but she was as determined as I was to get her back.

I grinned back at her. "It's a deal. We're staying out as long it takes."

Gambrill Park Road, where Jess had been reported, runs for approximately ten miles through Gambrill State Park and the watershed forest, with a small number of properties mostly set back amongst the woods. The forest setting makes it a beautiful place to live but it made our task harder. Despite having the address of where Jess was last seen we'd be lucky to find her; I feared we wouldn't be able to see the dog for the trees.

The property we were headed for was about nine miles down the road. I was getting more and more impatient but finally we saw the mailbox with the right house number on it. The house was set quite a way back from the road. We pulled into the driveway with forest either side of us and drove down towards the house. And then I saw her, walking through the woods on the passenger side of the van about 50 feet away.

"It's her, it's Jess!" I exclaimed, not quite believing what I was seeing. "Oh Jess, you gorgeous clever girl!"

Call it fate, call it serendipity, call it an act of God but that crazy, deranged husky had not only kept herself alive in the wild for nearly five weeks but was now walking through the correct bit of the forest at the exact minute we showed up. I don't think I ever loved her more than I did in that precise moment when I saw her all alone, still unaware that her Jenni had found her.

Officer Norris braked gently to a stop and turned off the engine. Jess stopped too, looking over at the van with interest. She looked lean but her eyes were bright and alert and she stood tall, clearly confident in the wild. Officer Norris grabbed her bag of cat food balls and opened her door quietly. Jess stayed where she was, still regarding the van intently.

"Ok, now remember, stay in here," urged Officer Norris as she slowly got out and went round to the back of the van. She opened the rear doors, retrieved one of her leads and then walked slowly out from behind the van where Jess could see her.

"Hey Jess," called Officer Norris in a calm, soothing, friendly voice. The effect on Jess was instantaneous; she immediately turned and sprinted away through the trees. That was my Jess! I wasn't in the slightest bit surprised. Despite my promise to stay in the van I knew it was up to me now. This was my opportunity, when I'd find out whether Jess and I had the bond I thought we had.

I opened the door of the van and without getting out, called loudly but calmly, "Jess, it's your Jenni!" The most incredible, amazing, life-affirming thing happened

– Jess skidded to a halt and spun round to face me. She remembered my voice!

At that moment I knew Jess had spent the last four and a half weeks searching for me and that doggy brain was telling her she'd found what she was looking for. She really did love me; she recognised my voice and didn't want to run from it. I knew I had to keep talking to her so I just carried on, saying anything that she was used to hearing me say.

"Easy Jess, good girl, walk nicely now. Take it easy for your Jenni. Who's my beautiful girl? Are you my crazy husky wolf? Oh Jess, you're such a good girl. Shall we go for a walk?"

With her eyes fixed on me, Jess tentatively took a few steps forward and I kept on talking.

"Where have you been Jess? What have you been up to? What a good girl, you found me! Time to go home now my crazy wolf, come home with your Jenni."

Jess gradually started creeping closer, seemingly trying to get a better view of me through the forest. It was an overcast day and the light amongst the trees was quite dim. Plus I had kept my promise to Officer Norris and was still sat in the van.

"Keep talking to her," urged Officer Norris who was stood perfectly still but I didn't need to be told. The sound of my voice was all that was stopping Jess from running off and I wasn't going to let that happen.

"That's it Jess, good girl. Take it easy. Any deer about? Any groundhogs? Where are those squirrels? Come on, let's go. Let's go Jess. Let's go home and see Steve. It's your Jenni and you're my beautiful girl, my beautiful crazy wolf."

"Get out of the van, let her see you," said Officer Norris softly. There was no ego about Officer Norris, no irritation that her plan hadn't worked – just an immediate and gracious recognition that I stood the best chance of getting Jess back.

I did as I was told and slowly got out of the van and took a few careful steps forward. I carried on talking, keeping my voice calm and steady so Jess wouldn't sense any tension. She was still edging closer but seemed a bit uncertain that it really was me. She was moving slowly from tree to tree, but gradually started to veer off to our right and her trajectory meant she was getting closer to the road too. I was acutely nervous that although the road was extremely quiet, we didn't want her to suddenly get spooked and go running across it and into the forest on the other side.

I kept talking and Jess kept moving, peering at me intently but still not completely sure, until she'd moved about ninety degrees from her original position and was standing at the end of the driveway. I didn't move but pivoted where I stood, not wanting to take my eyes off her for a second, determined not to break our connection.

"OK, go round to the back of the van," whispered Officer Norris, "You can do it, she's yours."

I walked slowly, still talking, not wanting to do anything wrong now.

"Take it easy Jessica, your Jenni's on the other end of this lead. No pulling, good girl."

Jess was only about 60 feet from me, so close but still with ample opportunity to run away from me if she decided to.

"Come on Jess, let's go home now. Let's go and see Steve. Come home with your Jenni."

I reached the back of the van and silently thanked Officer Norris for having had the foresight to open the rear doors. I always slapped the floor of the boot of our car as my signal to tell Jess to jump in; I hoped she'd remember that.

Jess now had a clear view of me down the driveway and slightly better light to see me in due to the break in the tree cover. Her posture seemed to change and I was sure I saw the moment she realised it really was me. She flinched slightly, as if taken aback, and seemed to hold her head a little higher.

My stomach lurched and I tightened my grip on the leads; what if this didn't work? I took a deep breath and focused all my energy on Jess, slapped the floor of the van three times in quick succession like I always did and called out, "Come on Jess, let's go".

Jess took a couple of steps toward me and stopped. I looked her right in the eyes, smiled at her and crouched down and slapped the floor of the van again.

"Jess, let's go," I called, louder and more confident now. And then Jess started running.

As she was halfway to me I knew I had her and yet I could still barely believe it. Surely she wouldn't stop now, yet was it really going to be this easy? I expected her to at least hesitate as she got closer but she didn't – she ran right to me and nuzzled into my face and neck. I gripped her collar, clipped the wire lead to it and then put the noose of the slip lead over her head. I had her. It had been five and a half weeks since she'd last seen me, and four and a half weeks since she'd escaped from the shelter and I had her.

"Oh Jess, you came back, you came back to me, I love you so much."

I was crying with relief, one arm around Jess's neck, the other hand stroking her beautiful head, my face right in front of hers, breathing in her wonderful doggy breath. Jess pawed my arm and gently touched my face with her nose, giving me those heart-melting husky kisses that I'd missed so much. She smelt awful but I didn't care.

"You came back, oh my Jess, you came back," I couldn't stop crying. I'd dreamed of this moment for so long and it had actually happened. I ran my hands down her sides. She was painfully thin and her ribs were showing. It was nothing that regular meals and a few treats wouldn't fix though.

"Do you have her?" called Officer Norris. From where she was standing she would have seen Jess run nearly all the way up to me but the van door obscured her final view.

"Yeah, I have her!" I called back.

Officer Norris came round the side of the van, a huge smile on her face.

"I guess she remembered me after all," I grinned, unable to hide a cheeky gleam in my eye. I meant this good-naturedly of course and Officer Norris understood.

She grinned back at me. "You must have spent a lot of time together!"

"Yes, we did", I said, stroking my beautiful girl. "All our time."

Officer Norris knelt down and petted Jess with me. I was surprised Jess tolerated this but she seemed to accept that I trusted this stranger who was dressed suspiciously like an animal control officer.

"Thank you Officer Norris, thank you so much. You were wonderful."

"Well you didn't really need me!"

That wasn't true. Officer Norris had been set on success right from the start. When Jess ran off initially she'd remained calm and when Jess stopped at the sound of my voice, Officer Norris adapted her plan instantly with not a hint of arrogance. All the time that I was talking to Jess and focusing on her, Officer Norris was appraising the situation. She was instrumental in gauging Jess's body language and advising me correctly. It had been a team effort.

The next challenge was getting Jess in the van for the ride back, however she obediently got into a large plastic crate in the back when I told her to.

"Can I ride in the back with her?" I asked.

We had only just been reunited and the passenger seat was simply too far away. Officer Norris laughed at me.

"Well you're not supposed to but d'ya think I'm gonna say no to you after that?"

So I squeezed in the back of the van amongst dog crates of various sizes. Officer Norris shut the doors and got in the front. I heard her get on the radio to FCAC and relay the news of Jess's successful capture with the great line, "We've just had a Kodak moment up here!"

During the ride back into Frederick I rang Steve, who was over the moon, and texted Carol who I knew would be anxiously waiting for news with the rest of the Monday morning spay and neuter team. She sent me a lovely message back saying she had never doubted me or my bond with Jess.

I'd already agreed with Didi and Linda that if we were successful in catching Jess, we'd take her straight back home rather than subjecting her to the stress of returning to the shelter. As long as she seemed ok, getting checked by the vet could wait a day.

When we pulled up outside our house Steve was waiting for us. He gave Jess a big hug when we opened the crate and then hugged me. Officer Norris laughed that she'd expected me to get a hug first. Steve had sensibly taken Duke and Lightning's crate upstairs to our bedroom and secured them in it. Doggy introductions could wait for the time being.

Jess clearly recognised the house and was obviously happy to be back. As soon as we were safely inside I removed the leads. She trotted over to the sofa, jumped up into her usual place and curled up with her chin on her front paws. My Jess was home.

As Steve was off work and could stay with Jess I decided to go back in to FCAC briefly. I needed to drop off Didi's wire lead as well as pick up a dose of Frontline, a flea and tick preventative. Whilst Jess was welcome back, parasitic hitchhikers were not.

Back at the shelter, I experienced a bit of a hero's welcome. Mr Domer high-fived me and was generous in his congratulations. "You always said she was still alive and you were right all along, great job!"

Carol hugged me and told me she knew I'd do it. And Dr C nearly made me cry when he simply said, "The Good Lord knew what he was doing when he gave these creatures a memory."

The reaction I got from the staff at the shelter was humbling. All of a sudden I felt like one of the team, not simply a volunteer. Jess had given me the best character reference I could have asked for and my fellow dog people respected it.

The moment when Jess ran up to me will forever remain one of the highlights of my life. Not only did she remember me, but also her reaction proved that she loved and trusted me without reservation. I had succeeded in forming a bond with an abused and scared dog that meant she chose to come back to me of her own free will and nothing else. She had no recall training and I had nothing with me to lure her in, such as her harness or the car that I felt sure she would have recognised. She came to me and me alone and it still feels like the greatest compliment anyone could ever pay me, and an irrefutable testament to the depth of the dog-human bond.

CHAPTER 13

POST TRAUMATIC JESS
SYNDROME

OVER THE NEXT couple of days we removed 23 ticks from Jess. She had various wounds on her paws and lower legs that looked like abrasions from barbed wire and she also had a weeping left eye. At my polite insistence she was prescribed doxycycline as a precaution against Lyme's Disease which she'd tested positive for when she first came to the shelter. One of the part time shelter vets was reluctant to issue it at first but I successfully argued that it was highly likely that one of those ticks was carrying Lyme's and after everything she'd been through she deserved to have that horrible disease stopped in its tracks. Jess couldn't advocate for herself; it was my job to do it for her.

Considering Jess had been living outside for a prolonged period and could go to the toilet whenever she wanted, I was expecting a few accidents in the house. Yet incredibly we had none at all. The first night back Jess slept in our room for the first time ever. At about 4:00 a.m. I was woken by her jumping up on the bed and barking. She then jumped off, ran to the door and barked again. The message was clear. I leapt out of bed and ran downstairs with her, hurriedly putting her harness on. Almost as soon as we got outside on the grass poor Jess had a big episode of diarrhoea. I was extremely grateful to her for letting me know she needed to go urgently;

cleaning that off the cream carpet would have been a nightmare.

To my great delight, Jess sleeping in our room became the norm. Steve's previous opposition to the practice evaporated and never returned. Jess loved it, I loved it and Steve admitted he loved it too. So every night I'd carry Jess's bed up to our room whilst feeling ever so slightly guilty that Duke and Lightning stayed downstairs in their crate. If they ever felt like second-class citizens then they didn't show it. They seemed quite content snuggled up together.

Jess seemed to take the presence of Duke and Lightning in her stride. We'd been especially cautious introducing her to Lightning as he was so small and I was worried she might think he was something she could eat. She did have a momentary gleam in her eye when Steve had brought Duke and Lightning downstairs soon after Officer Norris and I had arrived home with Jess. I held onto her firmly, conscious that she'd been foraging in the wild for weeks and was no doubt rather hungry. Yet once she'd given Lightning a thorough sniffing she relaxed and accepted he was puppy, not prey.

Linda and I agreed that we'd hold off on promoting Jess for adoption for a while and just let her settle back in. To my great relief there was no mention of Joe, the volunteer who'd applied to adopt her. To my knowledge he'd never offered to help look for Jess and he'd never even called the shelter to see how the search was going. This complete lack of concern was not exactly a glowing character reference and I agreed wholeheartedly with Jess – he didn't deserve her.

We never did definitively find out whether the stray dog at the farm had been Jess. Although the first animal control officer to respond to their report of a stray dog had shown Phyllis and her husband a photo of Jess, they'd only ever seen the dog at night or from a distance as the dog had always run away from them. It's entirely possible that the stray dog wasn't Jess but simply looked like her. On the other hand, there were no further sightings of the farm dog after Jess came back. The farm lay seven miles south-west of the shelter as the crow flies, and Jess was eventually found ten miles to the north. She could have covered those distances easily although she would have had to cross the busy Interstate 70 at least twice. Ultimately, like so much else about her, Jess's whereabouts during her adventure will forever remain a mystery.

Naturally a number of people assumed that after such a homecoming, Steve and I would definitely adopt Jess. We certainly discussed it – again – at great length. We both wished there was a way to make it work but all our previous reasons for not adopting her still held true.

I loved Jess hugely, more than I ever thought it was possible to love an animal. But love doesn't always conquer everything and our situation back home wasn't right for her. Steve and I came back to the same conclusion – we were not the right 'forever people' for Jess. I'll be eternally grateful to both Linda and Carol for never questioning our decision and assuring me that my reasoning was correct and a measure of how I always put Jess first.

As much as we wished our decision could have been different, we never doubted it and unfortunately Jess's behaviour on walks started to get even worse. For the first fifteen minutes of every walk she was barely controllable, jumping up at my face and barking continuously. She also started mouthing at me again although this only lasted a few days. I knew the barking and leaping around wasn't aggressive and I could put up with it but I doubted whether a prospective adopter who didn't know her good points would be so forgiving. Fundamentally, if Jess's behaviour didn't settle down then it made her practically unadoptable, despite her calm and affectionate persona when we were indoors.

Understandably I was terrified of Jess escaping again, particularly during her wild leaping around phase. She'd escaped from Joe the volunteer by wriggling out of her secure Ruffwear harness although I still couldn't fathom how she'd managed it and was convinced that Joe must have put it on incorrectly.

However thankfully for both of us, I had more confidence in Jess's escapology skills than in the escape proof harness. Just to be ultra-safe, I bought one of those lead adapters that allow you to walk two dogs on one lead. It had two short lengths of lead attached to a metal 'O' ring in the middle and a normal spring clip on each end. I put the harness on Jess as normal and clipped one end of the lead adapter to the robust grab handle on top of the harness and one end to her collar. This meant that Jess was attached to the harness whether she was in it or not and the harness was attached to the chain lead that she couldn't bite through and the chain lead was attached to the Light Blue Safety Lead that was clipped around my waist. For better or worse, Jenni and Jess were inextricably bound to each other.

It was a good thing I was so risk averse. A few days after her return, I decided to take Jess for a walk in Baker Park whilst Duke and Lightning were asleep. It was a gorgeous day; the trees in Baker Park boasted a full spectrum of autumn colours, the sun was shining and I had the best dog in the world at my side.

We had a lovely ramble along Carroll Creek once her mad phase was over and then sat down on the grass, a sufficiently anti-social distance from the path, watching the world go by. A number of other people were doing the same thing. After a few minutes I noticed a man and a woman approaching people and handing out leaflets. As they got closer to us I kept an eye on them and prepared to ask them to not come any closer. Jess had no interest in making new friends and neither did I. Then the woman caught my eye, smiled and made a beeline for me.

"Hey there, how are you?" she yelled over.

I held my hand up firmly. "Please don't come any closer," I yelled back, gesturing at Jess.

Maybe my British accent sounded too polite, maybe I looked too friendly but Leaflet Woman started jogging over to me. Jess didn't like this at all and scrambled to her feet. I yelled again, "Please stop, my dog doesn't like people."

Leaflet Woman was faster than she looked. She was bearing down on us and Jess was now pulling backwards frantically and barking. I leapt up to better control Jess; Leaflet Woman was only about twenty feet away. I turned around to try and shield Jess and calm her down and so I had the perfect view of what happened next – Jess pulled back sharply, ducked her head down and hunched her shoulders up, allowing her to slip her head, shoulders and front legs out of the first section of the harness and then the back section with the waist belt in one seamless action. It was exactly what she'd done with the flimsy step in harness at Gambrill State Park, except the Ruffwear harness was supposedly designed to prevent that kind of escape.

The move looked so easy it was as if Jess had suddenly shrunk or developed the mystical ability to shape shift. I swore, Jess kept reversing and then the lead adaptor that was clipped to the harness and to her collar checked her getaway. I silently congratulated myself for my paranoia – it had averted another disaster. I grabbed a still barking Jess by the collar and turned round angrily to Leaflet Woman.

"Seriously, go away," I yelled. She looked suitably shocked at the mad dog and the mad woman in front of her but did at least listen to me this time and left us alone.

After the rapid exodus of Leaflet Woman I sat down with Jess, told her what a good girl she was and apologised for taking her to a place where stupid people wanted to get within a mile of her. If she'd escaped from the harness and run off in Baker Park then the consequences didn't bear thinking about. Baker Park was long but narrow and she could have easily sprinted the width of the park to one of the roads that ran alongside. Then at one end of Baker Park were the busy Rosemont Avenue and the US-15, an interstate highway, and at the other end was downtown Frederick, neither suitable environments for any dog, let alone one who was scared of people and would instinctively run away from them. It would have been miraculous if she hadn't been hit by a car.

On the bright side, at least I now appeared to have a tried and tested Jess-proof harness and lead system. I didn't want to risk putting the harness back on as that would have meant unclipping the lead adapter and we were both rather shaky and stressed by what had just happened. So no doubt looking rather comical, Jess and I walked straight to the car with the empty harness swinging between the lead adapter and chain lead and headed to the sanctuary of home.

In addition to our unbridled joy at having Jess back, Steve and I were thoroughly enjoying our latest canine guests. Duke and Lightning were endlessly entertaining and full of personality. We loved watching them chase each other round the living room or fight over a tug toy. They could seem quite ferocious towards each other one minute and then curl up together in a bundle of brotherly love the next.

Unfortunately I soon discovered that Duke could be quite ferocious with me too. All puppies bite; it's completely normal behaviour and nothing to be alarmed about but Duke seemed to snap at me with real animosity and drew blood on more than one occasion. I began to be wary whenever I picked him up. Steve admonished me for this and told me Duke was biting me because he was picking up on my fear. I retorted that Duke had started it; I was only scared because he bit me so often. If his biting stopped then so would my nervousness. Duke wasn't like this with Steve or anyone else; there was just something about me he didn't like.

A few days after Jess returned, Duke made the mistake of snapping at my hand right in front of her. She immediately barked at him, swatted him over the head and then pinned him to the floor with one of her long front legs. Clearly it was okay for her to bite me in an affectionate, playful, slightly crazed way but any impudent pup who did it maliciously was in trouble.

This lesson in manners from an older dog was no bad thing and just as I'd done with the Magnificent Seven, I tried to give Duke and Lightning one on one time with Jess. However whilst she tolerated them it was clear she could take or leave them. She'd allow them to climb over her but never actively played with them. Maybe she was slightly ticked off that we got new dogs in her absence.

The following Saturday, when we'd had the terrier brothers for a week, we went out with Peter and Sandee who'd adopted Lewis, now Patrick. I didn't want to leave Duke and Lightning for too long so I suggested we took our desserts back to ours so Peter and Sandee could meet the new puppies. Sandee took one look at Lightning and fell in love. She decided he'd be the perfect little brother for Patrick and Peter had to talk her out of putting in an application on him. Needless to say Duke didn't snap at them either.

We never did solve the mystery of why Duke didn't like me. The most likely explanation is that during his short life he had been mistreated by someone who resembled me, most likely the wife or daughter of the man who surrendered Duke and Lightning to the shelter. If only dogs could talk to us. I didn't hold it against him and thankfully he remains the only dog who's ever disliked me.

The next weekend was our last with Duke and Lightning. We spent lots of time playing with them outside and Duke seemed especially affectionate towards Steve, frequently running over to where he was sat on the grass and jumping and snuggling in his lap.

"See, he's lovely," taunted Steve, fondling Duke's big ears. "I don't know why you're so scared of him!"

Duke's inexplicable vendetta against me hadn't abated and I was genuinely worried that he might fail his behavioural assessment at the shelter on Monday morning. All dogs and puppies had to undergo an assessment before being placed on the adoption floor and one of the tests involved being prodded with a plastic hand on a stick. I knew what Duke would have done to my real human hand if I'd prodded him and I was slightly concerned that he might be deemed too aggressive to be put up for adoption.

On Sunday night Steve was tired and went to bed early. I decided to stay up and watch a movie. Jess was curled up at her end of the sofa and Duke and Lightning were asleep in their crate. However I fancied some company so I plucked a sleepy Lightning out for a cuddle. I could be accused of blatant favouritism here but in my defence, Lightning had never attempted to maul my face off.

As I settled into a comfortable position on the sofa, Lightning snuggled down in my arms like a baby and went back to sleep. The sound of him breathing contentedly and the rise and fall of his tiny chest against mine was immensely relaxing.

Steve and I had been trying to conceive since the end of March but it hadn't happened yet. Conscious of the advice that if you're over 35 you should seek medical advice after six unsuccessful months, I'd made an appointment with my doctor on the base at the beginning of September. In the US, medical referrals happen fast and by early October we'd each undergone a number of investigations and I'd been issued with a fertility drug that would help stimulate ovulation. I had to take one of the tablets daily for five days from the start of my next period and then have sex every other day for two weeks.

Steve and I were in the early stages of that two weeks and this kind of directive was as romantic as it sounds. Nevertheless we'd been dutifully doing as instructed and hoped we'd soon be successful. But the process was weighing on me; what if this wasn't straightforward?

For someone who had previously never wanted children, the urge was now overwhelming. I don't think it was just my age and biological clock kicking in either. Notwithstanding my unwillingness to regard dogs as quasi-children, my foster puppies had nevertheless pricked my maternal instinct – they were small and helpless and completely reliant on me to feed them, keep them safe and show them love and affection. And I enjoyed being relied upon.

As much as I appreciated my cuddle with Lightning that night, he wasn't quite what I was after. I wanted to feel a little human body against mine, to feel a heartbeat and know I'd made it, to hear the sound of my own baby breathing. Yet I was beginning to think it might never happen.

CHAPTER 14

ORPHAN ANNIE

DESPITE BEING 'BIG dog' people, Steve and I had grown hugely fond of Duke and Lightning. Nevertheless, Steve felt that when they returned to the shelter we needed a break from fostering any dog other than Jess; I agreed. The night before I took the terrier brothers back to FCAC I promised my long-suffering husband that I wouldn't take on any new fosters for a while. I broke that pact less than twelve hours later.

Bright and early on Monday morning I fed Duke and Lightning for the last time and placed them in the travel crate for the short drive to the shelter. As it was so early in the morning, Carol and I temporarily placed them in one of the spay and neuter cages which meant I could periodically pop in and check on them during the clinic. Then once Lauren arrived at work they'd be processed, assessed and could go out on the floor in the puppy room.

When MaryJane arrived she wanted to meet my latest foster pups and was especially smitten with Duke. She got him out of his cage for a cuddle and he nuzzled into her shoulder like a baby. MaryJane rocked him back and forth and he purred with pleasure. This confirmed that it was just me Duke hated. And my fears about the behavioural assessment were misplaced – Duke passed with flying colours and was adopted a few days later by a family who already had a miniature Schnauzer, a great companion for Duke.

A couple of hours later, I was scrubbing surgical equipment when I heard two sets of footsteps come down the corridor and stop right outside the operating room. Then I heard Carol laugh.

I turned around and Lauren and Linda were stood in the doorway grinning conspiratorially. Linda was holding a small black puppy although the puppy's bottom was facing us so my first view was this little tail wagging furiously – I'd never seen a puppy tail wag that fast. Linda just looked at me and turned the puppy around and I saw the sweetest little face staring back at me hopefully.

"Now it's ok, I know you don't want another foster for a while," said Linda with a twinkle in her eye.

"Oh, look at her, of course I'll take her!"

It was that easy. Just show me a cute puppy bottom with a waggy tail and any pacts or promises I've made are rendered null and void. I didn't bother to ask Steve; I knew he'd be instantly won over as soon as he saw her.

Linda told me that the puppy had been picked up as a stray that morning in the grounds of a nearby high school. Puppies don't escape and go on the run; someone had intentionally abandoned her, not caring whether she lived or died. I decided to call her Annie after Orphan Annie.

Annie was a pit bull, a breed banned in the UK and controversial in the US. Many counties and cities had passed legislation banning pit bulls from their environs or mandating that they be muzzled in public. However pit bulls also had many defenders who were adamant that they were unfairly maligned and implored people to judge them by 'deed, not breed.'

None of this mattered to me because Annie posed no threat whatsoever. She was black with a white chest

and white paws and a rounded, chubby little tummy. Her
back legs seemed ever so slightly longer than her front
legs which made her adorably gangly. She had a sweet-
natured disposition and unsurprisingly, given the
circumstances in which she was found, just wanted to be
held the whole time.

I took Annie home after the spay and neuter clinic
and introduced her to Jess. Jess had accepted Duke and
Lightning but had never totally taken to them and had
never played with them the way she did with Scout.
Maybe it was because there were two of them or maybe
it was because they were boys. Annie was another matter
– Jess adored her immediately and it was clear the
feeling was mutual. Having Jess around worked wonders
for Annie's confidence and I have no doubt their
relationship served to help Annie bounce back from the
experience of being abandoned.

Satisfied that the two dogs were going to get on
well, I now had to confess my pathetic lack of puppy-
resisting willpower to Steve. I rang him at work.

"Hi babe, now don't be cross with me..."

"How many this time?" replied my poor husband.

I laughed. "Only one, she's gorgeous and I just
couldn't say no. You'll understand when you see her."

And of course when Steve got home later he fell in
love with Annie straight away. It would have taken a
harder heart than Steve's to resist those gangly legs and
waggy tail.

So Annie ingratiated herself into the Williams
family in a seamless fashion and just as Scout had done,
brought out a joyously playful side to Jess. Annie loved
to play and her idea of fun was to clamber all over Jess
and lovingly bite her ears, legs and face. She also
thought nothing of getting in to Jess's bed and playing
with Bear, a soft toy that I'd bought Jess when she
returned from the wild. Unusually for Jess she'd become

quite attached to Bear so I was surprised when Jess allowed Annie to take him from her. Jess didn't mind any of Annie's antics in the slightest and her patience with her new friend was phenomenal.

I loved having two dogs again. I'd sit and watch them for ages, not getting anything else done but thoroughly enjoying their natural interaction. In fact Jess and Annie proved a therapeutic distraction from the pressure of trying to conceive to a timetable.

Our failure to conceive, the month of medical investigations and resulting romance-sapping 'sex schedule' had taken a toll on me and Steve. During our last week with Duke and Lightning we agreed we needed a weekend away and decided to take Jess to Davis in West Virginia, about a three hour drive from Frederick. We'd been there for a ski weekend back in February, in between fostering Lily the Malinois puppy and Sam the beagle.

Davis was a small town of less than 700 people in West Virginia's Canaan Valley, situated alongside the Blackwater River and next to the Monongahela National Forest. At 3,100 feet, it had the distinction of being the Mountain State's highest town and boasted both downhill and Nordic ski resorts as well as extensive hiking and beautiful scenery. It was the perfect destination for a weekend of hiking when the fall colours would be out in force. As we were taking Jess on a trip to another state I had asked Linda's permission because if we lost her in deepest darkest West Virginia it would be difficult if not impossible to get her back.

"Of course you can take her, you've never lost her! Sounds like she'll have a wonderful time."

We'd booked our trip for the weekend after we got Annie but obviously long hikes were not suitable for a seven-week old puppy. So we dropped her back at the shelter on the Friday morning with the promise that we'd see her in a few days.

It was only late October but on the drive toward Davis the temperature dropped noticeably and the sky took on that close, grey quality that signals impending snow. We'd just crossed into West Virginia from Maryland and were about an hour away from Davis when the first white flakes began falling through the sky.

Jess had been curled up and sleeping in the boot but she must have either heard two excited snow-loving humans or smelt the snow because she soon woke up and stared transfixed out of the rear window. Our elevation noticeably increased and the white stuff kept coming and looked like it was settling. Steve and I were extremely happy with the unexpected weather. We'd been looking forward to an autumnal hiking weekend but now we were getting snow which was even better. And how appropriate to experience it with our wild at heart husky. Thankfully Steve and I had brought plenty of warm kit as we were expecting cold weather anyway so the fact there'd be snow on the ground wouldn't change our hiking plans.

The snow continued all the way to Davis and by the time we arrived at the Canaan Valley Resort it was clear it wasn't stopping anytime soon. The cabins were well spread out and felt suitably remote and the forest setting looked magical in the fading afternoon light. We'd booked a dog-friendly self-catering cabin – it wasn't luxurious but it was clean, cozy and comfortable and had a real fire. It was perfect.

The next morning we woke up to a thick covering of pristine snowfall obscuring all the vibrant fall colours that had been our original reason for visiting. It didn't matter – Jess was beside herself with excitement and so were her two people.

We'd always intended to hike up on the Bald Knob plateau where we'd been cross-country skiing the previous winter. The plateau offered spectacular views across the Canaan Valley and the Dolly Sods Wilderness and so we decided to stick with our plan and drove out to the trailhead, situated next to the ski lift. As it was only October the chairlift was closed and we were the only car in the car park. We later found out the chairlift should have been open but had ironically shut due to the unexpected weather. Not that it mattered as there was no way we'd have taken Jess on a chairlift anyway.

The trail that led up onto the Bald Knob plateau was only about a mile long but was quite steep in places. Add the deep snow and the need to wrangle an extremely animated Jess and it took almost forty-five minutes to get to the top. It was a stunning walk though. It snowed the whole way, the air was clean and crisp and we were the only people out.

Jess was in her element which also meant she was an utter pain in the backside. She wouldn't stop leaping up and down and Steve and I had to keep taking turns in order to save our arm muscles. It was impossible to be too annoyed at her however; she was having the time of her life. I only wished I could have taken her off the lead so she could bound through the snow to her heart's content.

The steep climb and a hyperactive Jess were well worth the effort as the view from the Bald Knob overlook was spectacular. The air possessed that enchanting quality that is forged by the combination of altitude and fresh snow and we had an amazing view of the Canaan Valley and beyond. It was our own personal winter wonderland. We sat down on our backpacks for insulation and shared a flask of hot chocolate and ate our packed lunch. Jess had a few treats, not that she needed any extra energy.

Snow, solitude, a pristine view and a cabin to go back to - life didn't get much better than this. It was a moment out of time – nothing mattered but the present, there was literally nowhere else I'd rather be and I forgot everything I was worried about.

After lunch we hiked around the plateau, trying to find the trails we'd roamed on cross-country skis the previous winter. Steve joked about how much fun it would be coming back with Jess and skijoring – skiing whilst being pulled along by your dog. I promised that if I didn't get pregnant this winter then we'd do exactly that, although I volunteered Steve to be the guinea pig and experience being pulled on skis by Jess first. If he survived then I'd try it.

We hiked for a couple of hours before heading back down the trail. By the time we got back to our car even Jess seemed relieved to get in and lie down. We'd achieved the impossible – we'd tired her out.

Back at the cabin we lit the fire and our tired but happy husky sprawled out in front of it, blissfully content. That night we had steaks, jacket potatoes, a bottle of wine and a roaring fire. We'd had a perfect day and the setting couldn't have been more romantic. Unsurprisingly something that we had to do became something we wanted to do so we left Jess sleeping by the fire and disappeared to the bedroom.

The next morning we hiked through the forest immediately surrounding our resort and also drove to the nearby Blackwater Falls, West Virginia's famous waterfall. There seemed so much more about this area to discover and we promised to return one day.

We drove back to Frederick later that afternoon. I remember feeling extraordinarily lucky. I'd had a wonderful weekend, staying in a beautiful place with Steve and Jess, the two loves of my life. And as amazing as Davis was, it wasn't an international tourist destination and wasn't the kind of place you'd know about unless you lived in the US. We were so fortunate to have the opportunity to discover these places that were off the beaten track. Years later, that trip remains one of my top five best ever weekends.

The next morning I was at the spay and neuter clinic as usual. Carol, MaryJane and Dr C were eager to hear about our weekend and thought it sounded like Jess's idea of paradise. After the clinic I was reunited with Annie. Her tail wagged non-stop as I picked her up and she covered my face in puppy kisses. Back at home, Jess and Annie were elated to see each other again. The weekend apart certainly hadn't diminished their bond.

During Annie's first week with us, I'd always felt a bit guilty that she slept downstairs by herself whilst Steve, Jess and I slept in the same room upstairs. Duke and Lightning obviously had each other to curl up with but Annie was alone. Maybe it was a realisation that I didn't have a huge amount of fostering time left or maybe it was my blossoming maternal instinct but that night I told Steve that Annie was going to sleep in her crate in our room from now on.

This proved to be a big mistake. Annie could now see Jess and there was no way she was going to settle down in a crate whilst her best buddy was sprawled wherever she chose on our bedroom floor. Equally I didn't have the heart to banish her back downstairs.

Admitting defeat, I decided to move into the spare room with Annie and got into bed with her. Annie snuggled in to me contentedly and immediately went to sleep. Arguably not the best habit for Annie to get into but I justified it to myself on the grounds that at her age she should have still been sleeping with her mum and littermates and my foster caring role to a seven week old puppy was primarily one of surrogate 'mom'. I lay awake for a while, humbled by the trust Annie was showing in me. Less than two weeks previously, as a six week old puppy, she'd been abandoned by someone who didn't care if she survived. And now she was sleeping soundly, her faith in me absolute. And bear in mind I'd returned her to the shelter a few days before and only picked her up again that morning.

Naturally Annie and I slept in the spare room together for the remainder of her time with us; I'm not sure who enjoyed it the most. It struck me later that it was an interesting coincidence that I began co-sleeping with a puppy that particular week; it wasn't as if I hadn't had numerous other puppies to choose from over the preceding months.

Despite the thick snow in West Virginia, November was proving mild in central Maryland and Annie's second week with us was warm and sunny. As with the other puppies, I took Annie out on short walks immediately by our house. I enjoyed taking her out onto the grass circle and letting her chase me around on her little frog legs. She loved being outside and would gambol ungainly along beside me with an expression of pure devotion on her face. She'd stick so close to me that she'd quite literally get under my feet and I accidentally trod on her paws a few times. This seemed to cause me far more concern than it did Annie.

"You need to give me a few inches of clearance Annie!" I'd reproach her but she'd just grin at me and wag her tail.

Annie wasn't the only one of my foster dogs benefitting from off lead exercise that week. FCAC had recently had a large and secure exercise enclosure constructed on the field behind the shelter. It was roughly 100 feet long and 70 feet wide, ample room for a dog like Jess to run around in. With Linda's permission I started taking her to the enclosure as I wanted to try and recall train her, as a precaution in case she ever got loose again and because all dogs should be recall trained anyway. But of course, in order to be able to practise recall, you have to have a safe and secure outdoor space and we didn't have that at our house. The shelter dogs were fed at 1:00 p.m. and so the enclosure was out of bounds from then until 2:30 p.m. as a precaution against bloat. However I fed Jess later in the afternoon so it didn't matter for her and using the enclosure at this time meant we weren't denying a shelter dog the use of such an important facility.

Jess looked nervous as we pulled into the car park at the shelter but as soon as I led her away from the building and towards the field she calmed down. And once we were inside the enclosure she realised that something fun was happening. As I took the harness off the thought crossed my mind that I had no idea if I'd be able to get her back. At least she couldn't go far although I didn't relish the prospect of having to phone reception and ask them to send Officer Norris or one of the other animal control officers on a mission to their own exercise pen.

Unsurprisingly Jess loved being off the lead and spent the first half an hour racing around in circles and tearing back and forth. Out of sheer joy she started running full pelt towards me, looking for all the world like a hungry but playful wolf launching herself at her quarry, except this predator swerved safely away from me at the last moment. It was a mark of my trust in Jess that I stood my ground, laughing at her with my arms outstretched, only to have her dodge the hug I was offering with a playful gleam in her eye. Jess ran all the way to the fence, whirled around to face me and charged all over again. This became known as the 'Race Full Speed at Jenni' game. After a while I could see Jess was tiring and thought now would be an opportune time to get her back on the lead. I held the harness up so she could see it.

"Let's go home Jess. Good girl."

Jess stayed where she was, looking at me uncomprehendingly. Surely I didn't intend for this fun to come to an end? The strange ways of humans must be ever so confusing to dogs sometimes. I walked over to her, holding the harness and lead up the whole time. To my surprise she lay down and allowed me to get her in the harness. Not recall as such but this was the first training session and I mainly wanted her to get used to this new space, enjoy herself and accept that we couldn't stay there indefinitely. This experiment had been a great success and I began taking Jess to the exercise pen two or three times a week.

Annie's time with us was fast running out. She'd grown in size and in confidence and I really felt as though Jess and I had fostered her together. The three of us rubbed along together so well and I was concerned how Jess would cope without her. And as for Annie, a puppy that had been cruelly dumped with not a thought to her safety, she had not only been rescued from that ordeal but had subsequently thrived thanks to foster care. What a turnaround in her circumstances.

Two weeks after her wagging bottom had greeted me in the doorway of the operating room it was time to take Annie back to the shelter and wish her 'happy trails'. She'd been a complete joy and we were all going to miss her hugely. Unsurprisingly she was adopted within days. Jess came to greet me when I got back from the shelter and seemed confused that I didn't have her buddy with me. For the rest of the day she seemed uncharacteristically subdued. That night I moved back into the main bedroom but I missed the presence of a warm little tummy and four little paws digging into me.

Annie was notable as the only one of my foster dogs that Steve and I couldn't adopt, even if it had been practically possible, as pit bulls are banned in the UK under the Dangerous Dogs Act. It's a controversial piece of legislation that condemns a dog on the basis of its breed, or even similarity to the prohibited breeds, regardless of whether the individual dog has done anything wrong.

On the other hand, it was enacted in 1991 after a spate of terrible dog attacks on children. One of the prohibited breeds, the Japanese Tosa, was specifically bred for dog fighting and is, depressingly, still legally used for that purpose in Japan. Tosas can weigh up to 200 lbs and it's difficult to escape the conclusion that anyone who wants a dog like that shouldn't be allowed to have one. Personally, I don't believe aggression is a natural dog trait; if a dog is truly aggressive then a human has made them that way, either through irresponsible breeding borne of an abhorrent motivation, or deliberate training, or both.

As for my own experience, I dealt with numerous pit bulls in the shelter, whether that was walking them, supervising 'meet and greets' or caring for them in the spay and neuter clinic, which included restraining them whilst they received their anaesthetic. I never once felt unsafe; on the contrary the pit bulls tended to be especially friendly and cooperative. The tabloid stereotype of the dangerous 'devil dog' certainly bore no relation to our sweet-natured Annie; the only danger she ever posed was taking up too much of the bed.

CHAPTER 15

SNIFFER DOG

A COUPLE OF days after Annie went back to the shelter and just over a week since we returned from our Davis trip, I started to notice that Jess was acting strangely around me. Whenever she could smell me but not see me, she seemed nervous, fearful even. Our downstairs was essentially open plan but with a partial wall between the kitchen and dining area. There was an archway on one side of the wall and it was fully open on the other, leading round a corner to the utility room, toilet and connecting door to the garage. So there were a number of scenarios where Jess could smell me before she could see me and when that happened she didn't seem to know it was me she was smelling. I'd walk around the corner and she'd be nervously backing away from me.

This behaviour had been going on for a few days when another incident made me wonder if there was something different about me. One of our walks took us along the security fence line, past the back yards of the houses that bordered Fort Detrick. For some reason Americans don't like solid fences so we could see in to each back yard through Detrick's chain link fence. One of the back yards contained two territorial Labradors who would always race right up to the fence, barking and growling furiously, with their hackles raised. Their behaviour never bothered me as they obviously couldn't get to me so I would always just ignore them. Jess always ignored them too, walking past like they didn't exist. She never seemed in the slightest bit troubled by them and I don't think she ever even glanced in their direction.

We hadn't walked that route for a few days, not since before Jess had started being weird with me. As we approached the yard the two dogs came racing up to the fence, barking and growling as usual. Jess's hackles immediately went up and she pulled sharply towards them and growled back. That was the first time I'd heard her growl out of anger rather than fear.

"Jess, it's okay! It's just those two silly dogs guarding their yard!" I reassured her, pulling her away from them.

Jess growled again, baring her sizable teeth. I was able to get her to keep walking but she kept looking back at the still barking dogs until we were well past their yard.

That's when I started to think I could be pregnant. I knew a few women who'd said their dog could tell when they were pregnant and this made perfect sense to me – dogs have evolved to be able to read our body language and our mood and a pregnant woman would naturally behave or walk slightly differently. Whilst I'd never heard of a dog who knew a woman was pregnant before they did, common sense dictates that the biochemical changes going on in a pregnant woman's body would be easily detectable to a dog's nose.

Dogs have 220 million smell receptors in their noses compared to our paltry 5 million. This superior olfactory ability has a life-saving application for people with certain medical conditions – dogs can be trained to sniff out an impending epileptic seizure, hypoglycemia in people with diabetes and even certain cancers. Medical detection dogs are now a legally recognised type of assistance dog. Of course a dog would be able to smell pregnancy with all of its attendant hormonal changes.

Did I smell different which was why Jess was nervous of me? And did she know what it meant which was why she was suddenly protective of me around unfriendly dogs? I didn't say anything to Steve but I began to get ever so slightly excited.

Another couple of days passed and Jess's behaviour continued. I was most intrigued by her reaction to the bad-tempered Labradors and repeated that walk on the Monday afternoon. Whilst Jess didn't growl at them this time, her hackles went up and she eyed them warily as we walked along the back of their territory.

When we got home, I worked out it would be a good day to take a pregnancy test. I hadn't had my period although that didn't necessarily mean anything, as my cycle was very irregular. Nevertheless I thought now was about the right time to take a test, not least because Jess's behaviour had got me thinking.

I also wanted to know for certain because if I wasn't pregnant, Steve and I were planning a 'Big Night Out'. I'd stopped drinking completely for three weeks of the month and Steve was only having the occasional beer. However we'd promised ourselves that if I didn't get pregnant this month we'd go out to drown our sorrows. We'd penciled in a night at Firestones, our favourite bar, on the Wednesday, and were going to get a taxi there and back so neither of us had to drive. Obviously the only way to be certain I wasn't pregnant was to have a period or take a test.

I had bought a pack of three pregnancy test kits in preparation. I read the instructions carefully, peed on the stick, placed it on the sink and started the stopwatch on my iPhone. Jess was lying just outside the bathroom as she always did. I went and sat down next to her and stroked her.

"Do you know already?" I asked her. "We'll find out in a minute. Two minutes in fact."

After an interminably long two minutes I went and retrieved the all-knowing white stick. There were two words on the digital display window - 'NOT PREGNANT'. I was surprised at how upset I was. I'd allowed myself to believe it had finally happened and I also thought it would be rather lovely if it was Jess who first detected the presence of a Baby Williams. But I wasn't pregnant after all. I threw the pregnancy test in the bin and smiled sadly at Jess.

"Oh well, at least I can drink on Wednesday night," I said to Jess who stared back at me impassively. "And I'm really going to go for it. It's just possible I'll manage three whole beers!"

I sat down with Jess again.

"So why are you being weird with me you crazy wolf?" I asked her, ruffling her head. "What's going on?"

Jess just smiled her inscrutable smile and said nothing.

When Steve got home I told him I'd taken a test but that it was negative. I could tell he was disappointed. I told him about Jess and her recent strange behaviour and how I'd started to feel hopeful. Despite our setback, we consoled ourselves with the thought of a night out. Then on Wednesday morning Jess nearly attacked me.

Jess was a big dog and she had a big dog bed. Ever since her return from the wild she'd slept in our bedroom but I'd usually bring her bed downstairs in the morning so she could lie on it during the day if she wanted. Her favourite sleeping position was curled up on the sofa but occasionally she liked a change of scene.

We'd just been out for our morning walk and I headed up to my bedroom to sort some laundry and bring Jess's bed downstairs. Crucially Jess saw me, her

Jenni, go upstairs. I collected the laundry, placed it in the plastic laundry basket and then picked up Jess's bed with my free hand. So when I was coming downstairs I had the laundry basket under one arm and was holding Jess's big bed up high in front of me so as not to trip over it. Coupled with the fact that our stairs had a solid wall on either side, this meant that Jess couldn't see me. In her doggy mind, her Jenni went upstairs but now this stranger who didn't smell like her Jenni was coming downstairs and her Jenni was nowhere to be seen or smelt.

I was almost at the bottom step when Jess started barking and growling aggressively in a way I'd never heard before. Jess would frequently growl when people came to the house but it was a low frightened growl that was always followed by her turning and running for the sanctuary of the farthest possible corner. This growling was different; this was fierce and purposeful. I could tell Jess was coming at me and she wasn't frightened – she was angry.

"Jess, it's me!" I exclaimed, swiftly lowering the bed so she could see me. Her behaviour changed in an instant – a momentary look of surprise crossed her face and then she came to me but now it was to rub against me and nuzzle in to me as if to say sorry. We had an affectionate, tail-wagging cuddle and all was okay again but she kept looking at me in a contrite way.

"I don't smell like 'me' do I Jess?"

Although the incident had only lasted a few seconds, there was no doubt in my mind that Jess was coming for me and was about to attack me, the odd-smelling stranger who'd made her Jenni disappear. I had to be pregnant; there was no other rational explanation.

So I took another test. I just knew this was going to be the one that confirmed my theory so when the screen said 'NOT PREGNANT' again I was totally perplexed. What on earth was making Jess act up?

I remembered reading about police, fire, and search and rescue sniffer dogs and how the handlers have a mantra, "Trust the dog". They believe that the dog is always right and if something doesn't make sense then it's the human handler who is misinterpreting what the dog is indicating. All afternoon I couldn't get that saying out of my mind – 'trust the dog.'

When Steve got home I told him everything that had happened and told him that despite two negative tests I was going to trust Jess and not drink that night. I could tell Steve thought I was being unnecessarily cautious but he didn't try and dissuade me. We had an enjoyable evening in Firestones but I remained an alcohol-free zone.

The next day I remained convinced that I'd done the right thing by not drinking and was still quietly confident. Then that evening we got some terrible news. We were driving to the cinema when I got a call from my fertility doctor at the Walter Reed National Military Medical Center.

"Hi Mrs Williams, we've looked at your blood test results and I'm afraid you didn't ovulate this month."

Obviously if you don't ovulate then you can't get pregnant. I must have looked as devastated as I felt because Steve immediately pulled over and stopped the car. The doctor explained that she would issue me a prescription for an increased dose of the fertility drug and we'd have to repeat the same 'sex every other day' routine after my next period. I got off the phone and burst into tears. I felt inadequate, a reproductive failure. Steve tried to be reassuring but I could tell he was upset too. We ditched the cinema and went home. We both felt crushed and worried. To not be ovulating, not even with the assistance of medication, meant there was clearly something wrong.

The following evening we were having a group of Steve's colleagues and friends round for a British Army style regimental dinner. Steve was going to wear his army mess dress and everyone else was planning to dress up too. We were doing roast beef accompanied by copious amounts of red wine.

"Well at least I can legitimately get drunk tomorrow!" I said to Steve.

The next morning, a Friday, I woke up feeling pretty depressed. Getting pregnant was clearly not going to be straightforward and all sorts of scenarios were going through my mind. What if the increased dose didn't work? We were approaching the point of having to think about IVF and I wasn't sure about that at all.

Amidst these negative thoughts, my mind kept returning to the one thing that didn't make sense – Jess. I knew that dog and she knew me. I hadn't imagined her strange behaviour and I certainly hadn't imagined her nearly attacking me. I looked at her lying on my bedroom floor with her chin on her paws, her usual position whilst she waited for me to shower and get dressed. I remembered the mantra - trust the dog, trust the dog, trust the dog.

I made a decision.

"Right, this is it, one more try then I'm going to accept I'm not pregnant," I announced to Jess.

I quickly unwrapped another test, peed on it and then put it to one side and spent the next two minutes defiantly pretending that I didn't care about the result. I brushed my teeth, got dressed and then picked up the test to throw it in the bin. I glanced at the display window, almost as an afterthought.

The digital display showed just one word this time – 'PREGNANT'. I looked at it for a few seconds, my brain trying to process where the word 'NOT' had gone. Then it sunk in – I was pregnant.

"Oh, no way!" I looked over at Jess who'd raised her head expectantly at the excitement in my voice. I was actually pregnant. Jess had been right and I wanted her to be the first I told. I went and sat down next to her and announced jubilantly, "Jess, I'm pregnant!"

Jess grinned at me. "Yeah, I know, I've known all along Jenni! I've been trying to tell you!"

I was ecstatic, shocked and really rather scared all at once. I can't deny I was relieved that Steve and I both 'worked'. And so much for not ovulating, expert fertility doctors at Walter Reed, the hospital that treats the President. The rebel in me found it fittingly unconventional that my slightly unhinged, down and out shelter husky had been right and they'd been wrong. Furthermore she'd been more accurate than a human-made pregnancy testing kit.

I also felt vindicated that I had read Jess correctly. I knew she'd been acting differently around me and not only was it satisfying to be proved correct, it was also a relief to know the reason why; she hadn't suddenly fallen out with me. And fundamentally it proved that you should always trust the dog.

After a few minutes of celebratory nuzzling with my personal fertility specialist, I made myself calm down and think. I was pregnant and I was sure that meant I needed to tell a medical professional. I rang my doctor at Walter Reed, the same one who had told me the previous evening that I hadn't ovulated.

"Hi, this is Jenni Williams, we spoke last night about not ovulating and increasing my medication. I just wanted to let you know that I took a pregnancy test this morning because my dog was being weird with me and it's positive. I'm pregnant."

"You can't be," replied Dr Sceptical flatly, "You didn't ovulate."

"Well I guess I must have done because the test is positive. It definitely says 'PREGNANT' in the little window."

Dr Sceptical clearly thought I was delusional but I insisted so she arranged for me to take a test at the primary care centre on Fort Detrick. I quickly drove down there and peed on one of their sticks. Plot twist of all plot twists – it was negative. I was momentarily thrown but the lovely nurse explained that HCG, the hormone that means you're definitely pregnant, is most concentrated in your first pee of the day. In the earliest days of pregnancy it wasn't unusual for subsequent urine samples to not contain enough HCG to get a positive result and so she sent me for a blood test which would be far more accurate.

A male phlebotomist took my blood. I explained I'd had a positive test that morning at home but then a negative one a few minutes ago. He told me that as far as he was aware you could get a false negative but not a false positive and repeated the nurse's explanation about HCG levels.

The blood test results would take a while so I drove home and walked Jess. My mind was all over the place, certain I was pregnant but still needing that final confirmation of a blood test.

After what seemed an age, my doctor on the base rang.

"Congratulations," she said, "Your blood results are positive. You're definitely pregnant."

It was finally official. We really were having a baby. Now I just had to tell the Daddy. I rang Steve at work.

"Hi babe, I'm just in the supermarket and they have a couple of interesting looking recipe cards for starters for tonight. Have you got a couple of minutes if I pop by work so I can show them to you?"

"Sure, meet me at the picnic tables outside work in fifteen minutes?"

"Great, see you then."

I waited for Steve in the warm November sunshine holding the pregnancy test stick instead of recipe cards. He came out and sat down.

"Close your eyes," I instructed and held the stick with the display window's wonderful message facing him. "Now open them!"

Steve opened his eyes, looked at the stick, looked at me, opened his mouth and looked at the stick again. He looked back at me and his eyes filled with tears.

"What the…?"

I laughed. "I don't have any recipe cards, I'm pregnant, I took the test this morning. I trusted Jess and she was right, she knew."

"But you didn't ovulate. The doctor said."

"Well she was wrong and Jess was right. She should be a fertility doctor!"

I watched Steve's face change as the news sunk in.

"I can't believe it – we're actually going to have a baby! You amazing, clever thing!"

It was a wonderful moment, telling the man you love that he got you knocked up. Steve gave me a gentle hug and then patted my tummy and said hello to our future little person. And when Steve got home that afternoon he was extra attentive to Jess, thanking her for her sterling work as a four-legged pregnancy test.

Obviously I couldn't drink that evening so we told our guests that I had an ear infection and was on strong antibiotics and couldn't touch a drop of alcohol. They all appeared to accept this and no one seemed suspicious. We found out much later that they all guessed immediately but kindly humoured us.

We had a great night with our friends and Steve and I were on cloud nine, stealing proud glances at each other when we thought nobody was looking. Everyone except me drank a lot of wine. I drank a lot of sparkling water.

So Jess stopped me from drinking on two occasions in the earliest stages of my pregnancy. I enjoy a beer or a glass or two of wine but I don't drink a huge amount. Even if I'd had a few drinks, it's unlikely that Baby Williams would have suffered any adverse effects. However Jess also prevented me from starting an increased dose of the fertility drug, which can be harmful to a developing foetus. Most intriguingly, as soon as I knew I was pregnant, Jess's weird behaviour around me stopped. She seemed to accept my new smell and never again acted as if she didn't know it was her Jenni around the corner or on the other side of a door. It was as if she'd been trying to tell me something important that I didn't know myself and as soon as I did know, she could stand down.

Years and a lifetime later, Eve has faced many medical difficulties and has more ahead. Every single night when I put her to bed, the thought crosses my mind that she might not wake up the next morning. I've lost count of the number of times I've had to call an emergency ambulance for her when she's had a seizure, or the number of dedicated and compassionate paramedics who've attended our house as a result. She's had her life saved by skilled nurses and doctors on more than one occasion, and her school staff and Steve and I do everything humanly possible to keep her safe. But this fact remains; the very first individual to protect Eve was Jess. Thank God I listened.

Always trust the dog.

CHAPTER 16

RESCUE ME

OUR HAPPY NEWS nonetheless threw up a rather large complication. Baby Williams's due date was 26th July 2012 and we were due to fly home on 27th July. That timeframe obviously wasn't going to work. Ironically sometime in October I'd said to Steve, "Don't worry, I'll get pregnant this month because it would be really problematic if my due date was next July!"

Our solution to this scheduling clash was simple – we would volunteer to stay in the US longer. Unfortunately Steve suspected that the army would decide to cut short his tour and warned me to prepare for that eventuality. It was still early days in my pregnancy and we weren't planning to tell friends and family yet, let alone the army. However the possibility of us returning to the UK earlier had a big implication for Jess – her foster home was not going to be around for as long as everyone thought. And if we did get sent home early then the latest I'd be able to fly would be late April.

So there was one person I did need to tell. On Monday morning I asked Linda for a quiet word and told her our news and what it might mean for Jess, that there was an outside chance we might be going home a few months earlier than planned. I stressed that my pregnancy changed nothing in terms of having Jess; we had absolutely no intention of giving her back to the shelter a day earlier than we needed to. However we should work off the presumption that Jess would lose her foster home sooner than expected. Linda was thrilled for us and agreed that it was now more urgent than ever to prepare Jess for adoption.

The biggest obstacle was still her behaviour on walks. Although the mouthing had thankfully almost entirely stopped, for about the first fifteen minutes of each walk Jess would jump up and down continuously, bark in my face and chew on the chain lead. The barking in my face had started a few days after her return from the wild. Unlike the mouthing it seemed frantic, a symptom of stress rather than playfulness. I did my best to ignore it which was exactly the right thing to do. The only trouble was that, once again, the right thing wasn't working.

I wondered if Jess associated being out on a walk with the fear of losing me again because she'd been on a walk with Joe when she'd slipped her harness and escaped. So when she finally settled down I'd stop and sit down with her and give her more attention than usual, rewarding the calmer behaviour and assuring her that she was safe and we weren't going to lose each other again. That didn't seem to work either and the cycle would repeat itself the next time we went for a walk.

I'd therefore been thinking that we needed an insurance policy, for Jess's sake. My ultimate fear was that she wouldn't get adopted and would go back to the shelter when we returned to England. Frederick County Animal Control had a low euthanasia rate but there could feasibly come a time when Jess was viewed as taking up kennel space that might benefit another dog. And eventually, if she was unadoptable, there would come a point where the shelter would have to take the tough decision to euthanise her.

That didn't bear thinking about and I needed to know it would never happen to her. I broached the subject with Linda who assured me that such a course of action would be a long way down the line and a last resort. I also knew that if that was on the cards then Steve or I would fly to Frederick, adopt Jess and fly her back to England despite the threat of the Dangerous Dogs Act. At least she'd be no worse off.

However a much more practical option was Jess going to a breed specific rescue, one with a 'no kill' policy that would keep her for as long as necessary. They would also be far more likely to attract people who specifically wanted a husky and therefore understood and tolerated their behaviour.

Linda agreed with me and contacted a specialist husky rescue that the shelter had used in the past, to explain Jess's situation and ask if they could help. Later that day Linda rang me to say she'd heard from the rescue's local coordinator and she wanted to meet Jess as soon as possible. This was great news.

I immediately emailed the coordinator, who was called Sarah, to tell her about Jess and arrange a meeting. I made sure to stress how far Jess had come and how impeccably behaved and affectionate she was in the house. I explained about her behaviour outside – there was no point glossing over it.

Sarah replied to say she'd like to assess Jess as soon as possible to determine whether she was ready to go into foster care with one of their breed experts. She also told me that she had an extremely friendly male husky named Rocky who was great with nervous dogs. Sarah and I agreed to meet at the shelter on the following Saturday, two days after Thanksgiving. This was much sooner than I expected and brought home to me that I needed to prepare myself to say goodbye. Yet as much as I didn't want to give Jess up, I'd always put her first and would continue to do so.

Steve, Jess and I arrived at the shelter early on the Saturday morning. Linda had reserved one of the larger 'meet and greet' enclosures for us so we went straight there and let Jess off the lead so she could be as relaxed as possible for her assessment. I was feeling nervous for her but did my best to stifle it.

Sarah and Rocky arrived about fifteen minutes later and unfortunately the play date did not get off to a positive start. Jess had been fine when it was just Steve and I in the enclosure but as soon as Sarah and Rocky appeared, Jess looked nervous and as they entered the enclosure she slunk under the bench I was sitting on.

After saying hello to Sarah I explained that Jess might need a few minutes to get used to them. However Sarah immediately stepped right past me and sat down heavily on the bench to offer Jess a treat. Unsurprisingly Jess backed away in fear. I was a bit taken aback that Sarah hadn't listened to me; surely she understood that forcing yourself on a timid dog was not the way to put them at ease? I explained that Jess wasn't particularly food motivated and couldn't care less about treats when she was outside and wouldn't have taken one from me either but I could see Sarah considered this a black mark against Jess.

Things got worse when Sarah let the celebrated Rocky off the lead. Rocky was a big, rather overweight, Siberian Husky but he wasn't friendly or playful. He seemed overbearing and bad-tempered and soon backed Jess into a corner and then snapped at her when she growled at him. I didn't like him and certainly didn't see any evidence of his alleged affinity with nervous dogs.

Sarah seemed to place far too much importance on the fact that Jess didn't like Rocky without once stopping to consider whether she had a point. Her whole impression of Jess seemed negative from the start and she didn't seem interested in listening to Steve or me, the people who knew Jess best. My optimism evaporated.

After about ten minutes of Rocky and Sarah refusing to give Jess some space and let her get used to them, I knew that Jess was completely stressed and wasn't going to improve. She'd had enough of them and so had I. However I wanted to salvage something from this disaster and thought it was important to demonstrate Jess's happy and playful side.

I suggested moving to the big exercise enclosure on the field behind the shelter that we'd recently started using, as it offered a lot more space and Jess loved it and felt relaxed there. I also suspected that she'd be able to outrun the rather rotund Rocky and put him in his place a bit and it would give her a break from Sarah's obsessive treat offering. Sarah reluctantly agreed but I could tell she was sceptical; I felt she'd already made her mind up and was determined to leave with a negative impression.

Moving to the exercise enclosure turned out to be a great idea. Jess relaxed straight away and ran around confidently, in marked contrast to her previous behaviour. To my amusement and pride she completely ignored Rocky who showed no inclination to join her, preferring instead to waddle around next to Sarah. Jess and I demonstrated our serious-injury-defying 'Run Full Speed at Jenni and Swerve at the Last Second' game. This was the real Jess, tearing around outside with her favourite person. I told Sarah as much and explained that this was how she was at home too.

However to my annoyance Sarah was still fixated on the fact that Jess wouldn't take a treat from her. She seemed to take it personally and wouldn't accept my explanation that Jess simply wasn't interested in food when she could be running around off the lead. Steve rolled his eyes at me behind Sarah's back and despite the stress of the situation, I had to suppress a smile. The whole experience was bordering on farcical. We were asking the specialist husky rescue to rescue our nervous husky and it seemed that Jess was failing some kind of mysterious test because she was nervous of Sarah, didn't like the sainted Rocky and wasn't hungry.

Sarah begrudgingly admitted that Jess was much more relaxed in the exercise pen and suggested going for a walk together in the next couple of weeks, so that she could 'assess' her some more. I didn't particularly relish the thought of spending more time with Sarah but for Jess's sake I had to play along and so agreed to meet up for a walk before Christmas. If it meant that Sarah agreed to help Jess then it would be worth it.

However the next day I received the following email.

> "After seeing Jess yesterday, I don't think she is ready to be adopted at this point. I don't see how an adoption could succeed right now. I have evaluated a lot of dogs, and she is the only one who wouldn't take a treat from me or who I was not able to pet.

> "The best thing would be to get her into a foster home experienced with Siberians and timid dogs. I will be talking to one of our volunteers this evening who is very experienced in working with timid and fearful dogs to see if she has any additional advice. I am also working on contacting other rescues to see if they have a foster home that may be a good fit for her and will be ready to work on her fearfulness.

> "I hope that when we go for a walk,
> since she won't be meeting us at the shelter
> first, she will be a bit less fearful."

Sarah's email riled me. I felt she was overly critical of Jess, placed far too much emphasis on the fact that she wouldn't accept a treat and neglected to acknowledge how Jess had relaxed as soon as we were in the exercise pen. Sarah had also spectacularly missed the point – we weren't asking for an opinion on whether Jess was ready to be adopted as we knew she wasn't. We were asking for a rescue place to give her more time to become adoptable and find that perfect forever home.

Nevertheless, I bristled at the sweeping generalisation that an adoption couldn't succeed. If our personal circumstances had been different then Steve and I would have adopted Jess a long time ago and the adoption would most definitely have succeeded. There was someone out there for Jess, someone who didn't expect her to be the life and soul of the party. Not all people were extroverts; why did Jess have to be?

However a portion of my anger was with myself because I'd let Jess down. Clearly I'd failed to prepare her for the world and ensure other people would see the dog I saw. I replied to Sarah, agreeing to meet up for a walk two weeks later and acknowledging that I hadn't done enough to enable Jess to give the right impression.

Perhaps Sarah realised how her first email had come across because her reply was much kinder.

> "Please don't feel like you've let her
> down. It sounds like she's already made a
> lot of progress with you. Jess is the most
> fearful dog I've ever seen. She's a difficult
> case and needs a lot of work.

"You've already brought her such a long way. She is so lucky to have you and Steve as a foster home! I'm amazed at how dedicated you are to her, most people would have returned her to the shelter by now."

That was a welcome compliment but clearly 'most people' were idiots. I still didn't agree with Sarah's assessment but I had to swallow my pride and accept that it mattered less and less what I thought. I was flying out of Jess's life in a matter of months and I needed to give her the best possible chance at finding another Jenni. Steve and I had successfully taught Jess to love and trust again. Unfortunately she only really loved and trusted two people – us. I was starting Jess on 'Socialisation Boot Camp' and I was starting right away.

I phoned up Kingsbrook Animal Hospital, explained Jess's situation and asked if I could bring her on a socialisation visit. They readily agreed and so a couple of days later Jess and I took a detour to Kingsbrook after a walk in Baker Park. Ironically Jess had never been to Kingsbrook before and was inevitably nervous to start with. However the staff were brilliant with her and gave her plenty of space and let her calm down before they interacted with her.

I'd emailed Nicky, the vet tech who'd adopted Scout (now called 'Mali'), to let her know we were going in and she'd agreed to bring Mali to work with her that day. Jess and Mali were over the moon to see each other again and had a great time playing together in the staff room. The presence of an old friend was hugely beneficial to Jess and she soon noticeably relaxed around the human staff and even took a piece of chicken from Nicky and one of the receptionists. It was a successful trip and I was hugely grateful to everyone at Kingsbrook for their concern for a dog who had never even been one of their patients.

I also got in touch with our friend Di, the wife of one of Steve's colleagues. Di worked shifts at a large retail store and had mentioned a few times about coming for a walk with me and Jess on one of her days off. So one morning Di came to Gambrill with us. Once Jess had recovered from her initial surprise that someone else was gatecrashing our walk, she seemed to accept Di quite happily. Over the next few weeks Di came walking with us whenever her shift pattern allowed. And once we'd established that Di was an acceptable person to have on walks, she started coming back to the house for coffee. Jess soon grew comfortable with Di's presence, both on a walk and at home, and even started to let Di pet her. Amy, Jan and Dick also started to drop by for a few minutes on their way home from work so that Jess got regular interaction with people she knew and felt relatively relaxed with.

The other big issue we needed to deal with was Jess's demented behaviour on walks and I have to admit that Sarah's breed knowledge proved invaluable on this issue. She had witnessed Jess leaping around and pulling when we'd walked from the meet and greet enclosure to the exercise pen during our meeting at the shelter. I'd also explained what an escape artist Jess was and how she'd managed to wriggle out of the Ruffwear harness. Sarah recommended we get a star collar, which she described as a humane and pain-free plastic correctional collar. I was adamant that I wasn't going to use a choke collar on Jess but Sarah assured me it wasn't a choke collar, simply a collar that tightened gently if the dog pulled, loosened when it didn't and didn't inflict any pain at all.

I had always ruled out using any kind of correctional collar on Jess but I had to admit that her extreme pulling and leaping around made her slightly less lovable, even to me. Furthermore it was hugely detrimental to her adoption prospects. Very few people would put up with it; it even annoyed me to the extent that in all honesty I didn't enjoy walking Jess. It wasn't a relaxing experience having her jump up in my face and then having to counteract her pulling for the duration of every single walk. Months previously the retractable lead had surprisingly alleviated the worst of her pulling but ever since Jess had bitten through it and we'd had to use the chain lead, that small victory was a distant memory and the pulling was as bad as it had ever been.

Sarah also assured me that the star collar was the only escape proof system she was aware of, an important consideration in terms of Jess's safety. I asked Linda her view and she was firmly of the opinion that if Sarah recommended it then it was okay.

So I finally relented and bought the star collar. It was made up of a length of interlocking rounded plastic 'teeth' with a loop of strong cord running through the two end teeth. The cord had a solid metal 'O' ring in the middle to attach the lead to. You simply unclipped two of the teeth, placed the collar around the dog's neck and clipped it securely together again. You could adjust the collar to the correct size for your dog's neck by removing or adding additional teeth. The plastic teeth weren't at all sharp, however I wasn't about to use it on Jess without testing it on myself first. I fitted the collar around my neck, took hold of the cord and yanked hard. It tightened noticeably but didn't hurt at all and I could still breathe easily. It merely felt uncomfortably 'too close', like a slightly small turtleneck jumper. Now I felt I could ethically use it on Jess.

Despite my overall experience with Sarah I'll forever be grateful to her for recommending the star collar; the difference it made was nothing short of miraculous. Jess's walking was instantly and immeasurably better and I realised with a tinge of sadness that this was the first time in weeks that I'd actually enjoyed a walk with her. She would still pull occasionally but it was much reduced, both in frequency and intensity, and the leaping up at me began to lessen considerably too. Jess still chewed the chain lead obsessively but you can't have everything. Finally I could relax and amble along and enjoy the scenery. And crucially, Jess was suddenly much more adoptable.

The thought subsequently crossed my mind that the harness had been the problem in that she'd been wearing it when she escaped and so associated it with losing me. That could explain why her behaviour got worse after she returned from her adventure in the wild and started wearing it again. I kicked myself for not thinking of this before. However that was in the past and thanks to the star collar, Jess's future looked a whole lot brighter.

A couple of weekends after we first met at the shelter, Sarah, Rocky, Jess and I met at Sugarloaf Mountain, a nearby state park, for a walk. Jess and I had never been there before and she was in high spirits, excited to explore somewhere new. The trail was steep and it was immediately apparent that Jess and I were considerably fitter than Sarah and Rocky, something that we used to our advantage. I made sure we stayed just far enough ahead of them that Jess was unbothered by their presence but just close enough that Sarah could see how much Jess was enjoying herself.

I thanked Sarah for recommending the star collar and praised the difference it had made to Jess's walking. The morning was a huge success and something appeared to have changed Sarah's mind about Jess. She told me Jess had made a lot of progress in two weeks and to my huge relief, agreed to consider Jess for a foster placement with the husky rescue. She also made a comment about promoting Jess to German Shepherd rescues as she felt sure she was a Siberian Husky-German Shepherd mix.

Ever since Steve and I started fostering Jess, we'd wondered about her ancestry as she obviously wasn't a pure Siberian Husky and a couple of people had commented that she looked part German Shepherd. My theory was that she was an Alaskan Husky, with a mixture of breeds plus an ancient line of generic northern sled dogs in her family tree.

Prompted in part by Sarah's comment I decided to buy a mail order dog DNA test, mainly out of curiosity but also in the hope that the results might make Jess eligible for other breed rescues. The test involved taking a swab from her cheek with a cotton wool applicator, screwing it into a plastic tube and sending it back to the lab. It was quick and painless.

A few weeks after Christmas an A4 envelope marked with the logo of the DNA company arrived in our mailbox.

"Hey Jess, come here, we're going to find out exactly what you are," I told her as I opened the envelope.

Inside was a certificate that told me that at least one of Jess's parents was a pure German Shepherd. Then it said, "No other dog DNA detected." I was confused. How could there be no other dog DNA? Then I realised there were a few explanations for this puzzling conclusion. It was possible that Jess was indeed a pure German Shepherd with slightly untypical markings and features. It was equally possible that the test was inaccurate and had simply been unable to detect the other breed or breeds. When I'd Googled 'dog DNA test' in order to purchase a kit, a number of consumer websites had popped up advising against using the DNA results for veterinary reasons in case they weren't correct. I therefore figured this was the most likely explanation. In addition, if Jess was part Alaskan Husky then that wouldn't have been picked up as it wasn't a breed that the test could detect.

Then another possibility slowly dawned on me – "No other dog DNA detected." What if Jess wasn't 100% dog? I had heard about wolf dogs but didn't know much about them. I did some research and discovered there were an estimated 500,000 wolf dogs (sometimes called wolf hybrids) in the USA. The website went on to list their behavioural traits, such as overly boisterous and unpredictable behaviour, extreme fear of strangers and stubbornness. This explained a lot.

Wolf dogs are illegal to own in many US states which wouldn't bode well for Jess's future. I didn't know what the law was in Maryland and didn't want to find out. I did the only thing I could do; I didn't mention the test and my theory to Frederick County Animal Control. Hardly anyone knew I was doing the test anyway and when one of the kennel techs asked, I simply said that the results were inconclusive and her ancestry was still a mystery. This was of course true. The test couldn't detect wolf DNA so it was merely a theory on my part. I put the test out of my mind and officially at least, Jess remained a husky mix.

However just over a year later, when we were back in the UK, a new friend of mine came round for coffee for the first time. Amanda was Canadian and knew that we'd spent time living in the USA and that I'd fostered dogs although I'd never specifically discussed Jess with her. She walked into my living room and saw a large framed photo of Jess and I in West Virginia that hung on our wall.

"Hey, nice wolf dog!" she said.

"Oh, is it that obvious?" I asked, a big grin on my face.

"Sure, we have loads of wolf dogs where I'm from."

Well that settled it as far as I was concerned. A Canadian recognised Jess for what she was and they should know. Like I said, it explained a lot.

In the run up to Christmas I decided to start crate training Jess to help convince prospective adopters that she was a well-trained, well-behaved, low-maintenance dog. Crate training is popular in the US and far more socially acceptable than it is in the UK. The rationale is that a crate is a dog's exclusive space, that they enter of their own free will and where they feel safe and cosy. The crate is not a punishment and must never be used as such.

I had never bothered crate training Jess before because in all honesty, I didn't like the sound of it. I much preferred the idea that she had the run of the house if we were out. However from the giveaway warm indentation that she left on the sofa, we knew where Jess spent most of her time when we weren't at home. I doubt it would have mattered if there were bars around it. Crate training would involve creating a space that she loved just as much as the sofa and would be something we could put on her 'doggy CV' that might just convince a prospective adopter to overlook all her other behavioural issues.

I borrowed an extra large crate from the shelter and a double duvet that I'd found in the laundry room. Generous members of the public often donated towels, blankets and dog beds to the shelter in order to make the kennels more comfortable. It was unusual to get a double duvet and this would be perfect for Jess's crate and would help replicate the comfort of the sofa.

I set the crate up in the living room, in front of one of the windows. I folded the double duvet in quarters so it was suitably soft and placed it inside. Then I left the door open so Jess could go in if she wanted. Jess watched me suspiciously from her usual space on the sofa whilst I was doing all this but once I'd finished and made no attempt to get her to go in the crate she seemed satisfied that life was carrying on as usual.

For the next week both Jess and I acted as if the crate wasn't there. Then one day I casually threw one of Jess's treats in to the far corner and went into the kitchen and started to make a cup of tea. Out of the corner of my eye I saw Jess slowly get off the sofa. I turned to see her to see her calmly stroll into the crate, eat the treat and then lie down with her head on her paws. I remained outwardly poker-faced about this major breakthrough but this was excellent progress. Jess had gone into the crate entirely of her own accord and seemed perfectly relaxed once in it. I sat down and drank my cup of tea and Jess remained in her new den, only coming out to follow me upstairs.

For the next week I'd occasionally throw a treat in the crate, especially if I was going out, to reinforce to Jess that it was a positive addition to the living room and signified good things. However at no point did I shut the door.

Then one evening Steve and I had been out for dinner. I was interested to see whether she went into the crate when we weren't there so when we came home I stopped the car on our road, just before our house, and we crept around the back of the house and peered through the living room window. Jess was sprawled out in the crate, fast asleep. I'd done it – the crate was now Jess's chosen place to sleep and she'd made that decision all by herself.

The next day I started throwing a treat in the crate and then closing the door for a few minutes when Jess went in there. The door being closed didn't bother her at all and she settled down perfectly happily. From then on I started asking Jess to go in the crate whenever I went out. I was relieved that Jess took to crate training so well but my decision to take things slowly had been the key to success. In doing so, I convinced Jess that the crate was her idea; I think this was the only time I ever managed to outwit her.

Despite having a few invitations from friends we'd decided to spend Christmas at home. It was rather bittersweet for various reasons; it was our last Christmas in Frederick, our last Christmas before becoming parents and our first and last Christmas with Jess who, despite not always being a good girl, received a stocking full of her favourite treats anyway. Like me, Santa obviously has a soft spot for crazy canines of indeterminate heritage.

The holiday period should have been a happy one but as New Year approached I found myself feeling uncharacteristically anxious about the future. 2011 had been a transformative year for me, packed with travel, adventure and dogs. I'd embraced living in the US and embraced a new 'career' as a foster carer. Yet I was conscious that the experiences of the past year weren't the start of something new; they had a shelf life and would be coming to an end in the forthcoming months.

Whilst nothing in life is ever certain, I knew that I'd be saying goodbye to Jess and Frederick during 2012. With the exception of Linda we still hadn't told anyone that I was pregnant and so the question of whether the army would let Steve extend his posting was still unresolved. Best case scenario, we'd be allowed to stay until the autumn. Worst case scenario we'd be leaving before the end of April which meant Jess had only four more months of a guaranteed foster placement. I could only hope that for all our sakes, our departure would be later rather than sooner.

CHAPTER 17

SAVING JESS

IN THE MIDDLE of January we had our twelve week pregnancy scan with a confirmed due date of 26th July. Safely reaching the twelve week milestone meant we were able to breathe a sigh of relief and at last share our news with friends and family. It also meant that Steve was obliged to inform his chain of command that I was pregnant and that Baby Williams was due to arrive the day before we were supposed to fly home.

Early indications that Steve would be allowed to extend his posting were promising. Steve discussed the issue with his American superiors and the British defence attaché at the embassy who all agreed it made sense for Steve to stay in post for a few extra months. Steve's American colleagues were especially pleased that he might be staying longer and that Baby Williams would be an American citizen. We hoped the UK chain of command would agree.

Although I was safely out of the first trimester, I was experiencing bone-aching levels of pregnancy induced tiredness. I'd go to bed early, sleep for nine or ten hours and wake up as tired as when I'd gone to bed. Despite this I was determined to give Jess the same amount of exercise she'd always had so I continued to take her to the exercise enclosure at the shelter a few times a week. Her recall at the end of our sessions was coming on and she'd begun to willingly trot towards me if I waved the lead at her. I also inadvertently taught her how to play fetch.

There were always various chew toys, Frisbees and tennis balls dotted around the exercise pen and Jess had always enjoyed it if I threw one of them for her; I think it activated her prey drive and she'd exuberantly race after whatever I'd thrown. One day I was chucking a tennis ball for her as usual. Normally she'd chase the ball down and then lie over it and I'd have to go up to her, get the ball out from under her and throw it again. However on this occasion, completely out of the blue, Jess picked the ball up in her mouth and then ran back towards me, swerving at the last second whilst simultaneously tossing her head and sending the ball surprisingly accurately in my direction.

"That was a good trick Jess!" I congratulated her.

I chucked the ball for her again and the same thing happened. My half-baked husky was playing fetch. This became our new favourite game. Given Jess's newly-discovered love of tennis balls, I again tried giving her one to take on walks to see if it would calm her down and divert her from mauling the chain lead. I'd tried this tactic a few times before and it had never worked. However on this occasion Jess took the ball in her mouth, gave it a gentle chew and then set off on our walk without jumping up and down or biting the lead. After about ten minutes she dropped the ball, gave the lead a single, cursory nibble and then carried on walking.

I picked the ball up, hardly daring to hope that we'd turned a corner. Yet on our next walk I offered her the tennis ball again and it had the same soothing effect. Finally, miraculously, it appeared that I'd succeeded in curbing Jess's lead-biting compulsion. This improvement turned out to be a semi-enduring one. Whilst Jess occasionally reverted to her old ways, such as when someone got too close to her or a section of

Baker Park seemed overly crowded, having the tennis ball to grind her teeth on instead of the lead made her look halfway respectable. This development couldn't have come at a better time.

Unfortunately, just as Steve had feared, the British branch of the chain of command disagreed with us extending our time in the USA and at the beginning of February Steve was informed he'd be posted early. We argued the case, citing my need for continuity of care during my pregnancy. However the British Army only pretends to care about its people and certainly doesn't care about their families. The answer remained an implacable 'no'. Our return date was set for 27th April, just under three months away and the last week I'd be able to fly without requiring authorisation from a doctor.

This had one extremely serious implication – Jess's situation was critical. Although we'd always planned for this as a 'worst case scenario' it still felt as though time was against us. We needed to find Jess her forever person or people as a matter of urgency.

I chased up Sarah, the coordinator for the husky rescue, and informed her we were definitely leaving at the end of April. She explained that Jess wasn't considered urgent because she was currently safe in a loving home but assured me that she'd find a foster placement nearer the time if necessary. This was beyond frustrating. Whilst I accepted the point that Jess was currently in a foster home, I feared Sarah wasn't thinking sufficiently long term and seemed to be refusing to plan ahead. In the meantime she did at least agree to share Jess's details with other rescues, including a German Shepherd rescue. However I decided to discount Sarah and her organisation as a serious option. It was going to be up to me and FCAC to find Jess her forever home.

So began a concerted and urgent adoption campaign. I wrote an updated piece for Petfinder, detailing the progress Jess had made in recent months. It was encouraging to look back on everything she'd achieved and I hoped prospective adopters would recognise the huge progress she'd made. I was conscious that Jess might be at a slight disadvantage by being in foster care because people who visited the shelter wouldn't see her in the flesh. Whilst sending Jess to live in the shelter full time would've been totally wrong for her and counter-productive, I did offer to spend a few afternoons or a Saturday sat in one of the cages with her. I figured she'd be fine if I was with her. Linda assured me she didn't think that was necessary just yet.

Instead, I produced a 'Jess advert' containing some of the best photos we had of her and a bullet point list of all her achievements and good points. I put copies up all around the shelter so that people who physically came in to visit the resident dogs would see Jess as well.

To complement the updated Petfinder profile, Linda wrote the following piece for Frederick's popular local paper, the Frederick News Post. It was published together with some action-packed photos of Jess in the snow that we'd taken during our weekend in West Virginia back in October.

Adventures with Jess

Frederick County Animal Control and Pet Adoption Center has a well-established Foster Care program composed of the most selfless volunteers in our county. It is a task that requires dedication, skill, and uncompromising patience to take less-than-adoptable animals and turn them into prospective pets. Foster Care animals are often sought after because of the one-on-one attention they receive and the information available from their foster family.

Jess is a beautiful Siberian Husky-German Shepherd mix who started her journey to the shelter in April 2011 as a posting on Craig's List. She was thin and very shy. Her situation includes a bit of a continental flavor—primarily the British couple whose home she's shared for the past 9 months. Her Foster Care parents have been her biggest fans and advocates. However, not unlike American Military families, their tour of duty in the States is concluding soon and they will be returning to England. As much as they would like to take Jess home with them, they are unable to.

Jess's Foster Mom has kept us up-to-date on Jess's progress via a series of writings I affectionately refer to as "Adventures with Jess". She writes: "I doubt Jess will ever win any 'Best Trained Dog' awards. However she now knows 'Sit' and will do so most of the time. I've taught her to play 'fetch' in the exercise pen at Animal Control - she LOVES this and will even bring the ball back and drop it in your vicinity. A retrieving Husky is a bit of a novelty! She also loves car rides and hikes through the snow.

"You will need energy, love, patience, time and a good vacuum cleaner for all that Husky hair. In return, you'll get great exercise, regular cuddles and the devotion of a beautiful dog who just wants to be loved."

For more information on Jess, or for more information on starting your own adventures as a Foster Care Provider, please contact Frederick County Animal Control.

As a result of Linda's article, a woman contacted the shelter to enquire about Jess and the shelter passed my number on to her. When she rang me, her situation initially sounded promising – they were an active family with a large and secure back yard. However she soon mentioned that her and her husband were planning to get Jess for their eleven year old daughter and wanted the daughter to be primarily responsible for walking her.

This was asking for trouble. Although Jess was considerably better behaved as a result of the star collar and the tennis ball, she still had the potential to misbehave at the beginning of walks and still pulled sharply if a squirrel or ground hog scampered past. If she ever pulled their daughter over and injured her then I suspected that Jess would be looking for a new home. I explained all this to the woman who said she'd discuss it with her husband and ring me back. She never did. I told Linda who agreed with me that we had to be honest – there was no point letting Jess be adopted by people, only to have them return her.

I was also obliged to veto a woman who was interested in Jess but who only had a three-foot high fence in her back yard and was adamant that she didn't want one higher. Jess would have laughed in the face of a three-foot fence as she vaulted gracefully over it to freedom.

Despite my readiness to discourage the wrong people, I was constantly thinking of ways to promote Jess and on the 18th February I wrote an email to Linda,

> "By the way, if you thought it would be a good idea to put her on the WFRE show then I'd happily go along with Didi. I don't think Jess would freak out (much!), she does fine when we go to the pet store now. I'd take her bed, her beloved tennis ball and plenty of treats for her. Let me know!"

As it happened, Linda did think that Jess appearing on WFRE would be a good idea and so arranged the infamous 'howling on live radio' interview.

I was proud of the effort everyone was making to get Jess adopted. In the last couple of weeks she had been advertised at the shelter, in the local paper, online and over the airwaves. Her forever home was out there and we were going to find it; failure was unthinkable.

CHAPTER 18

GOODBYE

A FEW DAYS after our starring performance on WFRE, Linda rang with potentially great news. A guy who'd visited the shelter had seen Jess's poster that I'd put up and was keen to meet her. His name was Sal and he lived by himself in a house with a fenced yard and he hadn't been at all put off by Linda's preliminary explanation about Jess. We arranged for him to come round and meet Jess on Friday after work. Sal was due at 5:00 p.m. and just before he arrived I gave Jess a little pep talk.

"Ok, this Sal sounds promising. I don't want to lose you Jessica but we're running out of time. Try and give a good impression for me, let someone else love you as much as I do."

Jess grinned her inscrutable, verging on unhinged, grin and I had no confidence whatsoever that she'd do as I asked.

At 5:00 p.m. I was impatiently looking out of the front window, feeling tense. What if this Sal was perfect? What if he wasn't?

A couple of minutes later a blue Mustang pulled into our driveway. At least he had good taste in cars. I heard a car door open and shut and went to answer the door with Jess following me at a suitably wary distance. I grabbed her collar firmly, opened the door and greeted Sal; right on cue Jess backed away from this stranger who had the nerve to visit our house. However she didn't bark or growl at him which was unusual.

Sal was in his mid-twenties and about my height with short dark hair. He had a quiet voice, a shy smile and seemed friendly but reserved. I liked him. Jess had retreated to the living room and as Sal followed me though she assumed her rightful place at the end of the big sofa. She sat up, warily eyeing Sal with suspicion. Interestingly she still didn't growl. Sal impressed me immediately because he ignored Jess and didn't try and approach her. I gestured to him to take a seat on the smaller two-seater sofa and offered him a drink. As I retrieved a couple of Cokes from the refrigerator I noticed Jess looking at him with what may have been interest. Sal had a calm and unassuming presence and I could tell that Jess was intrigued by him.

Sal explained that he had a senior role in his father's IT business. He lived in Thurmont near Catoctin Mountain Park where I sometimes took Jess walking and had a house with a big yard. He lived alone and didn't go out much. The fact he worked full time wasn't ideal but he did work from home regularly and his family lived nearby and were therefore able to help out with Jess if necessary. He did mention that he wanted a dog he could go hiking with which was a plus as I was adamant that Jess needed someone who liked the outdoors as much as she did.

I knew Linda had told Sal a little bit about Jess already and that obviously hadn't put him off. I was completely honest about what she was like and some of the issues we'd been through and Sal asked a lot of questions. Nothing I told him about her seemed to faze him. He explained that his family had had a nervous and fearful Rottweiler when he was a teenager. He'd been a rescue dog too and they'd got him when he was about the same age as Jess. They accepted this dog the way he was and they loved him, managed him and didn't try to change him. This sounded exactly the kind of approach that Jess needed.

After about three-quarters of an hour I'd decided that the visit was going better than I'd hoped and Jess had begun to relax. She'd moved from the sofa on to the floor, and seemed alert but not scared.

I asked Sal if he wanted to take her for a walk but he said he didn't want to rush her and would prefer to wait for another visit. Sal said he liked her but had to be certain that she would bond with him and that he could continue the work of dealing with her issues. I was touched by how considerate and patient he was and how he was determined to let Jess get used to him before making a decision. It showed he ultimately had Jess's best interests at heart. Neither Linda nor I had specified that potential adopters had to make multiple visits before their application would be accepted. This was something Sal had decided for himself and it showed him in a very favourable light. We arranged for him to come to the house again the following Tuesday evening and then meet us at the shelter on the Friday to see Jess in the exercise pen.

I rang Linda the next morning to tell her how the visit with Sal had gone and how we'd arranged two more visits. Linda was pleased about Sal and told me that there was another couple interested in Jess. This was great news; our marketing campaign was obviously generating some interest. We arranged for the other couple to come round on Monday evening. However Linda and I agreed that under the circumstances, the other couple wouldn't take precedence if they applied to adopt Jess before Sal had concluded his additional visits. Instead Linda would pick the most suitable home for Jess with my input. It amused me that after all this time there might actually end up being competition for Jess.

Monday came around and the couple, Brad and Jennifer, arrived just after 7:00 p.m. I immediately noticed that they smelled strongly of cigarette smoke. They were in their mid-twenties and seemed likeable enough to me. However Jess certainly didn't share my opinion; as soon as they walked through the door she growled at them and backed off to the living room. But then she didn't simply curl up and hide away like she normally did; for the next two hours Jess did not relax for a moment and spent the entire time circling the kitchen island and the sofa where they were sitting, barking every few seconds and looking at me and Steve as if imploring us to do something. I'd never seen her so stressed and the constant barking soon had me pretty stressed too. Maybe the strong smell of cigarettes reminded her of someone she'd rather forget but Jess was clearly upset and it was a marked contrast to how she'd been with Sal.

Brad and Jennifer kept saying how beautiful she was and how much they wanted to adopt her. Jennifer kept reaching out to try and pet her as she ran past but Jess was in no mood to oblige. I dutifully told Brad and Jennifer all about her, her wonderful traits and her more challenging ones. They both said they understood they would have to do a lot of work with her and were under no illusions about the effort and patience that would be required. Then I explained that Jess was an escape artist and checked they had at least a five-foot fence in their yard.

"We don't have a fenced yard," replied Brad casually. "I was thinking of one of those invisible fences and an electronic collar."

An invisible fence is a series of sensors demarcating an area of your choice, most likely a back yard, and a linked electronic collar worn by the dog. If the dog approaches the boundary of the 'invisible fence' then the sensors transmit a radio signal to the collar. At first this takes the form of an unpleasant, high-pitched sound and if the dog continues, it gets a small electric shock.

Firstly I'm against electrocuting your friends, especially your best and most loyal ones, and secondly, I didn't believe for one second that an invisible fence would contain Jess. The only fence that could keep Jess safe was a solid, visible and suitably high one. I could just imagine her defiantly shrugging off any electric shocks, however painful, and sprinting on towards freedom. And if Brad and Jennifer did find her after her inevitable escape, she was unlikely to run back into the arms of people she associated with pain and fear.

That admission did it for me, there was no way Jess was going to these people and I knew Linda would agree. It wasn't my place to tell them this however but I hoped they'd go soon. I could tell that both Steve and Jess felt the same way although Steve's body language was slightly more subtle.

Reading body language was clearly not Brad and Jennifer's strong suit. By the time they'd been with us for a couple of hours I was on the verge of telling them politely that we needed to conclude the visit. Then Jennifer asked if they could take Jess for a walk. Steve immediately looked at me and ever so slightly raised his eyebrows; I knew he was willing me to say no.

However I agreed because it would let them see Jess at her worst and hopefully put them off. I put Jess's star collar on her, clipped on the chain lead and explained to Brad and Jennifer that one of them would need to wear the trusty Light Blue Safety Lead around their waist.

"I won't need that," said Brad arrogantly, flicking his hand at the blue lead dismissively.

Now I was annoyed. The Light Blue Safety Lead was always attached to the chain lead and I wore it without fail whenever I took Jess outside. And she loved me more than anyone else in the world and always came back if she escaped from me. Steve was stronger than me, was Jess's No. 2 favourite human in the world and he always wore it too. And here was this guy thinking he could handle Jess better than we could after only knowing her a couple of hours.

"It's the rule I'm afraid, no exceptions," I said pleasantly but with a hint of steel in my voice. Jennifer caught my eye and took the Light Blue Safety Lead from me and clipped it around her waist.

"Come on beautiful, let's go," she said to Jess, taking a step towards the front door that Steve had opened now that Jess was safely secured.

Jess didn't move.

"C'mon Jess, c'mon girl," said Brad encouragingly.

Jess looked at me and pulled away from Jennifer.

"Oh, poor baby, don't be scared!" said Jennifer and I felt a bit sorry for her. I had to give them credit for not being put off by Jess's extremely cold shoulder.

"I'll try coming out with you," I said and walked forward in front of Jess with Brad and Jennifer following. We got to the end of the path with Jess trailing me nervously, clearly confused at what was happening. Then she started pulling urgently and biting at the lead.

"Wow, she's so strong!" exclaimed Jennifer, a note of doubt in her voice as she grabbed the lead with both hands.

Jess started barking frantically and pulling towards me again.

"I'm sorry, I don't think this is a good idea." I said, trying to sound disappointed.

In fairness to Brad and Jennifer they accepted this although when we were back inside they said they were definitely going to put an application in on Jess. I had to hand it to them, they obviously liked her. Then, thankfully, finally, at long last, they left.

We shut the door behind them and let a relieved Jess loose.

"I thought they'd never go!" I exclaimed.

"Yes, that was too much."

"Oh well, it was for Jess's benefit."

"Yes but she hated them!"

I laughed and stroked Jess reassuringly. She really had hated them.

"Don't worry Jess, they've gone and they won't be coming back!"

But Jess kept glancing nervously at the door so once I saw them drive off I took her for a short walk in order to demonstrate that Brad and Jennifer genuinely had left the vicinity. I had no idea what it was about them that Jess didn't like but her reaction was unequivocal and so was my decision – Brad and Jennifer were a definite 'no'.

I called Linda first thing in the morning and told her how Jess didn't like them and didn't relax at all during their visit. Then I explained about their fence-less yard and plans for an invisible fence and shock collar. Linda agreed with me immediately that ethical considerations aside, an invisible fence wouldn't contain Jess and therefore Brad and Jennifer weren't an option. She assured me that if they phoned up to put an application in then she'd explain this to them. I will always be grateful to Linda that she was as determined as I was to get the right person or people for Jess and didn't simply adopt her out to the first option that came along.

I began to pin my hopes on Sal and we had two more visits scheduled with him later that week. The Tuesday afternoon visit went well. Jess seemed to recognise Sal and gazed at him with an expression that verged on friendly. As with the first visit, Sal kept his distance and allowed Jess to get used to him. I was again impressed with his calm demeanour and his patience, two qualities that were exactly what Jess needed. Jess didn't feel the need to retreat to the sofa but sat on the floor next to me, not taking her eyes off Sal. After about half an hour I suggested he take her for a quick walk outside. He had to experience her behaviour at some point and it might as well be now.

I put Jess's star collar on her and explained about the Light Blue Safety Lead around the waist system; Sal didn't query it at all. And to my relief, Jess's reaction to going for a walk with Sal couldn't have been better – she wasn't just willing but seemed enthusiastic. As they strolled off together I saw Jess looking up at Sal with an expression on her face that seemed to say, "I like you." This was a huge step forward. I also noticed that she walked beautifully for him. As Steve and I watched them head off towards the fence line, I felt a mixture of pride and sorrow. I saw Sal reach out and stroke Jess's head; she didn't flinch. My crazy wolf was ready to leave home.

When they returned from their walk Sal seemed happy and so did Jess. I told Sal just what a big deal it was that she went with him.

Sal nodded. "I feel like we have a connection," he replied modestly.

We agreed to keep our appointment to meet in the exercise enclosure at the shelter on the Friday afternoon. I wanted Sal to see Jess at her most relaxed and give Jess the opportunity to continue to get to know Sal on her terms.

Over the next couple of days I was acutely conscious that this might be my last week or so with Jess. Maybe it was the pregnancy hormones but the prospect of Jess finding her forever home seemed to trigger a return of the low mood that I'd experienced over Christmas. I couldn't stop thinking about everything that was coming to an end – our life in the US, my time with Jess and me and Steve as a couple.

I was also downright scared about becoming a mother and was too ashamed to admit this to Steve. Having a baby is a leap into the unknown and it's an irreversible decision. Being responsible for the welfare of all my foster dogs had shown me that when you're caring for someone else, only your best is good enough. Thankfully I was undeniably good enough when it came to dogs. But what if I was terrible at looking after a baby?

Jess had been a constant presence in my life for the past ten months – even when she was on her adventure in the wild and wasn't physically with me. She was my canine soul mate, my rock and the only one I could confide in about this fear. Now I was about to lose her on the eve of the biggest upheaval, albeit a happy one, that I could imagine. Too many things were changing at the same time and I wasn't handling it well.

Friday's visit at the shelter went better than I ever could have imagined. Jess and I were already in the exercise pen when Sal arrived and when he came in she initially stuck to me like glue, perhaps unsure as to why Sal had joined us. I put the star collar and lead on her again and Sal walked her round and round the pen to let her get reacquainted with him. She soon relaxed and allowed him to pet her several times, sitting down obediently in front of him at one point, her beautiful face gazing up at him attentively.

Sal then walked her back to where I was sitting at the picnic table in the corner and Sal and I sat down for a chat. I let Jess loose and she once again glued herself to my legs, yet barely took her eyes off Sal. She seemed intrigued, verging on captivated, and after a couple of minutes moved closer to him. I'd never seen her so taken with someone she'd only recently met.

Then the most extraordinary thing happened – Sal started to tease Jess and she liked it. Out of the blue he suddenly leant forward and tickled her then abruptly turned away. Jess started in surprise. Then Sal turned around and tickled her again. To my utter astonishment this became a game that ended with Sal chasing an ecstatic Jess around the picnic table. Jess had the entire enclosure to escape to but instead chose to 'run away' from Sal by leading him round and round the table whilst looking back at him gleefully.

All of a sudden it was as if I wasn't there. There was a bond between the two of them that seemed to have materialised from nowhere. Sal had dropped his guard and was just a boy chasing after his dog and Jess seemed indifferent to my presence. She had a big grin on her face and her tail was wagging at full speed. I felt strangely emotional; this was what Jess's life without me looked like. I'd always known deep down that I couldn't keep her but to be confronted with the reality of her loving someone else the way she loved me tugged at my heart. Something had gone wrong in my universe; she should have been my forever dog. But she was going to be Sal's instead.

After a few minutes Sal sat down, grinning at Jess. She flopped down right next to him, letting him stroke her tummy and even 'kissed' him with her nose a few times. She looked happy and exhilarated, exactly how she looked when she played a game with me. I was now convinced that Sal was some kind of mystical dog charmer and I was a little bit in love with him myself.

Sal smiled at me. "So I've decided I'm going to put an application in. She's a great dog and I'd love to have her."

"That's fantastic," I replied, genuinely happy and relieved despite my sorrow at losing my best friend. I'd done it. I'd saved Jess. Her future without me was secure.

"I can tell she likes you. I'll let Linda know how this afternoon has gone and I'm sure you'll be successful."

Once Jess and I got home I emailed Linda. I told her how relaxed Jess had been, how she really seemed to like Sal and how I felt he was exactly right for her. I finished by saying,

> "I think he has a very nice way with her, he's incredibly patient, and clearly 'speaks dog'. Most importantly he seems to 'speak Jess'. He also finds her quirks amusing which I think is important. He's not under any illusions about what she's like and he shows the patience and confidence to deal with it. And I'm as sure as I possibly can be that Jess likes him."

That was the crux for me. I was Jess's advocate and I was certain that Sal was her choice. Linda phoned me on Saturday to say that Sal had submitted his application to adopt Jess and his interview was fixed for Monday morning. However if successful he wasn't planning to take her home straightaway because he had an immovable work trip on Tuesday and Wednesday. Instead he'd taken the Thursday and Friday off work in order to have a long weekend with her to help her settle in so was intending to pick her up from me on Thursday morning.

During the previous few days, when the prospect of Sal adopting Jess had started to look promising, the germ of an idea had formed in my mind. I didn't want Sal to be the person who took Jess away from her Jenni - it would be far preferable if her Jenni 'betrayed' her and

Sal was the guy who 'rescued' her. My plan was that I'd return Jess to the shelter a few days early so that Sal could take her home from there. As much as it broke my heart to give Jess up a minute earlier than I needed to, I believed it was the best way to help her bond permanently with Sal. And being in the shelter for a few days rather than a token few hours would reinforce to Jess that I really had abandoned her.

I told Linda my idea and she agreed that it made an unfortunate kind of sense. We decided that if Sal was successful at the interview, which we had no doubt he would be, then I'd return Jess to the shelter on Monday afternoon. Then Sal could rescue her properly on the Thursday morning.

That weekend Steve and I spoilt Jess rotten. We did our favourite walks at the watershed, Baker Park and on Fort Detrick and I cooked her an entire steak that I sliced up and fed her piece by succulent piece. I wanted Jess to feel completely loved before we let her go forever. Steve and I were both rather emotional and subdued that weekend and Jess definitely picked up on our mood. She seemed less relaxed and didn't want to let either of us out of her sight. We had to keep reminding each other to cheer up and act natural for Jess's sake.

On Sunday evening, Steve offered to come home slightly early the next day and take Jess to the shelter for me. I gratefully accepted. It was the coward's way out but I wanted to say goodbye to my best friend in my own house and I didn't think I could cope with seeing the expression on Jess's face when I left her at the shelter.

On Monday morning Jess woke me up with her gentle nose kisses for the last time. This was a life-changing day for both of us. Although Jess didn't know what was happening she definitely sensed something was afoot. She was especially affectionate and kept coming and nuzzling into me, seeking reassurance that I couldn't give because I was a bag of nerves myself. What if Sal didn't pass the interview or changed his mind?

My worries were of course unfounded. Linda called me just before lunchtime and confirmed that Sal had been successful and had signed the paperwork and paid the adoption fee. Linda told me how impressed she'd been by him and how much thought he'd given to Jess's needs. Apparently he'd been very touched at my decision to return Jess to the shelter early.

It struck me how we all simply wanted what was best for the soul lying at the opposite end of the sofa to me. Jess had been by far my hardest foster case but finally she was going to have the happy ending she deserved. I felt extraordinarily lucky to have been her foster carer and proud to have played a part in rescuing her. And I was proud of Steve, Lauren, Didi, Linda, Officer Norris and Sal too.

After lunch, Jess and I went for one last hike on our favourite trail at the watershed, the trail that had meant so much to us. We'd never be there together again. At one point along the trail, next to one of Jess's favourite watering spots, I decided we needed to leave a fleeting trace of Jenni and Jess for posterity. I started howling and Jess joined in, just a girl and her dog howling at the world together.

When we got home Steve was already there. We swiftly packed the car with all Jess's things – I was donating her bed, star collar, chain lead and Light Blue Safety Lead and ground stake, as well as the remainder of her food. Jess padded around us excitedly, rightly assuming that another outing was on the cards.

Then Steve looked at me. It was time. I knelt down. "Come here Jess," I said and my dream dog came and snuggled in to me for the last time. I ran my hands through her silky fur, trying to commit the smell and the feel of her to memory.

"I love you Jess, you're the best dog in the world. Thank you for being my best friend and thank you for coming back to me." My voice cracked and my composure crumbled. Jess looked at me, worried and uncertain, and pawed at my shoulder. None of my emotion was feigned of course but it did mean that I'd achieved my aim – Jess knew something bad was happening. Now I needed to let her go.

"I love you so much, I'm so sorry. Happy trails."

I hugged her one last time, kissed her beautiful head and walked away. I went and sat on the suddenly empty seeming sofa and listened to Steve start the car and drive off. Then I cried tears of sheer grief.

The ten months Jess had lived with us had been the best time of my life. She'd been an unadulterated joy and a frustrating challenge all at the same time; a constant source of wonder and worry, a dog who made me feel eternally bound to the timeless tale of dogs and humans. Enchanting, loving, adventurous, independent yet devoted, she'd embodied my childhood dream of what a dog should be and our friendship was the one I'd yearned for as long as I could remember. She'd taught me so much and I knew I'd never have the same bond with another dog because the circumstances could never be replicated. She was one of a kind.

My job had been to get Jess to trust people again and in terms of humanity as a whole, I failed. But then I'm not sure anyone could have succeeded. However I did get her to a place where she loved me and Steve, and months later, Sal. So out of seven billion people, I helped Jess to trust three of us. Maybe that was as good as it was ever going to get with her.

It's generally believed that dogs live in the moment but I don't think that's always true, certainly not for dogs who've been traumatised by abuse or neglect. I know Jess remembered her past but I also think she was conceptually aware of the future and was scared of one without me. That's why she slipped her escape-proof harness and ran away from the volunteer who'd intended to adopt her. Then along came Sal and something clicked between them; she seemed to know he was different and he broke through her fear in a way that was magical to witness.

Maybe she sensed a sadness in me, even in our happiest times, that signaled to her that we weren't meant to last; that I was never going to be her forever person. I wouldn't put anything past Jess – for all her craziness, she was a wise old soul.

CHAPTER 19

LAST DOG

THE FIRST COUPLE of weeks without Jess were awful. I missed her unbearably and this time I knew she wouldn't be coming back. Sal kindly emailed me a few photos of Jess sprawled on his sofa and playing in his backyard. She looked happy and relaxed, exactly what I'd hoped for. Sal assured me that she'd settled in to her new home really well and he was so pleased he'd adopted her. My sense of loss was at least mitigated by the knowledge that against the odds, I'd helped find Jess her perfect forever home.

One evening, Steve asked me if I intended to go and see Jess before we left Frederick. I had thought about this; Sal only lived about fifteen minutes from us so it was extremely tempting. Yet I'd reluctantly decided that it would be best for Jess if I stayed away. She needed to forget about me now and if I showed up at Sal's it would only confuse her. I'd always put what was best for Jess ahead of my feelings and I wasn't going to change now. Interestingly Sal had never mentioned me going to visit either. I think we both instinctively understood that for Jess's sake, Jenni needed to become a memory, not a visitor.

I did at least have a lot to occupy my mind and my time. Our USA adventure was rapidly coming to end, we were about to embark on a monumental new one and there was a huge amount to do.

I told Linda I was still keen to foster, however we were moving out of our house on 23rd April and spending our last few days in a hotel so we only had six weeks left. This was obviously not enough time for a long-term case but we agreed that a two-week puppy foster would be ideal. Linda assured me I was top of her list. I desperately hoped something would come up; the house felt terribly empty and I was apprehensive about going home as I didn't know when our circumstances would allow us to have a dog in our lives again.

The next few weeks flew by. We had to arrange the shipping of all our belongings, sell our car and close down our mobile phone and internet contracts. Selling the car turned out to be pleasantly straightforward; our friends Ken and Helen bought it. We'd had a lot of great times in that car and I was glad it was going to a worthy home. Ken vowed to never wash Jess's nose prints off the inside of the rear windscreen and he was as good as his word for the three years he had the car. Ken is now a Maryland state Delegate – his constituents should know they elected a politician who keeps his promises.

As the days went obstinately by, I began to doubt that I'd manage to fit in another foster. I volunteered at the shelter most days, even if it was just for an hour. I knew how much I was going to miss that place and I wanted to fit in as much dog walking, laundry folding and poop scooping as possible.

Then on Monday 9th April, exactly two weeks before we were moving out of the house and into a hotel, my phone rang. With exquisite timing it was Linda.

'Hey Jenni, I've got some great news for you. Would you like to take a husky puppy for us for two weeks?' she asked, knowing full well what the answer would be.

I arrived at the shelter less than ten minutes later. Linda took me down to the quarantine room and introduced me to the most beautiful puppy I'd ever seen, a tiny bundle of black, tan and white fur with stunning ice blue eyes. Linda told me that she had been found at the side of the I-70, a busy six-lane highway. What kind of person abandons a puppy somewhere like that? Linda said she thought it was fate that this puppy had shown up for my last two weeks.

I decided to call the pup Smokey after Smokey Lonesome, a character in one of my favourite books. Smokey Lonesome was a hobo, down on his luck, and I thought that was quite fitting for my little stray.

So for the last time I went through the process of preparing for the fun and chaos that a puppy brings to a house. I collected a box of puppy pads, several towels and a small crate from the shelter and took my last little hobo home.

I soon discovered that Smokey did not like being put down. Ever. She wanted to be on my lap or in my arms the whole time, understandable given her traumatic experience. Seeing as I liked nothing more than cuddling puppies, we were a perfect match. I decided it would be amusing to fail to mention the latest member of the family to Steve. When he got home that evening and walked through the door I simply held Smokey up and said, "Surprise!"

Steve was feeling as tense about leaving the USA as I was and he had the added stress of handing over all his work. His eyes lit up and he grinned at me, a mixture of happiness and good-natured exasperation that once again I'd surprised him with a four-legged houseguest.

"Wow, she's beautiful," he said, coming over and taking Smokey from me. Smokey immediately snuggled into his chest and his affections, earning herself an unexpected privilege a few hours later that no other puppy had been granted.

That night I set up the travel crate by my side of the bed so that Smokey could sleep right next to me; Steve didn't even attempt to dissuade me. Jess had slept in our room every night since her return and the 'no dogs sleeping in our bedroom' ship had long since sailed. I added some towels and a cuddly toy, then lifted Smokey in. She curled up in the corner closest to me and I turned the light out to go to sleep.

Straightaway Smokey started whining and pawing at the side of the crate. I did my best to ignore her so that she learned this wasn't the way to get attention. It didn't work. I decided she needed a brief moment of reassurance that I was still there so I turned the light on, gave her a quick cuddle and then placed her back in the crate. I got back into bed myself and turned the light off. Smokey instantly started whining again. It was unsurprising that she didn't like the dark. The previous night she'd been abandoned next to a busy highway, a frightening and dangerous environment for any dog, let alone a six week old puppy. Now she was being plunged into darkness again.

I confess – I crumbled and figuratively threw the positive reinforcement rulebook out of the window. I knew Smokey was going to be my last puppy for a while and I couldn't bear the sound of her unhappy so I brought her into bed with me. She snuggled into my neck and went quiet immediately. I waited a few minutes until I was sure Smokey was asleep and then started to ease myself up slowly in order to gently place her back in the crate.

"Oh, leave her, she's asleep," said a voice from Steve's side of the bed. The voice sounded exactly like my husband but surely he would never tell me to let a puppy sleep in our bed?

I started laughing softly. This was a bit of a turn around from the 'no dogs upstairs' policy enforced by that same husband less than eighteen months previously. "Are you sure?"

"Yes," replied Steve. "Don't disturb her. She's fine."

Having a puppy sleep in your bed is lovely if a little disruptive. Smokey slept beautifully for the first few hours, curled up between our heads. Then sometime in the early hours I was woken up by her pawing my cheek and chewing my hair. This went on for a while until she went back to sleep. It was endearing being woken up by her the next morning too. She woke me first and then began gently pawing at Steve's head. He woke up with a sleepy but contented smile on his face.

We couldn't enjoy this family bonding for long though. Smokey's pawing became a bit more frantic and prompted Steve to get up and take her outside. For obvious reasons our white bed linen was at risk with a puppy sleeping in the bed. However in the two weeks we had Smokey, she never once peed on the bed at night. I think she readily accepted it as her bed too and so kept it clean.

As Steve had so much to do in our final few weeks, and was also clearing out his office and bringing various items home, I had started driving him in to work and picking him up. On Smokey's first morning with us I didn't want to leave her at home by herself whilst I dropped Steve off. She had barely been out of my arms since I'd collected her from the shelter. So Smokey came with us, snuggled in to Steve's chest on the way there and then curled up on my lap as I was driving home. I accept this probably wasn't the most sensible way to drive but the speed limit on base was 25 mph and the roads weren't exactly busy.

Pregnancy was taking its toll on me and I was experiencing another phase of extreme tiredness. I spent a large portion of the day lying on the sofa. Having

Smokey's warm little body to keep me company was deeply satisfying. I knew I'd be doing this with Baby Williams in just a few months time and I hoped he or she would sleep as peacefully as Smokey.

But it wasn't just during nap time that Smokey wanted to be close to me. During her first week with us, if I was making breakfast, doing some laundry or cooking I had to do it one-handed because Smokey insisted on being tucked up in my other arm. I didn't mind at all; doing household tasks one-handed was good practice for me.

The days were disappearing too fast and I had mixed feelings about going home. I was looking forward to seeing family and friends and, deep-seated 'becoming a mummy' fears aside, I was naturally excited for the end of July when we'd finally meet Baby Williams. But I was also extremely sad to leave. I had grown to love Frederick and the US as a whole and felt completely at home there. I was also dreading the end of my dog-centric lifestyle. I had no idea when I'd be able to have a dog again as I was due to have a baby and would then be returning to work full time after a year or so. In dog terms, going home felt like a backwards step and I wasn't at all sure how I was going to cope.

Our final couple of weeks were filled with goodbyes. We had meals out with various friends and Steve's leaving do from work where his colleagues triumphantly presented us with a certificate they'd made declaring Baby Williams a citizen of Fort Detrick. Sadly I don't think this proclamation has any official standing. I also had a baby shower with my FCAC friends, hosted by Carol, where an excitable Smokey appeared to be under the impression that she was the guest of honour. She was probably right.

With the exception of Steve, I'd spent more time with dogs in the last eighteen months than I had with people. Nonetheless it was hard to say goodbye to our human friends. We'd embraced Frederick and Frederick had embraced us in return. Fostering dogs had enabled us to forge a deeper connection to our community, introduced us to people who remain friends years later and afforded me an identity and a purpose distinct from merely being Steve's 'dependent alien' wife.

This made one particular farewell especially memorable. Peter and Sandee, who'd adopted Patrick, invited us over for a doggy play date with Jan, Dick and Cali, and Nikki and Mali. Cali and Mali were of course two of Patrick's sisters from the Magnificent Seven litter. We'd seen Patrick, Cali and Mali individually since they'd been adopted but not all together and the three of them hadn't seen each other since I'd taken them back to the shelter. It was fascinating to see them reunited and we all agreed that they seemed to recognise each other. As I watched the three much loved dogs playfully chasing each other around Peter and Sandee's back yard, I contemplated how different their lives might have been without Frederick County Animal Control and the foster care programme.

Sunday was our last day in our house and our last day with Smokey. The next morning I was taking Smokey back to the shelter and Steve and I were moving out of our house and in to a local hotel. It was a beautiful April day and Steve, Smokey and I spent the afternoon playing outside. Smokey was in her element, running between me and Steve and basking in the undivided attention of both her people. Having Smokey around had made our final weeks infinitely more enjoyable. She gave us something else to focus on and helped to take our minds off the stress of packing up our lives again. She was a worthy last dog. That evening we barbecued steaks out on our patio and reminisced about the great times we'd had in that house and the fifteen dogs who'd made it a home.

Monday morning came too quickly and after breakfast it was time to return Smokey to FCAC. Linda greeted me in reception and took us to the puppy room where there was an empty enclosure all ready for Smokey. The woman who gave me my first dog smiled at me and I knew she understood the significance of this moment.

"Take your time," she said kindly.

"Maybe I'll just stay with her for a bit and settle her in."

I got in the enclosure with Smokey and cuddled her for the final time.

"Bye bye Smokey." I had tears in my eyes. "Thank you for coming to stay with us for the last couple of weeks." I took one last look into her glacial blue eyes.

"Happy trails."

And that was that. When I first applied to FCAC eighteen months previously, I thought I might get to foster a couple of dogs, maybe three if I was fortunate. I never imagined I'd foster fifteen in that space of time, or have one of them for ten months. Fostering those dogs had been a childhood dream come true, a dream that had morphed into a reality that felt like it was meant to be. The dogs had changed me and as I bid farewell to my final foster dog, I feared I was losing part of myself.

Back at home the removal people had arrived and were packing our belongings with brutal efficiency. Steve and I sat on the patio, literally on the patio as the chairs and table were encased in bubble wrap and packing tape, whilst our USA adventure was irretrievably dismantled. It seemed a forlorn end to the experience of a lifetime.

Four days later, we flew out of Washington DC and home to England and the impending adventure of parenthood. I left behind fifteen dogs who had received a second chance and were now living the lives that all dogs deserve. And as difficult as it was to give up every single one of them, I can't recommend fostering highly enough.

The beauty of fostering is this; I didn't save fifteen dogs – I saved thirty. For every dog I fostered, space was created in the shelter for another dog who got the chance to find their forever home. If you're reading this and thinking you'd like to try fostering, I hope this convinces you. Yes, it will break your heart getting attached to the dogs and then having to say goodbye. But your heart won't stay broken; a little piece of your next dog's heart enters and mends it again. So gradually your heart gets less human and more dog-like. And that can only be a good thing.

CHAPTER 20

HAPPY TRAILS

WE ARRIVED BACK in the UK at the end of April 2012 and our beautiful daughter Eve Jessica Williams was born at the end of June. Her middle name was chosen in honour of the individual who knew she existed before anyone else did. She certainly takes after her namesake in a number of ways – like Jess, Eve is bewitching, funny, stubborn, affectionate and determinedly independent despite her inherent vulnerability. I love her more than I ever thought possible.

However when Steve and I first received Eve's diagnosis of an incredibly rare chromosome condition, the news hit us both extremely hard. The first year was rough and I don't remember a whole lot. Eve's development was severely delayed, she rarely smiled and she faced a lot of medical problems, including a particularly evil form of epilepsy that threatened to take her from us.

Steve and I loved Eve, of course we did. But it wasn't a joyful, happy, carefree kind of love. Instead it felt like an unbearable burden, born of sadness impossible to articulate. We were grieving a child who never existed, gut-wrenchingly worried about the one who did and fearful for all our futures.

In the minutes after being told about Eve's condition, I realised with utter clarity that I wouldn't be returning to work. This little girl was going to need round the clock care and the best person to provide that was me. Yet it's a measure of the emotional turmoil I was going through that soon after that decision, I experienced crushing self-doubt about whether I could do it.

I had absolutely no experience of disability and during my pregnancy had taken all the recommended nutritional supplements and opted in to the routinely offered tests, the unspoken point being to avoid having a disabled child. Except no one ever puts it that bluntly.

As the enormity of Eve's difficulties and the impact on our life began to sink in, I couldn't see a way forward. I hated myself for failing to rise to the occasion in contrast to the inspirational parents I was seeing on Facebook disability forums, with their sunny-side-up blogs about life with a child with Downs Syndrome or cerebral palsy or autism. They were proper parents and I was a failure. I felt so sorry for Eve, being landed with me for a mum, and the thought crossed my mind that she'd be better off without me.

Despite being thousands of miles away, my foster dogs saved me. I've never agreed with the lazy adage that dogs give you unconditional love and the subtext that you can therefore treat dogs however you like with no consequence. Dogs are discerning; they don't love unconditionally.

Sam and Jess in particular had learnt that humans could be cruel and violent. As a result, both dogs were scared of people and certainly weren't inclined to show unconditional love. Then I came along and changed their minds. Sam and Jess loved me because I was kind and patient and always put them first. I honoured my side of the dog-human bond and was rewarded a thousand fold.

In some of my darkest times after Eve was born, when I doubted whether I had the ability and the qualities to be her mummy, the faith that my dogs had shown in me pulled me through. They'd all trusted me (well all except Duke!), with Sam and Jess giving me the biggest endorsement of all. I had to believe that they'd seen something in me that I currently couldn't. And when in doubt, trust the dog. I wasn't a terrible person; I could do this.

I began to believe in myself and gradually Steve and I found our footing. Eve's specific type of epilepsy was cured although she still has more general seizures, she started smiling and never stopped, and her hilarious little personality began to develop. We came to terms with how our plans needed to adapt and vowed to ensure that Eve would still have a life filled with fun, travel and adventure – it would just look a bit different.

But even as we emerged from the darkness of Eve's first year, it was apparent that we had another problem – we didn't have a dog. Life without a dog seemed unnatural now and I needed one more than ever. I needed to be the best version of 'me', the Jenni I'd become in the US when I had a dog by my side. I remain convinced that my reaction to Eve's diagnosis and my state of mind in her first year would have been markedly different if we'd somehow managed to adopt one of our foster dogs.

When Eve was almost two, we bought a house with a garden and were finally able to welcome another dog into our life, a Golden Retriever puppy called Scout. It had always been my favourite name and now I had a dog I could keep.

Scout's arrival made our family complete and she is the ideal dog for us at this stage in our lives. She loves people, is affectionate, playful and totally trustworthy but has enough of a stubborn and independent streak to make us laugh. So perfect is Scout that I remain convinced that my foster dogs somehow had a chat with her and told her all the ways I needed her to be the model Disney dog and all the ways I secretly wanted her to be a little bit naughty.

Finally getting my own dog revealed a helpful truth. In typical parenting, when you have a healthy and non-disabled child, the ultimate goal is seeing your child become increasingly self-reliant, move out of your house and in practical terms at least, lead a life independent of yours. Yet the gold standard of dog guardianship means committing to that dog for its entire life. A dog will never live independently of its human; it's our job to care for them for the rest of their days. And that's not a negative – it's the whole point.

The same is true for a child like Eve. She will never live independently and whilst I can't predict the future and have no idea how long I'll live or whether I'll physically be able to care for her when I'm elderly, I know that I'll always be heavily involved in her life and her care. And that no longer feels like a burden I can't shoulder – it seems like an adventure I feel lucky to have embarked upon.

I owe a huge debt to Frederick County Animal Control because without the experience of fostering those down and out dogs I wouldn't be the person or the mummy I am today. Those dogs showed me another side to myself; a softer and selfless side. They taught me patience, compassion and how you never ever give up on someone vulnerable who depends on you. And most importantly they taught me that being responsible for someone who will always need you, makes you the person you were destined to be.

Fostering gave me a unique insight into the ancient bond between dogs and humans, a relationship that has endured for tens of thousands of years and brought immeasurable benefits to humankind. I believe that dogs have impacted our evolution more than we'll ever know; they've certainly evolved me.

*   *   *

There's a lovely prose poem called 'Rainbow Bridge' which tells the tale of what happens to our dogs after they die. According to the story, the dog wakes up in a paradise of pristine meadows, tree-covered hills and sparkling streams. This land lies beyond our world and is connected to Heaven via the aforementioned bridge.

There is abundant food, water and sunshine and all the old, sick or injured dogs are restored to full health and fitness. Our friends spend their days running around, exploring and playing happily together. But ultimately they're not there to play; they're there to wait.

Every so often one dog suddenly stops, looks up and barks with unbridled excitement as they recognise the figure calling to them from across the meadow. Their human has arrived, the person they loved in this life that they had to leave behind. They run to you and you greet each other jubilantly, overjoyed to be reunited at last. Then you cross the Rainbow Bridge into Heaven together, never to be separated again.

On 13th October 2014 I was browsing Facebook when at the same moment I had two messages flash up – one was from Linda and one was from Sal. Both messages said the same; Jess had escaped from Sal's yard the previous evening and had been hit by a car and killed. Sal, Linda, Officer Norris and everyone at the shelter who remembered Jess were devastated.

I was devastated too. I'd always hoped I'd see Jess again, perhaps if we visited Frederick in the future when she was settled enough in her forever home that a visit from an old friend wouldn't confuse her. And now that we had a house, Steve and I had always said that if Jess ever needed us, if Sal ever gave her up (we had no reason to think he would but still), we'd adopt her and fly her to the UK. Somehow we'd make it work.

I know I gave Jess a chance at life that she wouldn't otherwise have had. I hope she knew how much I loved her and why I couldn't keep her. I hope she died instantly and felt no pain. I like to think of her running along, loving the feel of the wind in her ears and intoxicated with the sense of freedom as she answered the call of the wild.

If there is such a place as the Rainbow Bridge and if I did my job right, then Jess will be waiting there for Sal, not me. But it would be nice if she came to say 'hi'.

A few weeks after Jess died I was thinking about her when I realised there was a strange and wonderful coincidence concerning Jess and the members of the Williams family. Our names were Jenni, Eve, Steve and Scout. Our initials spelt 'JESS'.

That Christmas I bought myself a necklace with a pendant made up of two silver circles. On the smaller circle is engraved 'JESS' and on the larger one, 'HAPPY TRAILS', my final farewell to all my foster dogs. 'JESS' stands for all <u>five</u> members of the Williams family and 'HAPPY TRAILS' is our family motto; a celebration of all the happy times we've had together and all the trails we have to look forward to.

You can't always choose your trail but you can choose how you ride it and we ride happy.

Happy trails.

THE END

About the Author

Jenni Williams lives in the Surrey Hills in south-east England. She likes dogs, forests, craft beer and nice people. Her dream car is a blue pick up truck.

Get in touch –
Twitter: @jenniwdog
Email: jenni.williams.author@gmail.com